In Memory of Herman Kahn

THE
US
MARITIME
STRATEGY

Norman
Friedman

Copyright © Norman Friedman 1988

First published in 1988 by
Jane's Publishing Company Limited
238 City Road, London EC1V 2PU

Distributed in the Philippines and the USA and its dependencies by
Jane's Publishing Inc.
115 5th Avenue, New York, NY 10003

ISBN 0 7106 0500 5

Printed and bound in the United Kingdom by
Biddles Limited, Guildford and King's Lynn

Contents

Acknowledgements

I cannot list all of those with whom, for well over a decade, I have discussed US naval and national strategy, or for whom I have professionally studied aspects of that strategy. I can, however, thank those who read earlier versions of this manuscript, and some of whose comments are reflected in its final version: A D Baker III, Cdr John Byron, William Carpenter, Cdr Albert C Myers, Dr Thomas Hone, and Dr Michael Vlahos. I owe particular thanks to Captain Peter Swartz, a direct contributor to the strategy, its bibliographer and, so far as one exists, the historian of the modern US Maritime Strategy. All have been extremely helpful, and in many cases have helped me clarify my own thinking. I alone am of course responsible for whatever unclarity remains.

I do not think this book could have been written without the love and thoughtful support and encouragement of my wife, Rhea.

I would like to emphasise that the views reflected here are my own, and do not necessarily correspond with those of the US Navy, or of any other US government or private body with which I have been associated.

List of Abbreviations

AAW	Anti-air warfare
AE	Ammunition ship, in the US standard naval designation system (A for auxiliary, E for ammunition)
AF	Stores ship, in the US standard designation system (A for Auxiliary, F for stores)
AFS	Combat stores ship, carrying spare aircraft parts as well as provisions; would form part of an underway replenishment group
AMRAAM	Advanced Medium-Range Air-to-Air Missile (designated AIM-120A), replacing the current Sparrow (AIM-7).
AO	Tanker (O for oiler); this designation applies both to ships designed to refuel warships and to tankers carrying fuel from point to point.
AOE	Fast underway replenishment ship carrying both fuel (O) and ammunition (E). A "one stop" ship, to be distinguished from earlier single-purpose replenishment ships such as tankers (AO), ammunition ships (AE), and stores ships (AF).
AOR	Underway replenishment ship carrying fuel and ammunition, essentially a somewhat smaller and slower equivalent of the AOE.
ASUW	Anti-surface (ship) warfare
ASW	Anti-submarine warfare
CIC	Combat Information Centre, in which data from a ship's sensors (and from other sources) is correlated to provide an integrated tactical picture
ELF	Extremely low frequency (radio)
IFF	Identification, friend or foe
LCAC	Air-cushion (AC) landing craft (LC)
MAB	Marine Amphibious Brigade
MAF	Marine Amphibious Force
MOE	Measure of Effectiveness
ROTHR	Relocatable over-the-horizon radar

RPV	Remotely piloted vehicle, sometimes also referred to as UAV (unmanned air vehicle)
SIOP	Single Integrated Operational Plan, the US plan for largescale nuclear attack.
URG	Underway replenishment group
VLF	Very low frequency (radio)
VSTOL	Vertical and short take-off and landing (aircraft)

1. Introduction: Why a Strategy?

It is now about five years since the current Maritime Strategy was first formulated within the US Navy.[1] The strategy has shaped the current US naval expansion, and that alone makes it worthy of study and discussion. Moreover, to the extent that the idea of an *explicit* strategy has sunk roots within the US naval establishment, it can be expected to guide development for many more years.

The phrase "Maritime Strategy" has had several quite different interpretations. Is it a new US national strategy, placing maritime considerations above, say, continental ones (to the detriment, perhaps, of NATO)? Is it perhaps a totally new way of understanding naval or maritime warfare, explaining and justifying the substantial expansion of the US Navy during the Reagan Administration? This book is intended to describe and explain the current US Maritime Strategy, and above all to place it within its national and historical context.

That in turn requires a comparison with alternative maritime strategies, as they have been and are practised by other navies, and as they have been proposed by critics of the current maritime strategy. It is the contention of this book that the current US Maritime Strategy is the natural successor to earlier versions of US naval strategy, dating back as far as 1889. The outline of this strategy (as opposed to its detailed implementation) has a logic transcending the very considerable changes in naval technology over the past century. Because many of the strategic issues in naval warfare show this kind of constancy, historical examples will be used very freely.

That deserves comment. Since World War II it has been fashionable to imagine that technology is changing so rapidly that

1

historical experience is nearly irrelevant, and national military programmes are typically evaluated on the basis of computer models of future war. One consequence of this type of analysis is that new threats generate new weapons rather than new strategy or new tactics. The historical record, however, shows that tactics and strategy can often drastically modify the impact of new technology.[2] The closest available approaches to actual historical combat experience are fleet exercises and war gaming, since interactive exercises and games emphasise the impact of tactics and strategy. It is no accident, then, that coincident with the introduction of the Maritime Strategy (which seeks to achieve results by strategy as well as by technology), the US Navy showed drastically increased interest in gaming and in more realistic fleet exercises (and advanced tactical training, exemplified by "Topgun" and its strike warfare equivalent) as opposed to static computer modelling, which emphasises the competition of technology against technology.

The Significance of the Maritime Strategy

The Maritime Strategy is both more and less than its critics have suggested. It is more, in that it provides a stable framework within which hardware and tactics can be developed and evaluated, as alternative approaches to a commonly-understood problem. Thus to make US Maritime Strategy explicit is to seek unity within the US (and, hopefully, the Western) maritime community by making many more or less implicit ideas explicit, so that different elements of the community have a common language and can examine and understand those ideas. The formulation of the strategy is also an attempt to formalise the ideas and the elements of maritime warfare so that they are more comprehensible to the larger defence community, which often seems more comfortable with the concepts of land warfare and strategic nuclear warfare. In this sense the formulation of the Maritime Strategy is one more in a long series of attempts to bridge the very broad gap between air, land, and naval strategic thought.

In particular, the US Maritime Strategy envisages early forward naval operations as a means of dealing with a land-oriented super-power, the Soviet Union. Successful forward operations can prevent the Soviets from overrunning the flanks of NATO; they are analogous to the forward defence planned for the Central Front. In both cases, deep air strikes are needed to destroy Soviet offensive forces. In the maritime case, the early destruction or neutralisation of the Soviet naval threat will free maritime forces to more directly affect events on land. The Maritime Strategy is necessarily global because it uses the inherent mobility of maritime forces as leverage against the relatively much less mobile Soviet ground and tactical air forces. It is necessarily an alliance strategy, based on the needs and the capabilities of the allied navies and on the character of alliance geography (such as the positions of the choke points). Finally, it is perforce a joint (service) strategy, since it relies on ground and air forces to seize and hold (or defend already held) key geographical positions, such as Iceland and the Aleutians, and since events elsewhere on land can profoundly effect the overall naval geography of the Western Alliance.

Thus the Maritime Strategy is often summarised by the words forward, global, allied, and joint (service).

The strategy is less than its critics charge in that it is not intended to stand alone. It is part of a broader US national strategy. However, because that strategy tends to be implicit, its maritime component stands out. Moreover, the national strategic assumptions have been changing, in some important ways to the discomfort of many within the US and allied defence establishments. The current prosperity of the US Navy is to some extent a reflection of that deeper but unexpressed national change.

The Meaning of Strategy

Strategy means so many things to so many that it seems worth while to define it here. Given some context of conflict, a strategy is an overall plan to get from the present, or from some assumed beginning scenario, to some desired goal. In game theory, the alternative plans of operation are termed strategies. Others might term them alternative tactics. In a war, one might speak of the tactics of a battle within a campaign carried out to some strategic plan, or of the campaign as part of some grand strategy. For this book, strategy is planning on the most general scale, so that it becomes a way of understanding and evaluating alternative approaches to warfare.

Strategy is inescapably both political and military. A highly logical military strategy may be entirely impossible to execute because it violates the political constraints of the system within which it has to operate. This has been particularly apparent in cases of limited warfare, but it applies to all situations. In the case of the US Maritime Strategy, much of the controversy has surrounded its supposed political problems: its approach to nuclear forces and its application to the NATO alliance.

The game theory approach illuminates something very fundamental: the strategy which is followed, whether or not it is explicit, represents a choice among alternatives. To the extent that those alternatives are identified and understood, the strategic choice is a definite one. To the extent that they are not well defined, it becomes difficult to use strategy as a guide to other choices, e.g. in force structure and technology. The game theoretic point of view shows, too, that conflict is the confrontation of two strategies played out against a variety of circumstances. To the extent that the enemy's strategy is well understood, then, that should motivate a choice of one's own strategy. However, some particular choice, optimised for a particular enemy strategy, may perform disastrously against any other. A mixed strategy, averaged over various approaches, may seem better, given poor information concerning enemy thinking. This idea is typically expressed as the requirement to deal with enemy capabilities (i.e., with a variety of possible enemy strategies) rather than with supposed enemy intentions.

In the case of the Maritime Strategy, some very particular assumptions about Soviet maritime (and overall military) thinking have been made. To the extent that they are valid, they in turn present the United States with some extremely valuable opportunities. At this writing, the assumptions seem reasonable because they seem to reflect fundamental features of Soviet politics.

The Maritime Strategy in particular is a concept for operations against the Soviet Union in the context of general war. Because this context is considered the most stressing, it is generally used to measure the adequacy of American military forces. Thus the Maritime Strategy becomes a means of defining the desirable composition of the US Navy: it comprises those forces required to execute the strategy. Conversely, the strategy is designed to make the best possible use of an affordable level of US naval forces.

The Maritime Strategy must satisfy several other conditions. First, precisely because it is *not* intended as a US *national* strategy, it must fit the requirements of the larger US national strategy, which itself is integrated with the strategic requirements of the Western Alliance system (including, but not limited to, NATO). Thus it must function in the scenarios of greatest interest on an alliance-wide basis, involving more or less general war with the Soviet Union. The alliance element means that the Maritime Strategy cannot be unilateralist. It must seek to achieve the ends the alliance as a whole needs, and it can (and does) seek to incorporate alliance forces alongside US national ones.

On the other hand, the United States functions outside the Western Alliance, particularly in the Third World. Thus the forces the Maritime Strategy defines must also be effective in peacetime operations and in the more limited wars the United States often finds itself facing.

Third, the forces required to execute the strategy (in both contexts) must be affordable. That means that the *same* forces must be usable in both the general war and the limited war contexts. Similarly, the strategy must make optimum use of *existing* naval forces, since quick wholesale replacement is impractical. These two conditions are by no means identical.

Ideally, the strategy should be general enough to be able gracefully to accommodate likely changes in naval technology. That almost certainly translates to a requirement that it derive its authority partly from its clear relationship to long-standing fundamental principles of naval warfare, principles with which the naval community will be comfortable. After all, no matter how logical the strategy, it cannot survive if it is an alien growth.

Finally, the strategy is *public*. The Soviets (and other potential enemies) can be expected to read about it, and to watch aspects of it practised in exercises. The strategy must be effective *despite* such observation, which in any case is inevitable in peacetime. It must be general enough, and supple enough, to deal with the countermeasures the Soviets (among others) are likely to develop.

All of this must seem so obvious as to be trivial. However, much of modern military thinking is oriented towards the characteristics of particular weapon systems. The solution to a technological problem (e.g. quieter submarines) is generally taken to be a superior technology (e.g. better signal processing). The strategist takes a very different view. He does not eschew technological improvement, but he seeks advantages through the more clever application of existing forces. The ASW component of the Maritime Strategy is a prime case in point.

Roots of the Maritime Strategy

The Maritime Strategy had three complementary roots. One was a demand, voiced by then Secretary of the Navy John Lehman, that the Navy make its fundamental ideas more explicit so that they could be coherently presented to Congress. To the extent that the Navy's programme showed greater coherence, Congress would find it more logical and attractive. Earlier programmes, which seemed much more *ad hoc*, had often been attacked as such, and whittled down.

The strategy, moreover, was presented as part of the Reagan Administration's defence build-up. The 1980 Republican platform had called for the restoration of the Navy, and for its expansion to 600 ships, but it had not included any details of the new naval programme. It was up to Lehman to propose a programme which would make the best possible use of the money Congress could be expected to provide, particularly at the outset. Unless the new programme was clearly coherent, special interests could be expected to demand that their pet projects be funded, and the necessarily temporary largesse of Congress would soon be wasted.

Certainly Lehman later attributed much of his own success to the obvious coherence of his programme. At least to some extent, Lehman's demand reflected his own experience as an analyst during the Carter Administration, when civilian decision-makers clearly out of contact with naval thinking severely damaged the naval programme. For its part, the Navy of the 1970s failed to develop a public rationale for its desired force structure in terms the civilian decision-makers could understand.[3]

The explicit Maritime Strategy spoke to a major civilian (and ground forces) concern, the way in which investments in naval forces could help fight the great land battle to be expected in Central Europe in the event of a major war with the Soviets. The naval budget cuts of the Carter Administration were often justified on the basis of concentration on the NATO problem, as opposed to such peripheral problems as the limited war in Vietnam. The strategy (and its predecessors generated within the Navy) showed how naval projection forces would be expected to function in a major NATO-Warsaw Pact war.

Another root of the strategy was a need to evaluate the efficacy of US naval forces. Given a basic war-fighting strategy, alternative possible forces for a given budgetary period could be realistically compared. There was, therefore, a demand, first voiced by the Vice Chief of Naval Operations, Admiral William Small, about 1982, for a strategic framework to motivate the five-year programme. In this context the strategy was valuable as a common language for programmers, budgeteers, and for the operating forces.

This unifying effect might be expected to go much deeper. For many years, commentators on the US Navy have complained that it is really at least three quite separate navies: a carrier navy (with some semi-orphaned shore-based aviators in tow); a surface navy (more or less morosely tied to the carrier navy); and a submarine navy. The split between these "unions" is technological. However, actual naval warfare very clearly spreads across their boundaries. It can be argued, then, that to the extent the entire Navy is forced to think in war-fighting terms, the "union" splits will be at least ameliorated.[4]

The rise of explicit strategic ideas can also be traced to a resurgence in naval interest in tactics and operations, i.e., in war-fighting, which can be attributed in large part to Admiral Thomas

B Hayward. Hayward was responsible for the new forward strategy applied to the Seventh (Far East) Fleet in the late 1970s, and he
was also responsible for the formation of a Strategic Studies Group
(SSG) at the Naval War College soon after the beginning of the
Reagan Administration in 1981.[5] Although the SSG did not formulate the briefing usually associated with the Maritime Strategy, it
did study many tactical issues arising out of basic strategic concepts, and it trained officers who would later work on the evolving
explicit maritime strategy in the Pentagon.

Some have suggested that the turn towards greater interest in
naval tactics can be attributed in large part to the level of stability
reached by new naval weapon systems in the middle and late
1970s. Until then, so much energy went merely into making the new
anti-aircraft and anti-submarine weapons work that little attention could be spared for their broad tactical implications. Second,
naval technology reached a sort of plateau. Although improvement
was still rapid, the basic list of weapons was fairly well fixed.
Again, that made it possible for tacticians and strategists to spend
more of their time on methods of using the existing menu most
effectively.

What is New

The Maritime Strategy is novel for two reasons. First, the focus on
war-fighting strategy is unusual for the period since about 1950;
note that the word "strategic" is almost universally applied to the
application of long-range nuclear weapons, not to an overall concept of warfare. Second, it is unusual, in American history, for the
national or military strategy or even one of its components to be
made so explicit.

It might seem odd for a focus on just how to fight a war to be
considered novel. However, the reader might reflect that, at least
from the early 1950s onwards, the existence of nuclear weapons
made it difficult, at best, for the US military establishment to contemplate a protracted general war in which conventional kinds of
strategy would be very realistic. The split between services implicitly designed to fight a variety of wars can be traced back, first to

the intense rivalry of the early postwar years, and then to the ascendance of a civilian Secretary of Defense, particularly under Robert S McNamara.

The advent of nuclear weapons coincided with the rise of what seemed to be an overwhelmingly powerful conventional land military force, the postwar Soviet Army.[6] It seemed impossible for an exhausted West to mount a non-nuclear defence of Europe on the land. Joint war plans were developed, but they seemed to offer very little prospect of success, given existing US and West European economic and military conditions.

The newly-created Air Force argued that nuclear weapons could deter or roll back a Soviet land invasion. Within the US defence establishment, a demoralised army saw little alternative. The Navy was extremely sceptical, but the fiscal reality dominated, and by 1950 the United States was moving towards a national strategy largely dependent on the threat of nuclear attack – and little concerned with the details of how that threat would be executed. Moreover, the whole idea of the nuclear threat changed the concept of war, from a drawn-out struggle to a short prelude to a knock-out blow. Many in the United States still equate the Single Integrated Operational Plan (for large-scale nuclear attack) (SIOP) with a war plan, whereas in fact it is no more than a battle plan.[7]

In 1950 the outbreak of war in Korea demonstrated the limitations of the nuclear threat, and the Army and Navy recovered some of the ground they had lost in the fiscally austere late 1940s. From a national point of view, the Korean experience was important because it showed that in future the military would have to deal with two quite different classes of war, the big war against the Soviets, and a smaller war in the Third World. Smaller wars would be limited by political decision, primarily to avoid escalation into the kind of unlimited nuclear conflict which might be expected if the Soviets were directly involved.

As for the big war, nuclear weapons still dominated, because it was assumed that the West (by this time, primarily NATO) could not, in peacetime, maintain the sort of land forces which the Soviet command economy could support. At best, NATO ground forces could slow down a Soviet offensive for long enough to make the war-ending threat of nuclear escalation credible. This slowing-down operation might be a single battle or a connected series of battles, but it would not last very long, and it would have little to do with classical ideas of military strategy. Certainly it would not be designed with the classical goal, victory, in mind; that (usually described as "war termination on favourable terms") would come, if at all, as the result of the nuclear threat.[8]

The emphasis on nuclear weapons had another important conse-quence. Civilian theorists of nuclear warfare achieved very con-siderable influence, and civilian leaders of the US defence establishment were much taken by their views. Nuclear issues were considered sufficiently grave (and sufficiently comprehen-sible) that civilian decision-makers established an effective mono-poly over US declaratory strategy.[9]

The postwar nuclear period was marked by the rise of an aca-demic discipline of strategic analysis, practitioners of which find their way into government. They are taught to expect explicit doc-trine where, often, none has been formulated. They are so well aware of the advantages of explicit strategic doctrine that they find its absence puzzling. To some extent, indeed, one might regard the formulation of an explicit strategy for maritime warfare a result of the collision of academically-trained experts (including expert operators in uniform) with the older strategic tradition.

Perhaps the epitome of the postwar period of US strategic thought was the US performance in Vietnam, in which a non-nuclear version of nuclear escalation theory was applied so unsuccessfully. Given the steep decline of strategic thinking in much of the uniformed military establishment, there was little articulation of basic strategic questions: of an explicit US war aim, or of a consequent path to attain that aim, or, for that matter, of the resources consonant with that aim.[10]

The effect of the official nuclear focus was that the services developed several generations of new technology with little explicit attention to how they might fit together in a major war. The service, particularly naval, view seems always to have been scep-tical of claims that the mere existence of nuclear weapons would eliminate the possibility of an old-fashioned protracted non-nuclear war. One might see the Maritime Strategy as the first explicit example of a reversion to an earlier concept of strategy.

The rise of the Office of the Secretary of Defense (OSD) was the other important event of this period. The history of postwar US defence can be seen in part as conflict among the services, mediated by a civilian secretary placed over all of them. The sense of a unified US defence policy naturally grew with the focus on nuclear weapons wielded by the three services, since the details of land, sea, and air combat seemed less and less important. Secretary McNamara was determined to gain efficiency by lumping service elements in functional categories, to achieve the best mix among the services within each category.[11] Perhaps his most enduring achievement was the notion that such mixes could always be compared programmatically, so that the optimum mix of weapons among the services could be determined. McNamara could reasonably claim that his task was urgent: the postwar military technological revolution was bearing very expensive fruit, and it was by no means clear that even the United States could afford all of the weapons it was developing. Not only was the overall budget limited, but as McNamara entered office in 1961 it seemed increasingly likely that the United States would be drawn into a series of small limited wars, the first since Korea. They in turn required further new technology.

Unfortunately, the systems analysis which McNamara introduced had no overall agreed and explicit strategic or tactical framework, and therefore little if any concept of force employment. It focused on Measures of Effectiveness (MoEs), which were too narrow to be realistic. This was not a new idea; the US Navy used a form of MoE analysis (in limited forms of war gaming) before World War II to evaluate proposed new types of ships and weapons. However, the prewar Navy had the saving grace of using full-scale exercises (Fleet Problems) to test its operational concepts. The reality learned in the big exercises was fed back into fleet-scale war games. In all of these cases, moreover, the interactive character of the analysis fed in such realistic factors as individual initiative and the accidents of war. Moreover,

participants in the prewar planning process seem, in retrospect, to
have been well aware of the limitations of their work.

The current situation is very different. Computation has become
far more sophisticated, and therefore it seems (apparently very
deceptively) to promise precise results. However, in fact it is often
much less sophisticated than prewar practice. The analysis is
"static," i.e., friendly and enemy forces are compared, generally by
computer, but "strategies" (in the game-theory sense) are selected
beforehand, and they do not change as the battle progresses. Typical
battlefield effects such as shock (which can cause troops to break or
run even though few have been killed) are difficult to model math-
ematically, so they are omitted.[12] There is little sense of the effects of
accidents (the "fog of war", for example), which often dominate real
battles. It is difficult to represent morale, or the state of training. Nor
can the static analysis really evaluate the effect of foresight (or its
lack), or tactical brilliance (or gross stupidity). The problem is not
that these are marginal limitations, but rather that they are so often
the central issue in real wars. In effect, then, systems analysis, both
as it was defined in McNamara's time and as it functions two decades
later, omits some of the dominant considerations in combat.

The villain seems to be an emphasis on technology per se and hence
on the objective characteristics of weapons, often to the extent of
ignoring basic operating practices, which determine how close
weapons can come to their theoretical performance. The threat
defined in such apparently objective (but actually inadvertently
deceptive) terms are too often used to drive budgeting and force
planning. Similarly, the nominal characteristics of weapons do not
give an accurate indication of the capabilities of our own systems.
These problems surface (and are often burlesqued) as absurdly optimistic predictions of weapon performance.[13]

The alternatives, greater attention to historical analogy (which
would bring such human considerations as shock and accident into
focus), and fleet exercises and gaming (which focus on dynamic tactical interaction and take account of accident), have not totally
replaced static analysis because (like war itself) they do not produce
sets of easily reproduced comparative numbers suited to the budget
process.[14]

Typically a small number of scenarios is developed specifically to test existing and projected forces. This requirement in itself makes for some considerable unreality, because the scenarios are designed to be the most stressful possible. That makes sense if there is a one-dimensional scale of stress, from (say) the relatively simple case of a limited border clash in Berlin up to a full-scale Warsaw Pact *blitzkrieg* across Europe. However, the reality is that different scenarios stress military forces in different ways, not merely at different gross levels. For example, the Warsaw Pact *blitzkrieg* scenario tests those NATO forces in place at the beginning of the war, or mobilisable within the few days of available warning. One can envisage a very different scenario, in which both sides are sucked gradually into a war, and in which both mobilise in parallel. In this case what counts for NATO is a combination of medium-term mobilisation potential and the ability to keep producing material, so that the Soviets cannot easily break the stalemate. The role of naval forces in the two scenarios differs radically.

The choice of scenarios, moreover, is affected by the degree of analysis computers can accomplish. That means, for example, that it is much easier to deal with short than with protracted conflict, in effect with single battles rather than with campaigns.

To the extent, then, that strategy is about the cumulative effect of a series of operations on the will of an enemy government, the modern technique of analysis tends to evade strategic questions, and to avoid the advantages which an effective national strategy can provide – and, for that matter, the advantages which an enemy can derive from his own strategy.[15]

An Explicit Strategy

The explicitness of the Maritime Strategy is very new, at least for the post-World War II period. It would be absurd to imagine that the United States Navy has lacked strategists in its past – after all, Captain Alfred T Mahan, one of the founders of modern naval strategic thinking, was an American, and indeed an early lecturer at the Naval War College. However, note that there was relatively little public discussion of basic strategic ideas after Mahan. His writings reflected a new fundamental strategic consensus on basic issues. Later discussion (some of it termed strategic) was actually concerned with tactics and grand tactics, within the context defined by Mahan.[16]

Public discussion arose again only when US strategy had to adjust to a radically different world order, after World War II, as a consequence of both the newly dominant position of the United States and of the appearance of nuclear weapons.[17] By the late 1950s a kind of strategic consensus had been reached, at least as regards the problem of a major European war. It might be argued that the current intense discussion of US war-fighting strategy reflects yet another set of fundamental shifts: the rise of more and more independent allies (so that the United States is no longer in anything like so dominant a position) and the perceptibly declining impact of nuclear weapons, as both sides have become heavily armed (and hence mutually deterring).

For the most part, then, the US military tradition has been to avoid detailed discussion of strategic concepts, except when those concepts change radically. As in Britain, the basic issues are rarely explicitly addressed, with the result that it is sometimes difficult to respond to radically changed conditions in a manner consistent with classic strategic ideas, i.e., comfortably. On the other hand, explicitness could be embarrassing. To adopt an explicit strategy implies a process of choice; such choice creates winners – and losers – within the bureaucracy, both in kinds of forces supported and in kinds of technology purchased. Second, an explicit strategy is generally justified in terms of a particular scenario or class of scenarios. The more optimised it is, the more embarrassing when history does not call those particular scenarios forth. Finally, the more explicit the strategy, the more sharply drawn the underlying assumptions – which may themselves be unattractive, either at home or in allied governments. Recent history reveals examples of all of these pitfalls.

Perhaps the sharpest of all US explicit strategic choices was the postwar decision to depend heavily on strategic deterrence, as exemplified by the air force and its Strategic Air Command. The navy was the major loser, a defeat demonstrated by the cancellation of the super-carrier *United States* in 1949. The implicit scenario was World War III, a Soviet attack on Western Europe which would justify a US nuclear counter-stroke. When war actually came in June 1950, in Korea, it became obvious that the global nuclear strategy was irrelevant there: history had been, and would be, full of surprises. It is only fair, however, to point out that the threat of US tactical nuclear weapons helped to guarantee the Korean armistice of 1953. This threat in turn was credible because the United States had overwhelming strategic nuclear firepower, so that the North Koreans and their Soviet patrons could not hope to match US nuclear escalation.

These considerations recall the conditions which define the shape of the Maritime Strategy. For most of the postwar period, the basic design of the US Navy has been a matter of controversy. To the extent that the Soviet naval threat in major war is considered largely a submarine threat, it is argued that the US Navy should be designed primarily to defeat those submarines.[18] However, a purely anti-submarine navy would not be effective in many lesser (but more likely) conflicts; it would not satisfy the important condition stated.

The adoption of an explicit strategy has several important advantages. It provides a theme for tactical and technical development. The statement of the strategy is also a statement of problems to be overcome, and it encourages those within the service to address the urgent problems thus illuminated. Alternatively, it might be seen as a means of distinguishing urgent from less urgent problems; the less urgent problems would otherwise soak up scarce talent and funds.

In theory, then, the basic strategy should guide both tactical and technological development. It should serve as a measure of the value of proposed tactics and weapons, and thus as a means of achieving maximum effectiveness on a necessarily limited total naval budget.

In theory, a nation (or a service) chooses a strategy, and uses that strategy to select appropriate forces. Certainly, if a strategy is stable enough over the time scale during which forces are renewed, that can happen. The development of the US Navy between wars illustrates this process. Basic US policy – national strategy – was to keep one power, Japan, from dominating the entire Far East. This national strategy defined the naval and military strategic problem, to thwart a Japanese offensive 8000 miles from the American mainland. The ORANGE war plan was the proposed solution. It shaped the US Navy which fought World War II. That was partly because so much of that navy was built up during the interwar period, after the basic naval strategy had been formulated, and while it remained very much in force.

The Maritime Strategy cannot be expected to shape a navy many of whose ships predate it. It reflects very basic and quite traditional naval views, but the conditions in which it can be expected to operate are relatively recent. The strategy, then, cannot be expected to shape the designs of the ships laid down or ordered during the Reagan Administration.[19] It could, however, decide the relative numbers of different types ordered, and some of the features of ships now under design.

One might say, then, that existing forces constitute a limiting condition on the development of any new strategy, in that the strategy should make economical use of them. That is not, however, entirely true. When the US Navy was forcibly reoriented largely towards anti-submarine warfare after 1945, war-built ships (including numerous carriers) not immediately relevant to the new strategy were laid up. Many were never recommissioned, although the mass of existing hulls did represent a potential – which was later realised – to espouse a radically different strategy.

To the extent that the academic idea of explicitness has had enormous impact in the larger world of government, the existence of an explicit naval doctrine has enormously helped the Navy in selling its ideas, to the extent that the other services, which have decided not to develop comparable strategy, have complained of their disadvantage. It seems unlikely, however, that they will be able to formulate strategies of their own, for two reasons. One is that their operations are much more closely tied to particular geographic and tactical situations, and hence much more difficult to generalise into a simple and broad formulation. A second is that, in a major global war, they would be much more closely integrated with allied forces, so that land and air strategy cannot really be formulated from a national point of view (that is less true of combat doctrine). The US Navy is so much the senior maritime partner in NATO that its ideas are much more dominant there, even though in many theatres it expects to be closely integrated with allied forces.[20]

Strategy and Creativity

Why, then, should the Navy need an explicit strategy? The answer has to be that the choice of a strategy focuses interest and creative energy within the Navy on the solution of the tactical and technical problems associated with that strategy: on how to fight. Failing such a selection of a particular strategy or a class of strategies, the Navy expends much of its energy in more abstract debate. Without some basic choice it is impossible for the Navy to place relative values on its various programmes; evaluation is necessary if, given limited funds, intelligent choices are to be made. Elaboration of the strategy can, moreover, reveal significant gaps in naval strength which might otherwise be considered unimportant. Only third would one add that, by adopting a particular strategy, the Navy can explain itself most effectively to the public which assigns its resources.

All of these considerations mean that, as long as it fulfils the basic requirements of US national strategy, the choice of some particular maritime strategy is far better than none. The strategy which is chosen may not be the best which could ever be devised, but that is beside the point. The strategy need only be good enough – and stable over time. Many naval officers have criticised the Maritime Strategy, suggesting that it was extremely high-handed for any such doctrine to be enunciated. The suggestion here is that the importance of a particular choice (essentially between the power-projection or maritime supremacy school and the ASW/sea control school) greatly overshadowed the merits of any particular strategy, although this book will argue that the boundary conditions seem to limit choices to something close to what has been chosen.

An explicit enough choice will tend to unify thinking within the service. That unity in turn should focus creative energy on the most pressing problems.[21]

The idea of having an explicit strategy or strategic goal carries with it a strong sense of self-discipline. Projects which are technologically attractive but strategically unimportant may die, while projects less efficiently carried through but strategically vital will have to prosper. In the past, technological competence was a much surer index of the survival of a given project; the new class of competent losers will not thank the strategists for their disasters. Yet the Navy almost certainly cannot afford all of the new technology it is currently developing. Choices must be made. The question is how that will be done.

Notes

1. Captain Peter M Swartz has compiled very complete bibliographies which trace the development of the public version of the strategy. See his "Contemporary US Naval Strategy: A Bibliography" in the Supplement to the January 1986 issue of Naval Institute *Proceedings* and his "The Maritime Strategy in Review" in the February 1987 issue of the Naval Institute *Proceedings*. An "Addendum" to the 1986 bibliography (updated to April 1987) is available from the US Naval Institute.

2. The Battle of Lissa, 1866, between the Italians and the Austrians, is a prime example. The Italians had the nominal advantage, due to the purchase of several powerful ironclads. The Austrians won by better tactics, and exploited Italian tactical confusion by ramming (which was the only way that they could overcome the new ironclad technology). The lesson usually learned was that the ram was the weapon of the future. The larger, and usually missed, lesson was that tactical skill could radically change the nominal balance of power. The victory of an outnumbered (and worse equipped) British ground force in the Falklands in 1982 would seem to teach a similar lesson.

3. Carter Administration thinking crystallized in a major national-security study called PRM-10. A Navy rejoinder, "Seaplan 2000," was sponsored by Secretary of the Navy Graham Claytor and was conducted largely at the Naval War College, led by Francis J West. Lehman was a participant. "Seaplan 2000" introduced ideas of maritime air superiority and the new potential power of surface ships equipped with the Aegis missile system and with towed arrays, but its impact was limited because it did not speak directly to the usual

concerns of the civilian policy-makers. See Swartz, "Addendum," p. 54.

The Carter Administration problem was partly a reaction to the gradual changes in US posture before and during Vietnam. As nuclear weapons became less credible in the late 1950s, the army and air force came to be identified with the "big war" in Europe, and Navy projection forces (including the Marines) with peripheral warfare – with Vietnam. The identification was simplistic but widely held. If, after 1973, a repetition of Vietnam seemed unlikely, the Navy was faced with the question of its relationship with the big European war. The Maritime Strategy can be seen as the explicit answer the Navy developed to this question. Ironically, as the answer has been developed, peripheral warfare once more seems likely.

4. An analogy can be drawn to the pre-1941 period, when US naval strategy was fairly explicit, and was directed towards the defeat of Japan. The big fleet exercises, which certainly forced officers to look across "union" boundaries, tested aspects of the ORANGE war plan, which in turn embodied the planned strategy. One result was that surface officers were quite able to absorb the potential of carrier operations. Admiral Raymond Spruance, a cruiser officer, was a good example: he won two of the major carrier battles of the war, Midway and the Philippine Sea. See Swartz, "Addendum," p. 62.

5. See Swartz, "Bibliography," pp 41–42.

6. One of Stalin's most successful bluffs was to convince the Western powers that, while they found themselves far too exhausted to maintain large armies, he maintained 175 first-class divisions. Only fairly recently has it become apparent that Stalin had indeed been forced to demobilise and that, moreover, his early postwar army suffered much too badly from a lack of motorised transport to contemplate an invasion of Western Europe.

7. The SIOP makes no provision for what happens *after* the big nuclear attack, i.e., for how the war is to be prosecuted or ended. It is not a strategy, in that it is not a plan towards the goal of a favourable end to the war. Rather, the *strategy* is to *threaten* to make a SIOP attack, in hopes that the prospective results will be so terrible that the enemy will prefer to end the war. The problem is that the enemy now has his own ability to mount such an attack, so the SIOP threat is now less credible, and the strategy less and less viable. This is *not* necessarily to say that nuclear weapons are unusable. The point here is that concentration on the mechanics and tactics of large-scale nuclear delivery necessarily obscures basic strategic issues. The US government said as much publicly in 1974 when it announced NSDM-243, a policy of developing limited nuclear attack plans for specific contingencies.

8. It was (and is) sometimes argued that, should they fail to win very quickly, the Soviets themselves would resort to tactical nuclear weapons. Since the mid-1960s, the official NATO strategy has been flexible response: conventional forces to deal with limited attacks but, more importantly, to provide initial resistance so that the West is not faced with the need to decide instantly to use nuclear weapons (and thus to accept the terrible damage which a Soviet nuclear response would incur). In theory, as the conventional forces are pushed back, NATO would threaten escalation: first to the level of tactical nuclear war, which would destroy large elements of the oncoming Soviet Army, and then to strategic nuclear war, which would destroy a large fraction of the Soviet Union itself. This kind of escalation became less credible as the Soviets built up their own nuclear weapons. However, the basic policy has not been abandoned, partly because the only obvious alternative is a massive (and extremely costly) improvement in NATO non-nuclear forces and war stockpiles (to fight a protracted war). Moreover, to abandon heavy reliance on nuclear deterrence might be to accept a much greater probability that a war could actually be fought in Europe. Dr John Mearsheimer has attempted to solve this problem by a theory of "conventional (i.e., non-nuclear) deterrence". He argues that the Soviets will not fight unless they think they can win very rapidly, and that it is well within NATO's power to convince them otherwise. Unfortunately, it is possible to imagine scenarios for war-outbreak in which both sides feel themselves forced into conflict. In most cases, these scenarios break down after a few days because both sides, fearful of the possibility of nuclear escalation, prefer to communicate and to terminate the war before it gets out of control. Conventional deterrence, based on a calculation of possible consequences, seems much less robust.

9. Ironically, most of the major shifts in declaratory policy appear to have had little or no impact on US strategic war-planning, in that it was virtually impossible to translate public policy pronouncements into changes in the value assigned to different strategic targets. The only major effective change was the demand, during the Nixon Administration, that the President be provided with limited nuclear attack options, so that he would never be faced with the alternative of either firing most of the nuclear arsenal or abandoning the use of nuclear weapons. *That* demand could be, and was, translated.

10. See, e.g., Col Harry G Summers, USA (Ret), *On Strategy: A Critical Analysis of the Vietnam War* (Novato, California: Presidio Press, 1982).

11. McNamara's view survives in the standard breakdown of US forces into their strategic and tactical elements. He would trade, for example, among long-range bombers, land-based missiles, and strategic

submarines. Detractors would suggest that such categorization ignores the flexibility of some important weapons, such as aircraft carriers, and hence tends to devalue them.

12. Static analysis was probably to blame for the decision not to build a specialist fire support ship during the Vietnam War. Historically, shore bombardment has probably been most effective for its shock and temporary neutralisation value, not for its ability to destroy specific targets. However, the usual models are concerned *only* with actual destruction; often they do not even care *when* in an engagement some particular target is destroyed (although this might be the decisive issue). It will be no surprise that static systems analysis generally shows that aircraft (particularly when they are armed with "smart bombs") are more efficient than naval gunfire in destroying point targets. Amphibious warfare is probably the most complex of all naval tasks, in the extent to which shock and surprise are important.

13. Published kill probabilities, for example, may actually be derived from the reliability of a homing device or even of a fuse. However, the net kill probability of a weapon system depends on the tactical situation, and is necessarily much lower. Combat experience, which reflects real kill probabilities, suggests that no weapon is ever nearly as lethal as expected on the basis of simple calculation. This is not an argument against sophisticated weapons, but rather a caution against any belief that very small numbers of weapons will suffice in wartime. Unrealistic kill probabilities do allow planners the luxury of imagining that they can buy sufficient numbers of expensive weapons, whereas wartime experience suggests that expenditure rates will be far beyond anything conceivable in peacetime. Lest the reader imagine that this is intended as condemnation of modern fools, he should be aware that Britain, France, and Germany very nearly ran out of artillery ammunition in 1914–15 because before the war all had grossly underestimated rates of expenditure.

14. The Naval War College at Newport, Rhode Island, was an early centre of US wargaming. Prior to World War II, it tested not only the evolving US war plan against Japan, but also a wide variety of projected new types of warships, including the aircraft carrier. War gaming results were used to determine the characteristics and, often, the numbers of warships of various types. For an example, see the chapter on USS *Ranger* (CV 4) in N Friedman, *US Carriers: An Illustrated Design History* (Annapolis: US Naval Institute, 1983)

15. The current writer would hardly claim to be alone in this perception. Col William Boyd, USAF (Ret) has offered one of the more striking examples of the effect of cumulative attacks, in his theory of *blitzkrieg*. Col Boyd suggests that *blitzkrieg* was effective because the Germans were able to mount successive operations before their

opponents could react to earlier ones in the series; in his words, inside their opponents' "observation-decision-reaction" cycle. As the reactions became less and less relevant to what was happening, the victim government or general staff suffered what amounted to a collective nervous breakdown, and gave up. Col Boyd argues that this model is particularly applicable to France in 1940. The French began with more, and better, tanks than the Germans, i.e., with a considerable technological (or nominal) advantage – and then lost to grossly superior strategy and tactics.

16. The Mahanian strategy was actually publicly introduced by the January 1889 report of a Policy Board convened by then Secretary of the Navy Benjamin Tracy. It called for a US battle fleet powerful enough to threaten European enemies in their home waters, and thus to deter them from adventures in the New World. This official report was widely attacked, because it represented so obvious a shift in US national strategy. Tracy disavowed it, but built the sort of fleet the board had recommended.

17. During the prewar quarter-century, US naval strategy had been directed at a single object, the defeat of Japan. The political context had been US isolation in a world of roughly balanced great powers. After 1945, there was no longer a major maritime enemy, but on the other hand the United States was by far the strongest power, linked to her potential allies by the seas. It was by no means clear how US military forces could reach the most probable future enemy, the Soviet Union. Nor was it clear how the advent of the atomic bomb affected existing strategic ideas.

18. The present writer would (and will) argue that this is too simplistic a formulation, and that Soviet anti-ship bombers are at least as important a threat as Soviet submarines.

19. Ship design takes too long for that. For example, the new carriers are modified versions of the original *Nimitz*, which was designed during the mid-1960s, and whose design incorporates some features reflecting the strategy of the 1940s and 1950s. See, e.g., N Friedman, *US Aircraft Carriers: An Illustrated Design History* (Annapolis: US Naval Institute Press, 1983).

20. Paradoxically, NATO national land forces operate relatively independently of each other, because the front is broken down into specific areas of responsibility due to language and interoperability problems. Thus it is indeed possible for US, British, German, etc. armies to have their own tactical doctrines – within limits. The limits are set by the fact that the forces must match at their Corps boundaries. Because no such neatly defined boundaries can exist at sea, the US Navy must be closely integrated with allied navies sharing the same sea areas, and the same operations. However, the huge relative size of the US

Navy often gives it a dominant voice.

21. The conflict between the air, surface, and submarine communities is legendary. It seems likely that by emphasising the way the fleet as a whole fights the strategy (and its associated tactical extension) helps to unify the communities. Currently (1987) the Office of the Chief of Naval Operations is being reorganised to emphasise warfare-area rather than platform orientation. The Deputy Chief for Naval Warfare (Op-095), responsible for overall fleet tactics, will now outrank the three warfare-area "barons", now reduced from Deputy (three-star) to Assistant (two-star) Chiefs of Naval Operations: Op-02 for undersea warfare (rather than for submarines), Op-03 for surface warfare (rather than for surface ships), and Op-05 for air warfare (rather than for aircraft and aircraft carriers). Each warfare area crosses platform boundaries. The reorganisation may, however, be cosmetic. For many years, Op-090, responsible for constructing the overall programme, was the most powerful three-star admiral, even though he was never a Deputy CNO.

2. National Strategy

US national strategy is the most important limiting or defining condition which any maritime strategy the United States may evolve must satisfy. Matters are complicated in that the national strategy is almost necessarily largely implicit. Explicitness would demand that US national interests be distinguished from current major alliance interests. Although it is certainly true that nations have "no permanent friends, only permanent interests" (mainly based on geopolitics), it is also true that making those permanent interests too explicit may tend to undermine important alliances, and so may tend to act against current national interest.

Thus containment, which was first defined soon after World War II, is probably the closest approach to a US national strategy. The basis of containment was that the United States would be faced, for the foreseeable future, by a hostile Soviet Union. The United States could not expect to defeat the Soviets, but it could try to prevent the Soviets from winning the cold war by keeping them from taking over the major world productive centres not already in their hands: Western Europe and the Far East, principally Japan.[1]

The primacy of Western Europe was predicated on two considerations: the sheer size of the Western European industrial potential (compared, for example, to that of Japan) and the greater vulnerability of the land mass of Western Europe, close to the centre of Soviet military and industrial power, compared to the lesser vulnerability of Japan, an island nation.

There was some hope that a Soviet Union permanently blocked from military success would eventually become less hostile, but the basic aim of the strategy was (and is) US national survival, coupled with the survival of the Western political and economic system.

Containment is a real strategy in that it involves real choices. It eschews pre-emptive war against the Soviets, and thus accepts drawn-out hostility. US military forces, then, must be affordable in the long-term, a condition which imposes very real limits on military spending. That might seem quite unexceptional, but it can be contrasted with US policy in the late 1930s and early 1940s, when war with Japan seemed imminent – and when spending could be allowed to rise far above what could be sustained on a steady-state basis. Containment was, of course, an ideal, and it could never be assumed that the Soviets would eschew a pre-emptive war against the West.

The long-term character of the Soviet threat made it difficult to justify any immediate military build-up, since almost by definition that build-up could not be sustained for very long. Given radically changing military technology, the product of any build-up would soon become obsolescent. Moreover, excessive military expenditure would further depress badly damaged Western European economies, and thus would make Soviet political success more likely. These considerations explain why the Truman Administration so adamantly rejected increased military spending, even after the Soviets showed their continued hostility by seizing power in Czechoslovakia (1948) and by blockading Berlin (1949). Strategic nuclear weapons seemed to square this particular circle.

At this time the US and British governments assumed that Stalin might well strike in the short term. They defined a "year of maximum danger" by expected Soviet progress in producing atomic bombs, sufficient numbers of which it was assumed Stalin would require before attacking. In 1948 the estimate called for war in 1957. The British, for example, planned to modernise their armed forces by that year, foregoing any major production of what they termed "interim" systems. When the Soviets exploded their first bomb in 1949, the "year of maximum danger" was brought forward to 1954, and a rearmament (accelerated or peak spending) and seminal foreign policy plan, NSC 68, was circulated within the US government.

The outbreak of war in Korea seemed to indicate that Stalin did

indeed intend to fight, and the subsequent mobilisation (and creation of defensive alliances around the Soviet periphery) reflected
the recommendations of NSC 68. Ironically, it turned out that the
US economy could sustain very nearly the increased spending level
which resulted on a steady-state basis.

The other important aspect of the ongoing postwar Soviet political threat was subversion in the Third World, the source of Western raw materials. Anti-colonial wars, such as the conflicts in – to
some extent – China, Indo-China and Algeria, seemed to show that
the Soviets could export ideology and weapons even though they
could not possibly intervene militarily. The Western counter to
such wars had to be military, however, and generally it had to
come by sea.

US military development since the late 1940s has been compatible with containment in that forces – and, for that matter, alliances – have been designed to counter Soviet expansion, whether
by direct armed force or by political subversion. The political problem limited (and limits) steady-state Western defence spending.
Postwar economic recovery and growth, naturally opposed to high
taxation and high defence budgets, was the obvious way of overcoming the attractions of Communism. The issue (not always
recognised) has always been how credibly to contain the Soviets at
a minimum price. Changes in Soviet strategy and in the balance of
military power have changed that price and so have changed the
outward manifestation of the basic national policy.

Containment was necessarily a vague strategy. When the boundaries of US vital interests were defined, in 1949, to exclude Korea,
that definition may have led directly to the North Korean attack.
The lesson derived from that experience was that the Soviets and
their allies had to be rigidly contained behind the borders which
they had reached in the immediate postwar period. The United
States entered into alliances throughout the world. This period
culminated in John F Kennedy's inaugural address: the United
States would defend freedom anywhere, without reference to the
strategic importance of the area to be defended. Containment was
too ill-defined to discipline government decision-makers. In the
absence of any more definite or better-understood overall national

political strategy, it was impossible, for example, to decide how much the defence of South Vietnam was worth or, for that matter, how disastrous the loss of South Vietnam has been. Nor has any substitute for containment been developed since the fall of South Vietnam. The basic idea still motivates US policy, but the policy still lacks any obvious or explicit means of comparing the importance of various parts of the world.[2]

Without a detailed explicit national strategy, it is very difficult for US decision-makers to confront new conditions in a consistent way. Examples of such conditions, which are either current problems or are likely to become important in the near term, are the declining utility of strategic nuclear weapons; the decline of the Western European economies relative to those of the Far East; the rise of truly independent regimes in the Third World; and the rise of new industrial powers, such as Brazil, outside Europe and Asia. On the other hand, US strategy shows considerable stability, because the dominant consideration of international affairs is still the hostility and power of the Soviet Union.

The US government is ill-equipped to seek out and study long-term issues, particularly strategic ones. For example, policy-makers in any one administration tend to find themselves submerged in short-term problems. Particularly since the end of the bipartisan consensus on foreign policy during the Vietnam War, major shifts (in response to changing conditions) by any one administration tend to come under attack by the opposition party (which charges inconsistency); for its part, the incumbent administration tends to charge the opposition with undermining its (stable) policy. All parties tend to avoid especially clear-cut policy statements for fear of the trouble they will cause, since they will surely offend some important interest groups, either domestic or foreign. Official statements of US national strategy, then, tend to be anodyne, useless as measures of the real priorities of the government.

Shifts in strategic policy tend to come as the result either of electoral dissatisfaction (itself the indirect result of foreign policy surprise) or as the direct result of foreign policy surprise. The election of Ronald Reagan, on a strong defence platform, might exemplify the former. The underlying surprise was that United States national power could deter neither the Soviets (from sub-nuclear Third World adventures such as Afghanistan) nor Third World revolutionaries (such as the Iranians which held US diplomats hostage in Tehran). In an extended sense, the rejection of President Carter might be equated to a rejection of his policy of relying heavily on limited nuclear deterrence against the Soviets and of reducing the US military presence in the Third World.

The outbreak of war in Korea in 1950 was the classic foreign policy surprise. A more recent example might be the rise of terrorism, which is clearly not always directed by Moscow and so which cannot be stopped by threats directed against Moscow. Finally, the shifting economic balance in the world is reflected in rising US electoral dissatisfaction with the continued US role in defence of Japan and Western Europe. That role clearly made sense when both regions were prostrate. Now they seem more prosperous than the United States. Is it still as essential that the United States contribute so heavily to their defence? There is no question but that their conquest would still be attractive from a Soviet point of view since, even given the Soviet recovery from World War II (i.e., its rise relative to them), they remain valuable prizes in their own right. The question is how the burden of defence is to be distributed, especially if an uneven burden seems to hobble the economy of the United States herself.

Official responses to such stimuli tend to be couched in terms of current policy, but they must also respond, ultimately, to the major realities of the US position. Thus an understanding of those realities helps project forward shifts in the (unexpressed) US national position.

The Role of Nuclear Weapons

The central question is the probable role of nuclear weapons. In the late 1940s, they were the ideal mechanism of containment, which is primarily a deterrent or war-avoiding policy. That is, by threatening to destroy Soviet assets – be they military or civilian – the United States could hope to prevent Soviet attempts at expansion. In this context the outbreak of war would itself be a failure of containment, a defeat. In the event of that failure, US or NATO tactical nuclear weapons could be used to stop a Soviet military advance, and thus to limit damage to the West.

Thus US strategic nuclear doctrine began with the use of the threat of nuclear attack itself to dissuade the Soviets from considering an attack on Western Europe. It has never been clear that an actual nuclear attack on the Soviet Union would stop a Soviet invasion of Western Europe; indeed, it is sometimes argued that the Soviets would try to seize Western Europe as a "recovery asset" for a post-attack revival. The motivating question, then, has always been what happens if the Soviets call the nuclear bluff. At first the answer was literally to defeat them by using a combination of tactical and strategic nuclear weapons while denying the Soviets the ability to attack the United States (through, for example, the construction of the North American Air Defense Command and through a programme of counterforce strikes). From the mid-1960s on, however, the Soviets began to buy hardened strategic attack forces of their own, which could not be defeated by counterforce strikes, and which could not be countered effectively by air defences.

The character of nuclear deterrence began to change, because the United States could no longer hope to win by escalating a local contest to the intercontinental strategic level. Such escalation would only increase the scale of destruction on both sides. US and NATO nuclear weapons were increasingly usable only to deter the Soviets from using their own nuclear weapons. The "extended deterrent," the use of a US nuclear threat to protect allied nations from any Soviet attack (including a non-nuclear one) thus became less and less credible.

Soviet strategic goals were by no means symmetric with US and Western Alliance goals, in that the Soviets had no desire to maintain the *status quo*. Their ideology predicts the expansion of the "Socialist Camp" which they lead. To the extent that expansion was indeed the Soviet intent, nuclear weapons had a very different meaning. Expansion implies the seizure of usable or at least salvageable resources. Pure destruction (which would now be termed countervalue) is counter-productive. The Soviet position, then, was always to try to neutralise Western nuclear weapons, at least in Europe.

Soviet views of the position of the United States are a matter of some debate in the West. Western Europe can clearly be occupied by a large Soviet army. The United States almost certainly cannot be occupied in that way. However, Soviet strategists cannot ignore the leader of the coalition they face. If they cannot expect to occupy and exploit the United States, they can choose to destroy it. That in turn would require a combination of a prompt counterforce (disarming) strike and a later series of destructive (countervalue) attacks.

It is by no means clear that the Soviets have, or expect to have, the requisite capability. If the prospect of nuclear winter is discounted, analysis shows that it is extremely difficult actually to destroy a modern industrial state. Even substantial numbers of nuclear weapons leave vast resources, and people capable of utilising them, more or less intact, and recovery is possible and even inevitable.[3] Permanent destruction, then, requires that the attacker retain large numbers of weapons (such as reloads for missiles in silos) for later strikes, to kill off the recovery (or, more likely, several cycles of recovery). The necessary numbers are boosted further because many weapons intended for later use will be destroyed in the initial nuclear counterattack. Full destruction also demands that the attacker maintain (probably under unspeakably terrible conditions in his own country) the reconnaissance and command and control resources (which go far beyond surviving national leaders) to map out the nature of the recovery and to attack it. The Soviet ability to reload missile silos points in this direction, but only feebly.

It seems much more likely that the Soviets have been driven towards a situation in which their own nuclear weapons are valuable mainly as a means of neutralising Western nuclear weapons. They are, however, keenly aware of the potential value of a nuclear monopoly or near-monopoly, and their doctrine pushes them to try to destroy enemy nuclear weapons from the beginning of a war. This pressure also derives from their perception that "weapons of mass destruction" present the only mortal threat to their political system (see below), hence that they cannot really lose any war which does not escalate to the point of using such weapons. Dr Michael MccGwire has pointed out that for the Soviets the price of admitting that nuclear warfare is unlikely to be practicable is to accept that no war can be decisive: the Soviets can win Western Europe, but they cannot hope to defeat the United States, their ultimate enemy.

Thus neither side can really expect to use nuclear weapons in war, although any war will certainly fall under their shadow. In particular, it seems likely that the fear of nuclear attack will keep both sides from pursuing such ultimate goals as the fall of the Soviet state, or the surrender of the United States; only *in extremis* might a government readily contemplate the suicide-murder situation which seems to be inherent in strategic nuclear attack.

This kind of consideration would seem to extend to minor powers. The Chinese government has argued that the wide proliferation of nuclear weapons might enhance world stability, since it would deter the Soviets from adventures; would they have invaded a nuclear-armed Afghanistan?

This shift is continuing, and only incompletely recognised. A world in which nuclear weapons are really usable is radically different from one in which they are very limited in their application. Geography almost ceases to shape national strategy, since a nation anywhere on earth can be attacked at much the same expenditure of effort. Ocean barriers make little difference, although it does seem that increased range, i.e., increased warning time, might make a considerable difference to some future defensive system. It might also be argued that the larger the target country, the less likely that a small nuclear attack can totally destroy or disarm it. However, governments seem to show relatively little interest in such distinctions. The fundamental fact of long-range nuclear warfare, as it is understood among civilian national leaders, seems to be that enough weapons will get through to atomise those same leaders.

Moreover, it appears that national leaders doubt that it is possible to limit nuclear warfare to the smaller tactical weapons.

They seem to assume that, once the nuclear genie has been released, it will grow uncontrollably. Thus, although both NATO and the Warsaw Pact routinely discuss and exercise the coordinated use of tactical nuclear weapons and non-nuclear weapons, it seems unlikely that political leaders on either side would be very willing to authorise that use. Nor is it by any means clear that the release of substantial numbers of tactical nuclear weapons would really further the goals of either side. NATO forces might destroy large numbers of Warsaw Pact attackers, but the nuclear counter-salvo would destroy many of them. From the Soviet point of view, the degree of destruction inherent in a large-scale tactical nuclear exchange would be unattractive, given that the goal would be conquest rather than pure destruction.

If nuclear weapons are not really usable, then all of the limitations of geography and, for that matter, economics come back into prominence. It can no longer be imagined that wars will be short, because there is no longer any simple way (like the threat of escalation) to imagine terminating them. As a result, mobilisation should again become important. Similarly, in a protracted war, the economic support of the West, via the seas, becomes a major factor. Politically, it would appear that the decline in the extended nuclear deterrent has been the major strain on NATO over the past decade.

Thus a European war, albeit a much less destructive kind of war than has been contemplated in the past decades, is now more conceivable. As a result, details of war-fighting (as in the Maritime Strategy) have become much more important. In turn, discussion of just such details is an unpleasant reminder of just how conceivable war now is. This is not to say that open warfare is imminent; wars occur not because deterrence fails, but because of intolerable political pressures – which do not now seem to exist. It is to say that pressures which in the past were carefully vented may in future lead to limited conflict between the superpowers.

Given these considerations, the United States in the late 1980s finds itself in a semi-non-nuclear world, in which the lessons of the pre-nuclear past may have gained in their instructive value.[4] The mere existence of survivable nuclear weapons is extremely important because it still inhibits the two superpowers from violent confrontation. However, it is no longer possible to argue that, should they come to blows, their war would end swiftly as each tried to avoid nuclear escalation. There is no credible war-ending apocalyptic threat.[5] Thus, where NATO has debated whether to build up seven or 30 days' worth of munitions, it seems more realistic to imagine that, should war come, it might well last months or, more probably, years.

Such a war would be extremely expensive, although it would not carry the apocalyptic potential of a nuclear exchange. To the extent that it is difficult to imagine a nuclear war actually being fought, the declining perceived utility of nuclear weapons translates into an increasing possibility that war might actually occur within NATO Europe, a possibility which, understandably, has not been particularly popular. The problem is complicated because the non-apocalyptic war, while quite thoroughly damaging Europe, would almost by definition avoid severely damaging either the Soviet Union or the United States. In the past, then, reliance on nuclear weapons has cut the cost of defence in two senses: it has cut requirements for stockpiling (on the assumption that the war, if it came at all, would soon be terminated to avoid escalation) and it also cut the perceived probability of war.[6]

These words may seem odd; the Reagan Administration has often been credited with, if anything, increased attention to nuclear matters. However, it is instructive to compare the rhetoric of the 1980 Reagan campaign with the structure of the post-1981 defence build-up. The campaign emphasised the "window of vulnerability" due to the Carter Administration's failure to deploy such weapons as the MX strategic missile. It was designed by Dr William van Cleave, a well-known strategic nuclear expert. After 1980, Dr van Cleave returned to his university post in California. MX is being deployed, but at a relatively low rate. Perhaps more significantly, the rate of new Trident strategic submarine construction is substantially lower than in the past, the funds thus released going into the sort of navy required to fight a protracted non-nuclear war.

In other categories, the Reagan Administration certainly did repair the strategic command system it inherited, but that could be considered a means of precluding the Soviets from a disarming strike through destruction of US command and control. After all, unless one accepts the vision of nuclear winter, nuclear attack is still attractive if one side holds a virtual monopoly. Most of the money provided by Congress went into conventional weapons and manpower.

Even the Strategic Defense Initiative (SDI, or "star wars") can be seen as an attempt to escape from the nuclear emphasis of the past, particularly given the frequent claims that the United States would share the technology, and President Reagan's argument that it is time to escape from the nuclear era.[7]

It is clear that these sentiments have not received unanimous support within the United States defence establishment. The current situation seems comfortable, and few have yet realised just how illusory it is. Moreover, the prospective shift away from reliance on deterrence cannot be comfortable, particularly to NATO allies. Nor can many welcome the increased costs of conventional military forces implicit in the strategic shift. However, the shift seems historically inevitable. The question is how the US government will adapt to its major implications.

For example, any devaluation of nuclear weapons profoundly affects the relative value of long- versus short-range missiles and aircraft. Because their payloads are inherently limited, the expensive long-range vehicles are most valuable when they are carrying nuclear weapons. It is sometimes suggested that current and future precision-guided ("smart" or even "brilliant") weapons will be the non-nuclear (hence usable) equivalents of nuclear weapons. However, they are unlikely to approach the area devastation promised by even the smallest nuclear weapons, and it is by no means clear that the destruction of even a substantial number of point targets is always what is needed. Most combat seems to require the sustained delivery of large tonnages of bombs, and that in turn requires some weapon system (such as a tactical bomber) close enough to the target area to attack again and again.

Another major surprise has been the rise of new industrial powers, such as Brazil, entirely outside the Eurasian land mass, and so outside the reach of Soviet military power. This is a continuing development, but it seems important because it may change the relative strengths of the industrialised areas. For example, at present, the United States obtains many essential military sub-components from the Far East; in wartime it would be necessary to guarantee the security of sea lanes from those areas. If, instead, the same products were available in the Western Hemisphere, then it might be easier to secure their transportation to the United States. It is even possible that the new industrial powers will come into conflict with the United States, and that the geographical alignment of US forces will have to change drastically.

On a more technical level, the newly industrialised nations will probably develop and sell guided weapons, such as anti-ship missiles, on a large scale, as a means of subsidising further development. Brazil already has projects for anti-ship and anti-aircraft missiles. Because these nations are unlikely to share American (or, for that matter, Soviet) views on limitations to be applied to potential purchasers, their entry into the world arms market should make for considerable proliferation of at least moderately sophisticated weapons. At present, the United States tends to collect data almost entirely on Soviet-bloc systems, not even on systems sold by friendly countries to potential Third World enemies. This data in turn forms the basis for automated tactics, such as electronic countermeasures. A proliferation of new arms manufacturers would greatly complicate matters.[8]

The most extreme example of a new weapon capability in the Third World would be nuclear proliferation. The United States has tried to prevent this development, but it has few effective options other than the physical destruction of foreign facilities, which course it has not followed. It has negotiated a draft treaty to limit exports of potential ballistic missile components and systems, on the theory that limitation of delivery vehicles limits the spread of weapons.[9] However, warships, particularly submarines, would also be effective delivery vehicles, and they are not limited in any way. For example, reportedly the first Soviet nuclear weapon which could be delivered against the United States was a nuclear torpedo.

Nuclear proliferation by Third World powers would substantially change US strategy, because it might well be impossible to

deter them from action. The United States might then find herself
spending enormous amounts on the physical defence of her sea and
air frontiers, perhaps withdrawing from overseas commitments in
consequence. In the case of a submarine, defence would be particularly difficult because the submarine would have to be intercepted on the continental shelf, where sonar ranges are inherently
short.

It is by no means clear that the United States has the most to lose
from nuclear proliferation. Nuclear weapons make it very difficult
for one nation to invade another, to disturb the *status quo*. To the
extent that it favors the *status quo* (as in the basic theory of containment), the United States would presumably benefit from anything which made armed intervention, either by the Soviets or by
their proxies, difficult or impossible. The Soviets might find it particularly unpleasant to be unable to exert effective pressure on a
ring of nuclear-armed states on their borders. On the other hand,
neither superpower would find much comfort in the existence of
nuclear weapons in the hands of governments which themselves
could not be deterred from using them.[10]

The other radical change in recent years has been the rise of
truly independent Third World states. In the past, the US government tended to equate Third World crises with operations by
Soviet proxies. It was assumed that the Soviets would gain what
they could from any one crisis, but that they would seek to maintain
some degree of stability by avoiding multiple simultaneous crises.[11]
However, despite considerable efforts, the Soviets have failed to
achieve more than limited influence in much of the Third World.
Underlying problems and political volatility remain, and with them
the potential for US involvement. Now, therefore, several Third
World crises can occur simultaneously, and there is no centre
(such as Moscow) pressure on which can have much effect. For
example, the United States maintains naval forces in and near the
Persian Gulf (to address the danger to shipping resulting from the
Iran–Iraq War), off Lebanon, off Nicaragua, and, from time to
time, off Libya. Only Nicaragua can be described as a Soviet proxy,
although the Soviets have assisted all of the others. Indeed,
perhaps the clearest indication of limits on Soviet presence was

the blatant Soviet acquiescence in the US raid on Libya early in 1986.[12]

The Return to Classical Concerns

One might say, then, that at present the United States finds itself rediscovering some classic truths of geopolitics and, incidentally, economics. What is ironic is that what seem to be radically new, and even very uncomfortable, conditions would really have been very familiar to any US strategist educated before 1945.

The situation of the United States shows instructive political and psychological parallels with that of Great Britain, although the analogy is clearly limited. The important parallel is that the United States, like the classic island power, Britain, shares no land borders with any potential enemy sufficiently powerful to threaten it directly. Thus its strategic culture – its approach to world politics – is more like that of Britain than of France or Germany. Although an island nation can be defeated in the course of a long drawn-out campaign, its outlook is very different from that of a continental power which can rapidly be overrun by invasion over extensive land frontiers.[13] Given this immunity, island powers tend not to maintain large standing armies in peacetime; they can hope to create armies in an emergency.

Anything which negates the water barrier tends to have profound political and psychological consequences. Britain, for example, was deeply shocked by German World War I air raids, which showed that the Channel was no longer an effective barrier. That was a major reason why the Royal Air Force replaced the Royal Navy as the primary service during the interwar period. For the United States, the parallel shock was the rise of very long-range strategic bombing, leading ultimately to the creation of Soviet intercontinental nuclear forces. In each case, the water barrier retained much more of its importance than was appreciated at the time. German air power never did suffice to support a crossing of the English Channel. As for the Soviets, deterrence has limited the efficacy of their nuclear forces. To the extent that the Soviets cannot expect actually to attack the United States using nuclear weapons, the oceanic barriers retain their force.

The island analogy can be taken too far. Economically, the United States is more like the Soviet Union than like Britain, in that it is potentially very nearly self-sufficient. Indeed, at the close of the nineteenth century some in Britain predicted the rise of autarkic land-states like the United States and Russia and the decline of the great sea-trading state, Britain. Britain seems to have been most successful when she enjoyed virtual monopoly status in overseas (Third World) markets without having to defend or administer those areas. Through the second half of the nineteenth century the British found themselves moving from preferred trading status in much of the Third World to colonial or protectorate administration, as other powers began to form their own empires. The cost of empire (both for administration and defence) began to rise, to the point where, in the twentieth century, it was often said that the cost far outweighed the profit.[14]

The United States might be described as the leading nation (even if sometimes only as a market) of a commercial and social league held together by overseas trade routes. The league character of the West is consonant with the postwar US containment strategy: the United States sought, not so much to gain power through control of her allies or associates, but rather to strengthen them so as to deny the main enemy, the Soviet Union, any additional power. As a result, it was US policy, from the Marshall Plan onwards, to strengthen allied economies, even though that has sometimes been at US expense. It is only fair to recall here that postwar US exponents of a full free-market system assumed that the entire West would grow together, so that strengthening the West European and Japanese economies was not seen as detracting from US prosperity.

The result has been interdependence, both economically and strategically. The Europeans and the Asiatics have a major stake in the US-based system, although the very success of that system may have allowed them to forget how important that system is for their future prosperity. This is a major strain on the league as a whole, the United States contributing proportionately more to overall defence (particularly global naval defence), and many Americans wondering, as the British did before them, whether the cost of global defence was worth the economic sacrifice it seemed to entail.

The sea barrier has another very important consequence, for an island state allied to continental powers. It can isolate the island element of the alliance from disasters on the continent. For example, a classic English characterisation was that a sea power "can take as much or as little of the war as she likes", sustaining herself by imports from overseas areas not directly affected by the war. In the European wars of the eighteenth century, the British prevailed by constructing a series of continental coalitions. Britain survived the collapses of several such coalitions, but because she survived she was always able to construct a winning combination. Similarly, Britain survived the disaster of the fall of France in June 1940.[15] However, perhaps the most important lesson of June 1940 is that an island power cannot be defeated by a single catastrophe on land, outside its own land mass. Unless it is invaded or starved, *it* decides the duration of any war it fights.

In 1940 Britain clearly did not herself have enough military power to defeat Germany. That was not a new situation; in 1805 Britain was not strong enough to defeat Napoleon. However, in each case there was reason to expect that, if the enemy were unable to end the war quickly, other states would ultimately enter combat. A crushing alliance ultimately would be formed – as long as Britain could hold out for that event. Meanwhile British sea control made survival possible, by keeping open the sea routes to the Empire and, in 1940, to the United States.

Conversely, it is relatively expensive for a land power to defend itself against invasion. In the past, that situation has explained the substantial size of, say, the French and German standing military establishments. This high cost of national independence has also led smaller powers to seek accommodation with their larger neighbours. In an era of superpowers, it may lead Western Europeans to despair of successful defence, and so to seek some accommodation with the Soviets ("Finlandization").

The claim of relative economy may seem somewhat ludicrous in view of the size and cost of the modern American military machine, but it does help to explain why the United States is not compelled to spend anything like the share of national income which a major continental power, the Soviet Union, spends. Moreover, the perceived (and deeply understood) possibility of avoiding massive peacetime expenditure explains the widespread popular feeling that current US military expenditure is unnatural and excessive, and it may point towards future change. British unwillingness to maintain a peacetime draft (in contrast to continental nations like France and Germany) is, similarly, a consequence of island status. It reflects long-held traditional positions, not current British economic limitations.

An island nation typically projects its political power overseas by establishing outposts abroad, outposts which must be nourished by sea lines of communication. Such outposts may be foreign bases, but they can also be semi-permanent: ships on foreign stations, or cruising off foreign shores. To the extent that the foreign outposts are extensive, they may require large garrisons which in turn require a substantial standing army. The most important current example is probably the US Army in Germany; the British Army in India (largely protecting a land frontier against Russian attack) is the classical historical example.[16]

It may be instructive to consider how these factors applied to Britain, the classic island power. During the Napoleonic Wars, British policy had two objectives: to keep Napoleon from so uniting the power of the continent as to be able to threaten Britain directly, and at the same time to preserve the source of British wealth overseas, particularly in Asia. Napoleon understood the inherent conflict between these two objectives, and invaded Egypt specifically to threaten India, and so to concentrate British attention outside Europe. The British problem was complicated by Russian ambitions in Asia. The Russians had to be attracted into the coalition the British built to counter Napoleon, but that in turn required some agreement in Central Asia.[17]

Almost a century later, about 1905, British policy had to deal with three parallel threats. On the one hand, Germany threatened to dominate the continent. On the other, the alliance of France and Russia threatened both India and the trade routes to the Empire. A rising Japan directly threatened the Empire in East Asia. The

British chose to come to terms with France and Russia (and, incidentally, Japan) so as to be able to concentrate on their European problem. Matters were somewhat simplified by the Russian defeat in 1905, but even so a few years later the British had to negotiate spheres of influence in Central Asia.[18] Note that when Britain came to fight in Europe, her Empire provided large contingents of men as well as vital material support. The loss of the Empire, then, would have been felt on the Central Front.

British state documents of the interwar period show a similar conflict between the two policy objectives, the defence of the homeland and the defence of the overseas Empire, which was a major source of British national wealth (although it was also extremely expensive). Germany threatened Britain directly; Japan threatened the Empire. The British knew that they could not afford to fight both, and also that they could not depend upon the other major Pacific power, the United States, to help them fend off Japan. They tried to appease first one, then the other, threat. Ultimately they had to defend the United Kingdom directly, with unfortunate consequences for the Empire in the East.[19]

As in World War I, bare British survival required free access to overseas resources, both in the Empire and in the United States.

By analogy with Britain, classical American policy has always been twofold: to prevent the formation of any sufficiently strong hostile combination and at the same time to maintain free access to the vital markets and raw materials of the world. Although its application has, of course, changed very considerably over time, the fundamental policy is quite recognisable. The Monroe Doctrine, essentially the announcement that the Western Hemisphere is an American sphere of influence, might be seen as an attempt to maintain the island power status of the United States.

Beyond these strategic considerations, US national strategy has always had an important idealistic or ideological element, the belief that a world of democracies is likely to be fundamentally friendly and almost necessarily peaceful. The Monroe Doctrine, for example, was originally justified as a means of preventing the European powers, particularly Spain, from reimposing their tyranny on newly-freed republics. To the extent that the United States sees itself as having a democratising mission in the world, then, it has tended to become involved in the internal affairs of nations beyond what is required to maintain free trading access.

It seems, too, that it is in the US national interest to defend similar political systems; that the United States would find it difficult to maintain its internal system if it were the only democracy left in the world. To this extent the defence of Western Europe, a region bound so strongly to the United States, might be said to transcend the logic of *realpolitik*. Certainly, many Americans found it difficult to accept the cold national-interest logic espoused by Henry Kissinger. However, note that, before 1940, many Americans were quite willing to accept the fall of the Western European democracies; they regarded participation in a new world war as an excessive price to pay for democratic solidarity.

Before about 1880, US policy makers could reasonably assume that the several mutually hostile European powers would tend to balance each other off. Only Britain was strong enough to pose a realistic threat, particularly since (through Canada) she presented a land threat. US naval strategy, such as it was, was designed to deter Britain through the threat of trade warfare. The key argument in US naval reconstruction, from 1880 on, was that, with changes in technology, individual European powers could present a credible threat.[20]

The US *naval* strategy, developed from 1889 on, supported this national strategy. The United States would build a fleet which, by threatening attacks on an enemy's territory, would deter him from operating in the New World. The cost of dealing with this US fleet would be beyond any but the most powerful European navy. The US strategy was validated in the War with Spain in 1898: the threat of US naval attack on Spain herself kept the Spanish from moving their fleet against US territory, in this case the newly-conquered Philippines.

The free access element of US strategy was the Open Door policy in China. It might also be argued that the United States' position in the Philippines was justified largely because it provided a market in Asia.

On this basis, US entry into World War I on the Allied side was inevitable. Were she victorious, Germany could assemble precisely the kind of coalition which the United States wanted to preclude. Later it became evident that Germany had, in fact, contemplated naval aggression in the New World.

The United States opposed Japanese aggression on the mainland of Asia partly in defence of the US trading position there. Ultimately, by attacking US territory in both Hawaii and in the Philippines, Japan forced the United States into war. However, it can be argued that the prewar hostility reflected in the war plan against Japan (ORANGE) plan was largely due to the Japanese drive to a monopoly on Far Eastern trade and raw materials. In 1941, too, there was a real fear of the combination represented by Japan and Germany. Moreover, US policy during and immediately after World War II carried a strong undercurrent of dismantling the existing colonial empires, precisely in order to open up the world to US trade. While the United States was helping Britain, Holland, and France to survive in Europe, it was also working to restrain them from reoccupying their Asian empires.[21]

Conditions changed after 1945 in several important ways, but the basic ideas remained the same, and were reflected in the containment concepts described at the beginning of this chapter.

Soviet National Strategy

What of the Soviets? From the beginning, their ideology has posited a fundamental conflict with the capitalist West. The Soviets hold that the tide of history is sweeping them forward, and that conflict occurs when the West tries to resist, to impede its inevitable downward fall. Although it is difficult to reconcile this picture with reality as it is known in the West, the Soviet vision of reality is an important indicator of future behaviour. It also accounts for a particular flavour in Soviet military thinking. Soviet society tends to be pessimistic on a short-term basis: things tend not to work, the bureaucracy tends not to be efficient, etc. Yet this pessimism has essentially no effect on Soviet willingness to try very complex military manoeuvres, for example to contemplate ballistic missile defence. The Soviets are willing to try to do the best they can in the expectation that even poor efforts are worthwhile, and that they can improve towards some more ideal situation over time.

The reason is to be found in the fundamental assumption: if war occurs, it will not really be by Soviet choice. The Soviets may actually fire the first shot. However, they will see that shot rather as a response to some Western aggressive design or even to what they may see as an inevitable Western strike which must be countered prudently *in advance*. Matters will, of course, look rather different from a Western perspective. In any case, if the basic initiative is left to the enemy (the West), then the victim must do the best he can.[22]

This type of thinking tends to puzzle Westerners. We generally decide whether to build or to abandon military systems on the basis of estimates of their capability; in fact, we often demand extremely high capability. Such demands killed off earlier US attempts at ballistic missile defence. The Soviet attitude would be that ballistic missile defence is one of several important wartime missions, to be accomplished as well as possible. It seems likely that in this particular case the Soviets signed the ABM Treaty on the theory that they would actually achieve more with no defence but with a more certain offensive capability.

This kind of reasoning applies to strategic ASW. For many years Western analysts have argued that it is pointless for the Soviets to attempt to sink Western ballistic missile submarines, because their chance of success is so low. Quite possibly the Soviets would agree on the estimate of their odds; but their conclusion would be radically different. The prize would be so valued that they would be willing to take their chances. Similarly, they would attack NATO nuclear weapon storage sites early in any war, even though they could not hope to destroy all of them. The mission would be attempted, and less than optimum results would have to be accepted.[23]

Stalin expected war with the West, and Soviet historians sometimes ascribe the 1941 German attack to a capitalist attempt to destroy the world revolution at source. Stalin's explanation of World War II had another, very important twist. Because he was (by definition) infallible, he had to argue that Hitler's achievement of surprise had not been potentially fatal. Stalin therefore developed a theory of "permanently operating factors", such as the sheer size of the Soviet Union, which made the country impossible to defeat by surprise attack.

Khrushchev's great contribution was the assertion that nuclear weapons were different: that they could actually be decisive, even in the context of a very large country like the Soviet Union. Khrushchev called his theory "The Revolution in Military Affairs", and many in the West concluded that the Soviets would begin any future war with the enthusiastic use of nuclear weapons. However, taken in the context of Soviet military and political theory, Khrushchev was saying that only through the use of nuclear weapons could the capitalists overcome Stalin's long-term factors: only through the use of nuclear weapons could the capitalists *defeat* the Soviet Union. If indeed a war to the death were inevitable, then surely it would be nuclear. Arguments as to the destructiveness of nuclear weapons were irrelevant, since the opposition would surely not shirk from using its only decisive weapon.[24]

The next step was for Khrushchev to realise that the threat of *his* nuclear weapons could actually deter the West. The final world war might not, indeed, be inevitable. Instead, Khrushchev might be able to enforce "peaceful coexistence" while attacking the West on a sub-military basis, largely in the Third World. He could export revolution and, when revolutionary governments were installed, military hardware and expertise.

As in the West, Soviet military policy had important economic overtones. Khrushchev had to find the money to pay for the new nuclear weapons to deter the West. He also faced severe demographic limits, as the effects of reduced birth rates in the prewar purge years made themselves felt. Khrushchev's approach, then, was to emphasise nuclear deterrence, just as the US Truman Administration had emphasised them a decade before. He encountered the same problem: nuclear weapons could not deter an adversary from limited warfare. Cuba was Khrushchev's Korea; it demonstrated the bankruptcy of his heavy reliance on nuclear weapons.

For the Soviets, the period from 1964 on was a retreat from the twin assumptions that future war would be general and that it would be nuclear. Under Leonid Brezhnev, the Soviets resumed investment in conventional military forces, although they continued to invest heavily in the strategic forces which, in their view, limited any Western enthusiasm for strategic attack. By the 1980s, they were contemplating non-nuclear warfare even in Western Europe, on the theory that their own nuclear firepower would deter NATO from its proclaimed escalation policy. They had to accept that any such future major war would probably not be decisive, i.e., would not touch US territory.[25]

This is not to say that the Soviets no longer consider nuclear weapons potentially decisive. Quite the opposite; they emphasise measures to tip the nuclear balance in their favour, in the course of a non-nuclear war. Indeed, the offensive element of the Maritime Strategy uses their concern with the nuclear balance to keep many of their submarines concentrated where they can do little harm, protecting Soviet strategic submarines. Western analysts have tended not to capitalise on the other aspect of this concern, the Soviet predilection for attacking Western nuclear assets during the non-nuclear phase of a war. To the extent that such attacks can be frustrated, they can become a way of pulling Soviet offensive forces away from otherwise more immediately harmful operations, or even of destroying those forces. The bait/trap carrier operations in the north might come into this category, but there seems to have been little discussion of the effect of Western SSBN operations on Soviet attack submarine deployment.

Note, finally, that nuclear weapons present the Soviets with a special problem. Distrust of the military is ingrained in their political system, yet by deploying nuclear weapons they are providing the military with the single type of weapon defined as socially decisive, i.e., as capable of destroying the Soviet system, or of backing a coup. A system of keys can ameliorate the problem, though it probably cannot eliminate it altogether.[26] The closest the Soviets can come to a solution is to assign the KGB responsibility for nuclear security. This control would be one of several reasons for the success of Andropov's accession, which amounted to a KGB coup, and which presumably required military acquiescence.

All of this leaves one point unexplained. If the Soviets find nuclear weapons so unpleasant, why do their ships seem routinely to carry them? After all, in 1981 the Swedes detected nuclear warheads aboard an elderly Whiskey class submarine used for training. The best explanation would seem to lie in the basic Soviet scenario, which has not changed since the Revolution: war begins out of a surprise all-out Western attack. In that case, the very few Soviet warships at sea will badly need an "equaliser," and the only available one is a nuclear weapon. In a more limited (and more plausible) situation, nuclear weapons would be withdrawn to prevent inadvertent use – as appears to have been the case during the October 1973 crisis and war in the Mediterranean.

The Future of US National Strategy

Where does all this leave US national strategy? Clearly the Soviets are still fundamentally hostile, and they are still the only fundamentally hostile national system in the world. They still covet the industry of Western Europe. However, the Far East seems increasingly to be the primary focus of US trade. It also would seem a far richer plum for the Soviets, a point perhaps reinforced by recent increases in the Soviet Pacific Fleet. In this context, just how central is the Central Front?

The other question, increasingly heard in the context of a troubled US economy, is whether the United States should continue to deploy abroad a scale of forces initially justified by the weakness of the Western European and Japanese economies.

This question is complicated by the changing character of the Third World. Both the United States and Western Europe wish to maintain free access to its resources. Much of the Third World was colonized by the Europeans, and European powers still retain considerable influence. Apart from the French in Africa, they are reluctant to support military intervention, which might destroy that residual influence. The US position tends to favour direct intervention, as there is little or no residual influence to lose. As a result, to the extent that the Third World, rather than Europe, is a focus of conflict, the United States finds itself without effective allies, and often without bases it has built up for European defence. Thus the West European demonstrations against the US raids on Libya in 1986 tended to cause Americans to question the value, and the cost, of the investment in European defence. In turn, it is US seapower which allows the United States to intervene independently of the Europeans, since US warships are essentially mobile pieces of US territory.

The Europeans tend to wonder just how strongly the United States is committed to their protection. The weakening of the nuclear guarantee suggests to them that they may not be nearly as secure as in the past. The new US emphasis on power projection seapower must inevitably increase US independence of offensive action outside Europe (as the Libyan raids demonstrated). The Europeans must know that US sea control would permit the United States to fight on even if Soviet troops reached the Channel in some future war. To an American, that would be an advantage: the Soviets could never be sure of the quick victory they needed, hence they might find even conventional war quite unattractive in the first place. To a pessimistic European, however, it might well mean that not even surrender would necessarily stop the destruction of his country (as, say, in the case of France in 1940–44, when Allied bombing did substantial damage in the years after the surrender).

This fundamental divergence is based partly on culture and partly on geography. A continental power must either accommodate itself to its neighbours, or it must build up sufficient military power to overcome them, and overcome them rapidly enough to avoid unacceptable damage. Two world wars proved to most Europeans that the latter option was beyond their means; in their perception only a superpower like the United States could balance another like the Soviet Union.[27] Moreover, the individual West European economies are so small that they must all live by trade; rigid national policies have bought only economic disaster in the past. An island power, difficult or impossible to invade, can take a much stiffer line. A large island power, potentially nearly autarkic, can take a stiffer line yet.[28]

In 1987, then, Western Europe and NATO are still the focus of

US defence, but there is some question as to the viability of the current form of the relationship.

Notes

1. This formulation is based on arguments presented by J L Gaddis, *Strategies of Containment: A Critical Appraisal of Postwar American National Security Policy* (New York: Oxford University Press, 1982). Gaddis in turn derives his account from State Department papers of the late 1940s.

2. It is, however, clear that various administrations have approached just such evaluations. The Carter Administration came very close to withdrawal from Korea and concentration on Europe, leaving the Third World to its fate – until it discovered that such a choice had real consequences. More recently, the relative priorities of Southwest Asia and the Pacific Rim have been debated. The United States government has, however, tended to retreat from explicit strategic evaluations of different regions.

3. In the late 1970s, seeking a new basis for deterrence, the US government decided to threaten to deprive the Soviets of the resources required for their recovery after a nuclear war. US analysts were surprised to discover that there were no such resources: recovery is possible because the structure of a modern industrial country is so vast and so complex. The actual character of the recovery is unpredictable; it depends upon details of what is destroyed and who is killed, and upon the way the surviving government functions. None of this is intended to suggest that life after a nuclear attack would be particularly attractive; however, unless a severe nuclear winter set in, there would be some life for many millions of people.

    Over the course of a lengthy non-nuclear conflict, enough strategic weapons might be destroyed (e.g., by special forces or *spetznaz* sabotage) to reduce very considerably the penalty for some ultimate nuclear exchange. The success of the Strategic Defense Initiative (in either a US or a Soviet version) would also complicate matters. Even so, nuclear weapons present so terrible and so immediate a threat that deterrence will probably remain stable.

4. The flavour of the past may become even stronger in the future, if the current bipolar situation begins to break down as NATO Europe and Japan see their strategic priorities different from those of the United States, and as China modernises into great-power status. Historically, true bipolarity has been very rare in international relations. Loose and shifting coalitions have been much more common.

5. General Hackett's *The Third World War: August 1985* (London:

Sidgwick & Jackson, 1978) is very instructive here. Having brought about a very credible stalemate in Central Europe, Hackett is unable to end his war except by resorting to a bizarre and quite incredible limited nuclear exchange, one of the consequences of which is revolution in the Soviet Union.

6. British defence policy after 1957 is a major example of the economies nuclear weapons can bring. Faced with the need to cut costs and yet to be able simultaneously to meet a severe Soviet threat and to police much of the Third World, the British decided to deter the Soviets with the minimum possible number of weapons, while spending their limited resources on the Third World mission. This idea seems to have originated in the Royal Navy, and it was first set out in an internal Navy memorandum about April 1954. It then became the basis of the 1957 White Paper; much of the money saved was to go into a new generation of missile weapons, which were needed to deal with a later (presumably undeterrable) Soviet missile threat. See ADM 205/99 in the Public Record Office, Kew (London) and N Friedman, *The Postwar Naval Revolution* (Annapolis: Naval Institute Press and London: Conway Maritime Press, 1986).

7. Some of these points might appear to be negated by the extent of the security being applied to SDI. However, note that the Soviets are spending a great deal on much the same technology, and that one might argue that they will eventually gain access to much of the US technology through espionage. In that case the extent of the SDI security could be explained as an attempt to avoid giving the Soviets a lead which they might see as a crushing advantage over the United States.

8. During the Falklands War, it was claimed that HMS *Sheffield* had been unable to detect the incoming French-made Exocet which disabled her because her ECM library did not include non-Soviet missiles. A perusal of the major Western reference books will reveal just how little is said (or known) about the new Third World weapon systems.

9. An agreement with Britain, Canada, France, Germany, Italy, and Japan was announced in April 1987. The limits are 1100 pounds and a range of 190nm, designed to cover small strategic ballistic weapons but not tactical systems. Note, however, that for some years Israel has been credited with a more capable system. Other countries seeking space capability, such as Brazil and India, would almost have to develop the necessary hardware.

10. Recent experience in the Middle East (as in suicide bombings in Lebanon) suggests this possibility on an individual level. However, it is not clear to what extent a Middle Eastern *government* would find the total destruction of its nation an acceptable price for the destruction of its enemies.

11. On the theory that the Soviets would fear irrational behaviour by a sufficiently angered United States. The Soviets have always found it difficult to predict Western behaviour, because Western polities (particularly in the United States and Britain) will take enormous abuse before suddenly (and unpredictably) turning aggressive. It is sometimes suggested that the Soviets particularly feared President Richard Nixon because he was able to convey this apparent irrationality in foreign affairs.

12. This refers to the Sixth Fleet raids early in the year, in connection with rejection of Libyan claims to a 200-mile sea frontier in the Gulf of Sidra. The Soviets explicitly denied a defensive agreement which Colonel Gadaffi claimed; Soviet defensive missile crewmen (who were "playing soccer") did not man their weapons. The Soviet issue did not arise in the later raids, when the United States retaliated for Libyan terrorist acts against Americans in Europe.

13. This situation can change radically. If Mexico were to become a major security problem, that development would transform US strategic culture. This consideration explains US sensitivity to instability in Central America, which could, in theory, convert the United States from a relatively safe island-like power into an exceedingly unsafe continental power with a long and almost unprotectable frontier (with Mexico).

14. The transformation from informal to formal empire is described by Paul Kennedy in The Realities Behind Diplomacy: Background Influences on British External Policy 1865–1980 (London: George Allen & Unwin, 1981). As Britain declined economically after World War I, the idea arose that the Empire could operate as an autarkic economic unit, and that Britain could maintain her industries (increasingly uncompetitive in the world market) by reducing trade outside the Empire. This idea is illustrated in a remarkable collection of official posters issued by the Empire Marketing Board, designed to encourage the transformation: S Constantine, Buy & Build (London: Public Record Office, 1986).

15. Aircraft could jump the water barrier, which explains why the German World War I air raids against Britain were so traumatic. Similarly, after World War II the combination of nuclear weapons and long-range bombers threatened to negate the water barriers, the oceans, protecting the United States. In each case, an independent air force, for a combination of deterrence and home air defence, suddenly became extremely important. Note that water barriers resume much of their significance in a post-nuclear era. Even at short ranges aircraft carrying non-nuclear weapons are limited in their destructive power. This consideration would seem to explain the recent revival of British air defence, which would have been of only the

most limited utility in the face of nuclear attack. Note, too, that surface-to-surface missiles, with their extremely small payloads, are virtually useless in a post-nuclear era (except for the destruction of very small point targets).

16. This discussion is based on a narrow (essentially military definition of national power, and an alternative view deserves mention. Economic power is clearly very important and very different. For example, Japan is currently a major economic power, although she has not had to invest in military power to protect her projection of that power. The United States and the league she leads have guaranteed sufficient internal stability for Japanese economic power to flourish. This is an interesting twist on the British informal empire. As long as no other state could disturb British trade with the Third World, Britain could function very much as an economic power, with only minimal investment in defence, largely sufficient to maintain peace along the major trade routes (the Pax Britannica). As soon as other European states began to seize Third World territory, Britain had to back up her trading arrangements with armed force, and the cost of economic power grew, perhaps intolerably. The central question has always been whether economic relations can overcome political/military decisions, whether, for example, East-West trading relationships can erode the Soviet bloc and overcome its inherent hostility. Advocates of *detente* and *ostpolitik* clearly believe that ultimately they can, by providing the Soviets and their satellites with stakes too valuable to risk. Others would argue that the Soviet system inevitably favours political considerations over truly economic ones, both internally (efficiency vs. Party control) and externally.

17 See, e.g., E Ingram, *Commitment to Empire: Prophecies of the Great Game in Asia, 1797–1800* (Oxford University Press, 1981). The "Great Game" was the Anglo-Russian rivalry over India, extending through the nineteenth and early twentieth centuries. Ingram argues that Britain always had to choose between Europe and her Asiatic Empire; his example was the British choice between concentration on Europe (after the collapse of the Second Coalition against Napoleon) and the defence of Egypt (and, at a remove, India) against Napoleon himself. He sees this choice as analogous to the choice between the Eastern Front and the Dardanelles in 1915.

18. For this point, I am indebted to Dr Michael Vlahos of the Johns Hopkins School of Advanced International Studies. It seems remarkable in retrospect that the British choice between alliances was by no means as obvious as we now consider it. However, once the Germans had attacked France, the British had to react to prevent them from dominating the continent. That was the significance of the British pledge to Belgium; the British could not tolerate German

domination of the Flanders coast.

19. The Australians have never completely forgiven the British for this choice, as is obvious from Australian accounts of World War II. The modern British view seems to be that, given limited economic power, it was essential for Britain to split the Axis by appeasing one partner or the other. Appeasement itself was mandatory. The disaster was that neither partner was appeasable, and, ultimately, that both partners combined. For a typical Australian view, see G St J Barclay, *The Empire is Marching: A Study of the Military Effort of the British Empire, 1800–1945* (London: Weidenfeld & Nicholson, 1976).

    It is unlikely that the British ever came close to developing a balance sheet of wealth generated by the Empire vs. the cost of defending and administering it. Rather, at least from the late Victorian period, the Empire came to define the British position in the world, to justify the British view of the country as a Great Power.

20. The argument was that they could hold US coastal cities to ransom, threatening their destruction by naval bombardment. This threat avoided the problems inherent in actual invasion.

21. Perhaps the most extreme example was the denial of merchant shipping for the invasion of the former Netherlands East Indies in 1945. Until 1950, the United States refused military aid to the French in Indo-China.

22. The need to deal with surprise attacks is central to Soviet military and strategic thinking. Surprise must be particularly frightening to a rigid and highly planned society, which almost by definition cannot quickly mobilise without paying a very high economic and perhaps even social cost. Reportedly, for example, the Soviets found it difficult to mobilise to deal with Hungary in 1956 and with Czechoslovakia in 1968; problems in mobilisation reportedly contributed to the decision not to invade Poland in 1981, although no doubt there were other weighty considerations. For their part, the Soviets seem to expect that they will be able to discern any Western decision to strike, and thus that a pre-emptive policy is realistic. Certainly the Soviets have been effective at espionage (the classic example is Richard Sorge in Tokyo in 1941), but it is by no means clear that their form of government, with its concentration of so many concerns in so few hands, is well equipped to use such information in a timely manner.

23. This Soviet attitude is not actually altogether different from that of most Western military men – who would agree that they cannot always have the initiative. The demand for perfection might be ascribed more to the postwar academic view of war, and to the belief that anything short of a perfect nuclear defence was not worth having, given the number of deaths any weapon leaking through could cause. Such reasoning, which may not be entirely rational even in the

nuclear case, has become relatively common in the non-nuclear case, to which it should not apply. In the case of defence against ballistic missiles, it appears that, besides the Soviets, both the United States and British military worked on this problem postwar, without any assumption that leakproof defence was feasible. The leakproof criterion (and deterrence theory) came later. The current SDI debate shows fairly clearly a collision between the "do the best you can" and perfectionist schools of analysis.

24. This evolution is described in detail in H S Dinerstein, *War and the Soviet Union* (New York: Praeger, 1962). This book was originally written as a RAND study.

25. I am indebted to Michael MccGwire of the Brookings Institution for this point; he bases it on an analysis of recent Soviet writings.

26. It is extremely unlikely that attempts to circumvent the key would result in an explosion, even of the non-nuclear components of a Soviet bomb or warhead. Therefore it is always conceivable that Soviet military men would clandestinely disassemble several weapons to obtain sufficient components to build one or more explodable ones.

27. A greater degree of political union could, in theory, give the Common Market much greater military potential than the Soviet Union, but Western Europe still lacks strategic depth.

28. It may be significant that in recent opinion polls of the major Western populations, only the United States and Britain showed strong national identity.

3. Sea Power

All the applications of sea power flow from a single fact: the sea is the greatest of all highways. It is much easier to move a ton by water than by land and air, and there is no new technology in prospect which is likely to change that fact. Moreover, the seaborne highway is much more flexible than any pathway across the land; it has no natural shoulders, no lanes, and must evade few hazards. There are no equivalents of steep mountains and deep valleys to affect passage by sea, although different areas of the world do show radically different maritime conditions.[1]

The fundamental question in naval strategy, then, is whether the free use of the sea highway can be secured in wartime and, on the other hand, denied to an enemy. The combination of free friendly use and denial of enemy use constitutes command of the sea, the goal first enunciated a century ago by Mahan. Command of the sea is sometimes also called sea control. For surface ships, which can detect each other relatively easily, free friendly use generally requires that the enemy be limited in his own use of the sea, although it is never possible to exclude him completely. On the other hand, because they are so difficult to detect, the submarines of one side may freely use sea areas the surface of which the other side at least nominally controls. That was the basis of German operations in the Battle of the Atlantic in World War II. Conversely, it may be argued that free submarine operations do not require sea control in any classical sense. Thus Western strategic submarines enjoy free use, but their security is not considered to depend upon full sea control of their operating areas. By way of contrast, the Soviets do consider full sea control necessary to assure the security of their strategic submarines, which is why their form of naval strategy requires them to construct elaborate "sanctuaries" or "bastions" for these craft.

NATO is a maritime alliance, held together by the broad highway of the North Atlantic and, to a lesser extent, by the Mediterranean, the Channel, and the Baltic. Its wartime survival as an alliance requires, then, that it achieve and maintain command of those vital seas. One might even see the bare existence of NATO as an affirmation that sea control is a practicable wartime goal. To the extent that the Western Alliance as a whole includes the major industrial centres of the Far East (such as Japan, Singapore, South Korea, and Taiwan), it is even more clearly a maritime combination. Indeed, given the extent to which the West depends on these Far Eastern states for critical industrial products, command of the Pacific is required for survival in any protracted war, even a war limited largely to Europe. The current US Maritime Strategy is a means of securing command of the vital seas, and it implies a prescription for the use of that command.

By way of contrast, while seeking control over limited sea areas, the Soviets concentrate on denying the United States and her allies the free use of the sea, particularly near the Eurasian land mass. To the extent that the Western Allies effectively seized sea control from Germany and Japan in 1944–45, one might see post-World War II US naval policy largely as an attempt to defend sea control.

Continental powers, such as the Soviet Union (and Germany before her), have generally considered sea control an impractical objective. Instead, they have followed a negative strategy, sea denial, seeing the oceans more as jungles than as highways.[2] Sea denial strategy in turn has affected (and is reflected in) Soviet building programmes.

The difference between sea control and sea denial strategies is sometimes attributed to geography. Britain, the first sea control power, was successful partly because by her position she blocked the North Sea exits, and hence the Dutch, and later the German, fleets. In modern terms, the English Channel and the passage north of Scotland were "choke points", narrowly defined (hence easily patrolled) waters through which an intruder would have to come. The British fleet could blockade France and Spain (though less easily), ensuring a large measure of sea control. Britain lost this favourable position with the rise of the two great overseas sea powers, Japan and the United States.

It can be argued that, similarly, it is natural for the Western Alliance to follow a sea control strategy because it controls the choke points through which Soviet naval forces must pass before they can attack the sea routes of the world.

Some historical examples will show how choke points can work. In 1914, Admiral Sir John Fisher, the First Sea Lord, could look with comfort upon British (or friendly) control of the major choke points, the "keys which lock up the world": the exits from the North Sea (the English Channel and the passage around Scotland); the Straits of Gibraltar; the Suez Canal; Aden, at the entrance to the Red Sea; the entrance to the Persian Gulf; the Cape of Good Hope (the alternative way between the Atlantic and the Indian Ocean); the Straits of Malacca (the passage between the Indian Ocean and the China Sea); and the Panama Canal. The Germans could slip a few ships through almost any choke point, but they could not pass through very easily, and they had to go out of their way to evade British patrols. As a result, although German surface raiders were effective early in World War I, most of them were soon hunted down. Effective raiding was left to submarines, which, almost by definition, could evade control of the choke points.

The choke points became particularly important in World War I because the alternative sea control strategy feasible at the time, close blockade, had become quite dangerous due to the presence of German submarines, torpedo boats, and mines, all of which would be present near any major German base.[3] The British feared that losses incident to close blockade would tip the balance of sea power, so that the German main fleet would be able to come out and defeat the British fleet, and thus destroy British sea control. The British chose to exercise sea control at the choke points, the Channel and the northern approaches to the North Sea (which is why the Grand Fleet was based at Scapa Flow), accepting the loss of full control over the North Sea itself.[4]

By the end of World War I, control over choke points and been extended well below the surface, in an attempt to blockade

German submarines as well as surface ships. Examples included a mine barrage across the northern exit of the North Sea (largely contributed by the United States) to complement a tight barrier thrown across the exit of the English Channel, and a mine barrage across the Straits of Otranto, which seal the Adriatic.

The Allies sought a similar choking effect in World War II, but were unable to enforce a northern barrage. Even so, until the German victories of 1940, U-boats had to spend considerable time passing well north of British patrols based in Scotland, and so lost time in their operational areas. The *blitzkrieg* provided the Germans with bases directly on the Atlantic, in France and Norway, and that move alone substantially increased the percentage of available time which a U-boat could spend usefully, on patrol. As a result, the rate of sinkings by U-boats rose in the autumn of 1940, quite apart from any increase in the number of boats in commission.

This experience is still relevant. The West finds itself extremely well situated with regard to choke points, as everywhere the Soviets' main bases face closed seas. The Soviet Northern Fleet is based in the Murmansk area, and its ships and submarines must pass through the Greenland-Iceland-United Kingdom (GIUK) Gap before they can enter the North Atlantic. The Baltic Fleet, at Leningrad, must pass through the Danish Straits. The Black Sea Fleet, at Sevastopol, must pass through the Dardanelles. The Soviet surface fleet in the Mediterranean is part of the Black Sea Fleet, and thus depends for its support on free passage through the Dardanelles. The submarine fleet, however, is almost entirely supported by the Northern Fleet, so that the Straits of Gibraltar remain an important anti-submarine choke point.

Finally, the Soviet Pacific Fleet is based at Vladivostok and at Petropavlovsk-Kamchatsky. Vladivostok is inside the Sea of Japan. Petropavlovsk faces the open North Pacific, but it is so close to the Aleutians that movements are easy to monitor.

In this context, the historic Russian push towards "warm water ports" might be read more as an attempt to break out of the ring of natural choke points to reach the open sea.

In some cases substantial amounts of NATO or neutral territory lie on the Soviet side of the choke point. In the case of the North Atlantic, the Gap lies south of most of Norway. In the Baltic, the Danish Straits lie outside the German Baltic coast and much of the Danish and Swedish coasts, including Copenhagen and Stockholm. Turkey has a long Black Sea coast outside the Dardanelles. At least in the cases of the Norwegian Sea and the Baltic, Soviet seizures of territory beyond the choke point might provide air bases which in turn might make defence of the choke point, or even of points well beyond it, difficult.

Although the choke point directly limits only surface ships and submarines, it also imposes subtler limits on hostile aircraft. Clearly aircraft can try to overfly any territory. However, flight over unfriendly territory (e.g., territory bordering a choke point) requires either escorts or special measures, such as flight at very low altitude (to evade radar detection). Since modern bombers cannot fly very far at high speed at low altitude, it is often argued that they, too, will be channelled through choke points in wartime, and therefore that they will be vulnerable to defences concentrated in the choke point areas.

The Special Character of Naval Warfare

Naval warfare differs radically from land warfare. The area encompassed by any naval operation tends to be immense compared with that covered by a land battle, because ships are so mobile. Yet the number of discrete units involved tends to be extremely small: naval forces are very thinly scattered over the sea. Even in an era of satellite reconnaissance, they may well be difficult to find, and communication among them, and between them and their base, may be uncertain.

Apart from a few choke points, the sea shows no particularly strategic places to occupy. On land, victory goes with occupation of the contested area. At sea, occupation is meaningless, because there are so few ships scattered over so vast an area. That in turn determines the nature of naval strategy. On land, there is generally a choice between seeking to occupy land (e.g., by infiltrating or outflanking enemy units) and seeking directly to destroy the enemy

army. At sea, infiltration is meaningless. The offensive objective is
to destroy or immobilise (i.e., neutralise) the enemy's navy or his
merchant ships. Similarly, although one may speak of defence of
the "sea lanes", what that really means is the safety of particular
ships at sea. The battle moves relative to the ships, because empty
sea is of no particular importance.

Poor communication and vast spaces explain an important feature of US (and, for that matter, British) naval tradition. Until the
advent of long-range radio, a captain far from home could literally
begin a war or negotiate a treaty entirely on his own responsibility.
He had to rely very largely on his own initiative. The situation was
covered by a simple rule: the captain was given general directives,
and he was given a book of rules. His object was to achieve his
goals *without violating the rules.*[5]

By way of contrast, an army consists of large numbers of more or
less interchangeable units. Until quite recently, no general could
expect to maintain communication with his sub-units once battle
was joined, but he could certainly expect to distribute detailed
battle orders. The success of his battle plan depended upon the
predictable behaviour of his subordinates. The army's book, then,
was a book of allowed procedures. In the army, one did it by the
book.[6] This would seem to be an important observation, considering that the Soviet Navy is a direct outgrowth of a Soviet army
which goes "by the book" even more strictly than its Western
counterparts.

Vast areas and small numbers make reconnaissance extremely
important. A typical World War II convoy battle, for example,
might be fought over distances typical of those of entire European
land campaigns or even wars.[7] However, it would involve no more
than perhaps 10 escorts, a similar number of U-boats, and a squadron of long-range maritime patrol aircraft, all supported by land-
based intelligence and command/control. The battle would occur,
if it occurred at all, only because the U-boat commander ashore in
France was able to predict the course of the convoy and station
U-boats across that path.[8] Many of the successes of the Battle of
the Atlantic were successful examples of evasive routing: the
allies discovered the approximate positions of waiting U-boats,

and routed convoys around them.

On land natural terrain features would tend to define the possible battle area. The closest naval equivalents are ports and choke points. A blockader outside the port occupied by an enemy fleet need not search for it. Similarly, little reconnaissance is needed to engage an enemy who must pass through a narrow strait (a choke point) en route to his operational area.

In any case, to mount an attack generally involves disclosing the position of the attacker. If the attack fails, then, the attacker himself may be counter-attacked. It is relatively easy, in many cases, to destroy a ship or a submarine or a naval aircraft, *once that platform has been revealed*. Thus much of naval warfare has the character of ambush.

Convoy is a case in point. Submarines are relatively difficult to detect. However, they reveal themselves when they attack their targets. The idea of convoy was to concentrate the targets together with the anti-submarine ships, so that any submarine attempting to deal with the targets automatically made herself vulnerable. The advantage was threefold: submarines automatically brought themselves into range to be counterattacked; if the convoys were large enough, the targets were too numerous for any submarine to sink all at once, so the targets were protected; and, over the long run, submarine commanders tended to prefer not to chance attacks on convoys.[9]

Satellites have not really changed these considerations. Warships represent only a very small fraction of all ships at sea, even of all ships of a given size in a given area. Most schemes by which particular warships can be distinguished are subject to deception. Those which are not require that enormous amounts of data be processed. Above all, the ambush issue is still very important: he who masses to attack a false target forms a very attractive target himself.

The Sea as Highway

Changes in passenger transportation over the past century have tended to obscure the still-central role of the sea. First railroads, then highways, and then aircraft have all moved people much faster than ships or river boats. For example, due to the competition of jet airliners, ocean passenger ships have become very nearly extinct over the past two decades. However, goods still tend to travel by water, because such transportation is so very much more efficient. This development is unfortunate in that, for example, airline passengers who never see water tend to imagine that cargoes can do the same. The key issue is the capacity of the alternative means of transportation, in terms of tonnage delivered continuously per unit time. A second important issue is fuel: a given weight of fuel (per ton of vehicle) drives a ship much further than an aircraft, to the extent that fuel supply limits air transport operations.

The highway or transportation aspect of the sea makes itself felt in several ways. First, it confuses the usual military distinction between "interior" and "exterior" lines of communication: typically, an army fighting on interior lines can supply its front more easily than can another (say, an invader) operating at the end of longer supply lines. However, it is so much easier to move material by sea than by land that the sea is, almost by definition, an interior line of communication. That is why the United States found it easier to supply troops in Vietnam, thousands of miles away, than the North Vietnamese found it to supply their own troops in South Vietnam, only tens or hundreds of miles away. The US troops were supplied primarily by sea, the North Vietnamese, by land, down the tortuous highways of the Ho Chih Minh trail.[10]

Second, it is so easy to move great masses of material over the sea that substantial military installations can become mobile. The two principal examples are aircraft carriers and strategic submarines. Note that carrier strikes are often successful precisely because the land-based air force opposing them must be spread out to meet threats at many points; its supporting structure is not mobile enough to permit the degree of quick concentration required. Similarly, amphibious operations are feasible because it is relatively easy to move large numbers of troops (with their equipment) by sea. Amphibious operations succeed because seaborne troops can suddenly appear in such numbers that they overwhelm the limited defending force which can quickly be brought in over land. Suddenness is possible only because the troops can move so easily.[11]

Third, because sea transport is so easy and so cheap, it is easy to provide ships with substantial stocks of ammunition, fuel, and stores, so that they can remain at sea for extended periods, independent of bases or of port facilities. This is what makes peacetime naval presence effective: the coercing naval force need not depend upon the assistance of the local power. It can, instead, remain on station for an extended period. No other form of military power can do the same. Troops must occupy the area they defend or influence (or at the least they must occupy some nearby country). Aircraft can overfly, but that is transitory. To exert continued pressure without actually attacking, they require bases and support facilities.

The larger the ship, the easier she is to drive at a given speed, or over a given distance. For example, a 90,000 ton carrier can exceed 30 knots on about 250,000 shaft horsepower. An 8000 ton destroyer (less than a tenth the size of the carrier) requires about 80,000 horsepower (about a third as much) to achieve about the same speed. Moreover, the larger the ship, generally, the larger the percentage of her total size (displacement) which can be devoted to payload. These considerations explain the explosive growth of merchant ships since World War II, to (or perhaps sometimes beyond) the limits of structural strength in the case of supertankers.

Only in the last century or so has land transport achieved anything approaching the ease of movement by sea, and in much of the Third World rivers are still the major highways; that is why most cities in the world are built either on the coast or on major rivers. Even where land transport has achieved maturity, it still depends on fixed highways or railroads, and so cannot easily shift to meet changing military situations. By way of contrast, although references to "sea lanes" are frequent, there is nothing in the sea which defines those paths, and they can be shifted without any particular effort.[12]

This relationship reverses inland, where it is much more difficult to construct artificial rivers (canals) than to build roads or railways.

Aircraft can carry considerable loads, but those loads remain minuscule in comparison with those regularly carried by sea. The cost of transport, in terms of building and maintaining the aircraft and in terms of the fuel they require, is far beyond that imposed by seaborne transportation. Thus air transportation is still largely confined to the most urgent commodities: people above all, and, in war, materiel very urgently needed at the battlefield. In the past, for example, it has been a common rule of thumb that two pounds of fuel had to be expended for every pound of cargo carried by air across the Atlantic. Improvements in efficiency are unlikely to bring the figure much beyond bare parity between cargo and fuel.

Some Cases in Point

Cargo transport capacity can be compared in two ways: the speed with which a particular item is delivered, and the rate at which cargo arrives over the long term. For the individual item, an air-craft clearly provides the quickest service. Trucks on a highway or trains on a railway can move materiel fairly quickly, but their speed is of the same order of magnitude as that of a ship (generally up to about 50 knots compared to about 20 at sea).[13]

Cargo containers provide a convenient standard by which over-all rates of delivery over time can be compared. They were con-ceived as a standard (20 × 8 × 8 foot) package which might form the load of a truck or a flatbed railway car, or which might be carried as air or sea freight.[14]

The Boeing 747, the largest commercial airliner, can carry 10 standard containers at a speed of about 500 knots. Since a truck carries one container at about 50 knots, one might say that the 747 is equivalent, in load delivered over time, to 100 trucks travelling down a highway. This is quite apart from the fuel the 747 requires.

By way of contrast, a modern container ship may transport 1500 or even 2000 containers at about 20 knots. At that speed a 2000 TEU ship is equivalent to eight 747s or 80 trucks on a highway, in terms of cargo moved over distance in unit time.

These numbers considerably understate the limitations of aircraft. They are not nearly as serviceable as ships, and any system of moving cargo by air requires vast amounts of fuel. A 20-knot ship carrying 2000 containers requires about six days to steam to Europe. Counting turn-around time, one 747 can make six round trips (60 containers) in that time, so it would take something over 33 aircraft flying simultaneously to equal the ship's performance. These figures are bleaker than those above because they assume the aircraft must be turned around, and that they must return to pick up new cargoes, losing time on each return trip. Note, too, that aircraft are not always available, so the appropriate figure is probably closer to 50. Each one-way trip probably requires about 150 tons of jet fuel, for a total of about 60,000 tons of fuel. The container ship displaces no more than about 40,000 tons, of which no more than a few thousand is fuel. Air logistics tends to be dominated by fuel supply.

Amphibious Assault

Having said all of this, it is necessary to point out that the sea is also an effective barrier to invasion, because some considerable effort is required to mount a really large amphibious operation over a great distance. The attacker must cross the sea in relatively small numbers of discrete batches (ships), which can be sunk one by one, unless the attacker has secured some considerable measure of sea control.

Amphibious assault forces, moreover, must concentrate to overcome entrenched defenders. Much therefore depends on how quickly they can come ashore, and to what extent they can either evade or suppress those defending the beachhead. World War II experience seems to show that, in a conventional assault, it is almost impossible to dislodge an attacking force once it has established the beachhead through which supplies and back-up forces can flow, given the sheer weight which can be transported into the beachhead by sea. However, after World War II the very concentration which ships could achieve came to appear to be a liability, since it made an ideal nuclear target.[15]

All of this can be (and has been) done, but it is expensive. The historical record shows only one failed amphibious assault during World War II (the first Japanese attack on Wake, in 1941), but it also shows cases in which the obvious difficulties involved deterred potential invaders.[16] The abortive German attack on England, Operation Sealion, is the best known, but this category also includes Italian plans to seize Malta. This list would also have to include the abortive US projects for invasions of France in 1942 and in 1943.[17]

Perhaps most important of all, invasion by sea requires very considerable, and often very visible, preparation. The intended victim may be unsure of the date, or of the precise location of the attack, but he must be aware that something is coming, and he has time to prepare his defences. For example, in 1940 the British could watch the Germans assemble barges for the planned invasion, and when they were dispersed it was clear that it had been abandoned. In 1944, the secret of D-Day was not whether the Allies would invade (that was clear from the build-up of the necessary materiel), but exactly where and when, and elaborate deception measures were used to protect that information. Moreover, the mobility inherent in allied sea power made it plausible to the Germans that the invasion might fall almost anywhere on the Atlantic coast of occupied Europe, so that a deception ploy suggesting that the invasion would come in Norway was plausible.

By way of contrast, a land invasion over a border is easier and quicker to mount. Despite the record of successful seaborne invasions, the perception is that they can more effectively be resisted or deterred (not least by retaining sea control); that is what differentiates continental from island powers.

The Value of Command of the Sea

Given all of these considerations, the West would expect to derive several important wartime benefits from command of the sea:

1) It is required if military operations are to be sustained for any length of time, given the need to replace first ammunition, and then

spare parts. Although many NATO weapons and munitions are manufactured in Europe, virtually all require parts from overseas. The United States, moreover, still maintains a larger production base than any other nation in the alliance. As in the past, then, she would be expected to resupply the forces in the field. Note that an increasing percentage of vital military parts comes from the Far East, so that sea control in the Pacific becomes an element of successful warfare in Europe.

2) It is necessary to support US military operations on the continent. At present the United States maintains special dumps of materiel in Europe, which are to be matched up with troops arriving by air. However, these dumps might easily be sabotaged, or destroyed very early in a war. Moreover, any fruits of US mobilisation would have to arrive by sea. As noted above, aircraft cannot possibly supply the masses of materiel involved.

3) It is required if economic life is to be sustained for any length of time, since the West depends upon raw and manufactured materiels delivered by sea. At present Western Europe is largely self-sufficient in food, but it is not difficult to imagine the loss of much of the present capacity in the event of a major protracted war. In that case, as in the two world wars, the sea lane across the Atlantic would keep Europeans alive.

4) Given the inherent mobility of seapower, sea control can provide the West with the options of flanking attacks on a Soviet attacker. Instability on the seaward flank(s) of a Soviet advance might well force a retreat. Once a front had stabilised, flanking attacks might force diversions which might weaken Soviet forces on the main front, and so open up important opportunities. As suggested above, such flanking attacks can be extremely expensive. They become practical if NATO has sufficient maritime superiority to be able to risk major losses at sea.

5) The sea is the strategic depth of NATO. There is good reason to believe that the Soviets would find a protracted war uncomfortable. To the extent that the war would not necessarily end at the Channel, Western (mainly US) seapower denies them that option,

and thus tends to have a deterring effect in peacetime. The same consideration might have a war-terminating effect in wartime. Similarly, the existence of sea-based survivable tactical forces makes it impossible for the Soviets to disarm NATO in a quick air strike.

6) At the strategic level, NATO sea control equates to the survivability of NATO ballistic missile submarines. These craft in turn help to deter the Soviets from any escalation of their own, due, perhaps, to frustration at an inability to reach an early military decision on the continent.

7) In some important areas, NATO sea control can help prevent the Soviets from outflanking the alliance, e.g. by seizing northern Norway or the Danish Straits or the German Baltic coast.

8) To the extent that NATO command of the sea extends into Soviet operating areas, the NATO navies can present a threat which may affect operations on land, or may even encourage the Soviets to end the war. The chief current example is the threat, *as part of a non-nuclear naval offensive*, to destroy Soviet ballistic missile submarines, which are an important (though hardly the most important) element of the Soviet nuclear strategic force. To the extent that this force were jeopardised, the Soviets might see the balance of strategic forces shifting. Fearing that NATO could then achieve a favourable position by escalating to the threat or reality of nuclear warfare, the Soviets might (in theory) prefer to cease hostilities at a more rather than at a less favourable point in the conflict. It seems unlikely, incidentally, that this shift would, in itself, cause the Soviets to break off hostilities. However, if Soviet forces were achieving very little on land, the additional stress of losing nuclear supremacy might well affect their views.

Flanking operations are also likely to be important, at both the tactical and the strategic level. On the tactical level, it would be difficult for an advancing Soviet army to ignore an assault behind its seaward flank. If the front had stabilised, the Soviets might even find it necessary to pull back so as to clear their seaward flank.[18]

At the strategic level, once a front had stabilised in Europe, attacks around the flanks of the Soviet position might draw off

Soviet forces, or might even induce the Soviets to settle. It must be emphasised that, to be effective, these threats would have to involve extremely risky operations, such as assaults on the Kola Peninsula, or in the Black Sea, or near Petropavlovsk or Vladivostok.[19]

Much clearly depends on just how (and where) command of the sea is secured and maintained: there are alternative strategies leading to that goal. If sea control is achieved by the quick destruction of the main Soviet sea denial assets, then the surviving Western maritime forces can be freely used, even though they may still be at risk when operating inshore. The mobility afforded by the sea then makes flanking attacks possible, always assuming that the NATO maritime forces have the appropriate composition.

These are not new ideas. The sea provides extremely valuable mobility, and it can be argued that an inferior navy may best limit that mobility simply by existing, as a "fleet in being", and so by tying down a superior one.[20]

Alternatively, sea control might be assured by a continued blockade, e.g. by the use of the choke points, or by convoy operations. In any of these cases the NATO maritime forces would be tied down throughout a conflict, and risky enterprises might have to be foregone for fear of losing the balance of maritime power.

These are the two fundamental strategic choices for the West: the early assault on enemy sea-denial assets, vs. blockade or some other long-term sea control strategy. The extent to which they are practicable depends upon the available technology, and upon what each would be expected to cost. The choice also depends upon the boundary conditions imposed by national strategy, since a major war with the Soviets is only one of several important contingencies.

Notes

1. Perhaps the most important differences are in the type of waves encountered, which affect surface ship operations; in the acoustic structure of the water, which affects undersea warfare; and in radar propagation immediately above the surface, which affects surface and air warfare. Certainly one would expect ships to be routed to take

advantage of natural conditions, but the point is that such routing is not enforced to anything remotely like the extent seen on land.

2. The attempts to control "bastions" are an important, albeit limited, exception. The Soviets still do not seem to require long-haul sea lanes of communication, although from the mid-1970s on there has been speculation that they were coming to depend more on the Southern Sea Route from the Black Sea to the Soviet Far East. To the extent that land communication (primarily the Trans-Siberian Railroad) between the European Soviet Union and the Maritime Provinces is difficult and limited in capacity, one might see the Soviet Far East almost as an island cut off from its source of supply. This logic was used to explain Soviet interest in Aden and in the Indian Ocean and, for that matter, in Vietnam. However, alternative explanations are also possible. The Indian Ocean is the locus of the important tanker routes from the Persian Gulf to both Japan and Europe. Vietnam is near the great US naval base at Subic Bay in the Philippines, without which US operations in Southeast Asian and the Indian Ocean would have to be curtailed.

3. Close blockade was necessary because the only means of detection was visual: an enemy attempting to come out could be intercepted only if he could be seen. Even in excellent weather, a lookout aboard a ship cannot see objects on the horizon much beyond about 10 miles; he may be able to see a masthead 10 more miles away, or a total of 20. In daylight, then, scouts would have to be stationed within about 30 miles of each other, and to cover any very wide area would be prohibitively expensive. The closer the blockade, the less the total perimeter to be watched. Night blockade was even more expensive, in terms of number of ships per unit distance.

   Before the advent of naval aircraft, extensive open-ocean scouting (except in the immediate area of a fleet) was virtually impossible. For example, in 1898 the Spanish sent a naval force (under Admiral Cervera) across the Atlantic to Cuba to deal with the US Navy. There was little hope of detecting the fast Spanish cruisers in the open ocean, and there was some fear, in the big US coastal cities, that the Spanish would suddenly appear to shell them. However, once the cruisers had reached their base in Cuba, the US Navy could blockade them and ensure that a decisive battle would be fought. The US Navy did try to locate Cervera in mid-ocean by setting up a line of fast auxiliary cruisers (slightly modified ocean liners), in hopes that the Spanish would have to pass within sighting range of one of them. The Atlantic was much too broad for this to work.

4. They had to accept an intermediate situation, in which the Germans could operate relatively freely but could not begin to deny use of the North Sea to the British and their allies. The German battle cruiser

raids on Southern England in 1914–16 were a symptom of the basic problem. However, the British problem was somewhat simplified because codebreaking and other signals intelligence provided warning of German sorties. See A Hezlet, *The Electron and Sea Power* (London: Peter Davies, 1975) and P Beesley, *Room 40* (London: Hamish Hamilton, 1982) for examples. Given warning, the Grand Fleet could try to intercept the Germans at sea, as at the Dogger Bank in 1915 and at Jutland in 1916. There is evidence that the British would have done even better with better staff work. Their failures inspired the creation of the Admiralty's Operational Intelligence Centre in World War II. See, e.g., Patrick Beesley, *Very Special Intelligence* (London: Hamish Hamilton, 1978).

5. This ideal requires considerable self-control on the part of a modern government. Recent US administrations, with the signal exception of the current one, have tended to fear that any error at sea might soon cause a nuclear conflagration. As a result, during peacetime, they have tended to exercise extremely tight control, sometimes with disastrous results. Although the Reagan Administration has done much better, the results of excessively centralised control *within* the military chain of command can also be extremely unfortunate. US casualties in the carrier air raid on the Bekaa Valley in 1983 have been ascribed to excessive control exerted at the overall European command level. In turn, the success of the Sixth Fleet raid on Libya early in 1986 has been ascribed to the conscious decision not to interfere in tactical choices made by the man on the spot, the Sixth Fleet commander, Admiral Frank Kelso.

6. As fleets became larger, it became more important for the ships within them to follow standard procedures. Hence the development, in the eighteenth-century Royal Navy, of special fighting instructions. It is sometimes suggested that the Grant Fleet missed important opportunities at Jutland because its officers were too rigidly constrained by specific battle orders – which had been imposed precisely because the Grand Fleet had to be able to function predictably. The need to maintain independence in a senior officer still conflicts with the need to maintain uniform tactical procedures within a fleet under his command.

7. J D Brown, chief of the British Naval Historical Branch, likes to illustrate this point by comparing a typical convoy battle to a land operation. In European land terms, his transatlantic battle would have stretched from the Channel to Warsaw. However, the forces involved were tiny: about 2000 men at sea in the escorts and the U-boats (about a brigade) and a squadron of maritime patrol aircraft. On the other hand, the capital investment per man, in the ships, submarines, and aircraft, far exceeded what would have been seen on land.

8. In *The Decisive Convoy Battles of March, 1943* (London: Ian Allan, 1977) Dr Jurgen Rohwer has described one such encounter, made possible by code-breaking on both sides. The Germans were able to predict the convoy course, and the Allies changed its course as they picked up orders for U-boats to assemble.

9. Convoy was a success in the US and Royal Navies in both world wars. However, it could be turned on its head. The Japanese employed convoys during World War II. However, their escorts were ineffective, and the convoys themselves were small. They were also easy to track, given the successes of US code-breakers. As a result, they became valuable concentrations of targets, to be attacked with small risk of disaster. See W J Holmes, *Double-Edged Secrets* (Annapolis: US Naval Institute, 1977).

10. This is not to denigrate the value of naval bases closer to the theatre of war, only to point out how much more efficient sea transportation could be. Subic Bay and Yokosuka certainly performed valuable functions, and it was a rule of thumb of naval logistics that every thousand miles reduced effort at the front by about 10%. Even so, much of the supply to Vietnam came directly from US ports, on merchant ships directly crossing the Pacific.

11. In some cases, a defender may be unable to guess where, along a substantial length of coast, an amphibious force will strike. Given sufficient mobility, the amphibious assault may be made at an undefended point. That is the object of current US developments favouring amphibious mobility, the air-cushion landing craft (LCAC) which can cross a very wide variety of beaches, and the deep-penetrating MV-22 Osprey vertical and short take-off and landing (VSTOL) aircraft. However, an attacker can never be certain that a coast will be undefended, particularly when the potential landing area is limited, as in the case of an island. These considerations suggest the central importance of deception in amphibious operations, as in Normandy in 1944 – and in the Falklands in 1982, when the British deliberately landed far from fixed Argentine defences.

12. To a limited extent, and at a very high unit cost (and fuel cost), tracked vehicles and now hovercraft can operate without roads. However, it remains true that any large-scale movement over land is severely limited by terrain features such as roads, marshes, and hills and mountains. This is an important consideration in amphibious warfare.

13. The knot, the standard nautical measure of speed, is one nautical mile per hour, or 1.151 statute miles per hour. Although the nautical mile is 6080 feet, it is sometimes convenient to approximate it as 2000 yards.

14. Containers formed the basis of "intermodal" transportation, the

advantage of which was that freight did not have to be repacked for shipment beyond a port, i.e., by another mode of transportation. There are also 40 × 8 × 8 foot containers; ship capacity is usually defined in terms of 20 foot equivalent units (TEU).

15. In considerable contrast to World War I, which included the celebrated failed amphibious assault, Gallipoli. In that case the allies were able to get ashore, but they were unable to reinforce fast enough to make serious progress inland, partly because they lacked total superiority at the beachhead.

16. The current US position is that fast vehicles (helicopters and air cushion craft) shuttling between dispersed offshore amphibious ships and the beach or the objective area can solve this problem. Moreover, given the speed of the vehicles, the amphibious force can strike over so wide a stretch of coast that a prospective defender cannot be sure of the location of the beachhead until it is too late. Clearly much depends upon the extent to which geography limits the choice among possible beachheads.

17. The 1943 plans are described in some detail by J Grigg, *1943: The Victory That Never Was* (London: Eyre Methuen, 1980). Grigg argues that allied forces had been built to sufficiency by 1943, whereas the German coastal defences (the "Atlantic Wall") were as yet quite incomplete, so that the consequences of German errors (due in large part to allied deception) as to the actual point of invasion would have been far more serious than they actually were a year later. The counterargument would be that the non-events of 1943 and the real events of 1944 show both the problems inherent in amphibious invasion and the problems involved in defending against it.

In 1943 the Allies were only building up the forces they needed. Although they had something approaching the necessary numbers, they did not yet have sufficient experience, as problems encountered at Salerno showed. Nor had the Luftwaffe yet been ground down so completely as to assure the required degree of sea control on the English Channel. Finally, the Allies could not yet mount an invasion anywhere along the Norman coast, because they did not yet have the artificial ports used for D-Day. Thus the Germans *could* predict reasonably well where the invaders would strike, at or near one of very few major ports.

18. The classic historical example is the landing of British troops in Antwerp in 1914 to threaten the German flank. This threat did relieve some pressure on the main front, although in itself it could not be decisive. The British considered a flanking landing in Flanders in 1917–18, but could not afford the risks it entailed, because the German main fleet remained intact. The situation, then, was analogous to that which had inspired the retreat from close blockade.

19. The great historical examples are the failed assault on the Dardanelles and the allied operations emanating from the beachhead in Salonika. The latter are credited with severe damage to the Central Powers, and thus with helping to end World War I in 1918, rather than later. Churchill's insistence on attacking Italy as the "soft underbelly" of Europe falls into this category; in this case the Germans clearly were able to limit their losses, partly thanks to the difficult terrain they ultimately occupied. Italy tended to sop up Allied manpower and materiel, although it can be argued that operations in the Mediterranean were extremely important in keeping Turkey out of the war, and ultimately in inducing her to stop shipping valuable minerals to Germany. Moreover, the invasion of Italy secured the Mediterranean to allied shipping and so saved the large amount of tonnage otherwise needed for the longer route around Africa.

20. Historical examples abound. In World War II, the German battleship *Tirpitz* exerted enormous influence without ever firing at an allied surface ship (she did once bombard Spitzbergen). Not only did she keep much of the British fleet in home waters, but her threat forced Convoy PQ-17 to disperse, thus to become vulnerable to German aircraft and submarines, and so to suffer the worst of all the Russia-bound convoy disasters.

4. Tools of Sea Power

In Western navies at least, except for submarines, the basic tactical units of sea power are not the individual ships or aircraft, but rather organic mutually supporting combinations: carrier battle groups, amphibious groups, escort groups, underway replenishment groups. This organisation carries with it a distinctive style of command and control, in which group operations are controlled (on a detailed basis) by an officer flying his flag aboard a ship of the group. Submarines are generally excluded from this pattern because covert communication among nearby submarines is difficult; submarine operations tend to be centrally controlled from the land. Thus the single submarine is the basic tactical unit, whereas the single surface ship is generally part of a basic tactical unit, such as a carrier battle group.

The next higher level of command is, in theory, limited to more general instructions.[1] The higher-level command in turn may have access to "national [level]" sources of intelligence, information from which can be disseminated to the lower-level commanders, as an aid to their decision-making.

Such national-level sources are not new; as early as 1914, the British were using code-breaking and radio direction-finding to track the German High Seas Fleet, and even to predict its emergence from port. The fruits of this intelligence went to the centralised naval high command, the Admiralty, which then passed on what it considered relevant information to the much smaller staff of the Grand Fleet at Scapa Flow, or to other lesser commands. The structure made sense because the fleet at sea necessarily had less capacity to analyse raw intelligence than did the central naval headquarters. Moreover, intelligence flowing into the central headquarters might affect other naval activities.[2]

Modern successors to the British systems include SOSUS (the SOund SUrveillance System), the large fixed (now, with the addition of big towed arrays, semi-fixed) underwater surveillance system and satellites feeding stations ashore. Virtually all such systems are geographically limited. For example, SOSUS covers areas which would be important in an all out US-Soviet war, but it cannot cover areas likely to be involved in a limited naval war, for example in the Indian Ocean.[3] To the extent, then, that successful naval operations come to *depend* on sources of intelligence external to the inherently mobile fleet, the fleet becomes less mobile. The same might be said for dependence on bases, for example on air bases from which long-range ASW aicraft can fly.

The Soviets see matters very differently, exercising even detailed command from a very high level, outside of the operational group. The elements at sea, which may in principle be mutually supportive, have little direct contact; their cooperation is achieved largely by careful coordination of orders from above. Intelligence information is generally not disseminated to units at sea. Rather, it becomes a basis for centralised decision-making. Soviet style in fleet operation will be discussed in detail in a later chapter.

Mutual support in the Western style is possible (and useful) because the elements of the group can easily communicate with each other, dividing up defensive and offensive tasks. Effective communication makes for effective identification of friend from foe (IFF), to keep units within a formation or mutually supporting group from attacking each other. That is not to say that IFF is never a problem, for example in fleet anti-aircraft warfare.[4] However, note that submarines, alone of Western warships, generally operate independently: they present the most intractable communications (and therefore IFF) problems.

Ships (and aircraft based aboard ships, which may be considered integral with them) are distinctive for two reasons. First, at least in theory, they can be built and configured so as not to be tied to particular bases. They can be used on a global scale. They can respond to surprises. Moreover, they can exert pressure whether or not the local powers agree to their presence. Second, they can be built to keep the sea for a protracted period. For example, ship-based aircraft can be located near the merchant or naval vessels they are protecting, and can remain at sea with them, for a protracted period. By way of contrast, shore-based systems are generally permanent or at least very difficult to move; they are limited geographically, and reflect particular strategic assumptions. To the extent that a fleet comes to rely on such fixed assets, it loses its flexibility. To the extent that it depends on shore-based aircraft, it may suddenly discover that they are not present when needed.

Shore-based aircraft, moreover, depend on their own fixed bases. They may hop from airfield to airfield relatively easily, but sustained operation is severely limited by their needs for specialised support and for stocks of spare parts. Too, for them to occupy distant airfields demands the agreement of the local power, which may not be forthcoming.

The British experience in the Falklands (Malvinas) is a case in point. The Argentine occupation was certainly a surprise, although in retrospect there was substantial strategic warning. The British had little or no military infrastructure in place, but that did not matter: British warships certainly could steam 8000 miles, and the British had (or could obtain) enough supporting ships to keep them there, at least in a logistical sense. So much for the inherent flexibility of ships.[5]

From a military point of view, however, the British had surrendered much of their global flexibility when they abandoned their large-deck carrier force. The big carriers meant flexibility because only they could carry aircraft capable enough to support the fleet against all plausible threats; otherwise the fleet could not survive without the support of land-based aircraft. In particular, only a big carrier could accommodate both long-range radar aicraft and useful numbers of high-performance fighters.[6]

In the mid 1960s, then, the British announced that henceforth their navy would be limited almost entirely to a supporting role within NATO's Eastern Atlantic and Channel theatres, where it could be assured of support either by land-based aircraft, including fighters and their directing airborne radars or by US sea-based aircraft. Given such protection, it could be argued that the British fleet did not need its own organic airborne early warning aircraft or, for that matter, much fighter cover.[7] In this case, then, the fixed scenario (the NATO war) made it logical to rely on fixed assets, which in turn were not available in the surprise case.

The lesson would seem to be that a navy with potentially global commitments has to be able to carry with it what it needs to be self-supporting, both militarily and logistically. Fixed bases and other fixed assets are extremely convenient, but history suggests that they will rarely be appropriate to the scenario that actually arises.

This problem was hardly limited to the Royal Navy. In the United States perhaps the principal naval debate has been over the extent to which the navy should be designed specifically for the single scenario of the NATO war (and, within that scenario, close-in ASW). After World War II, for example, the new air force argued that naval forces were important only to support the overseas bases required for its (hopefully decisive) nuclear air offensive against the Soviet Union. Naval flexibility (which was associated with aircraft carriers and amphibious ships) was saved by a surprise: Korea. A quarter-century later, the Carter Administration tended to emphasise NATO Central Region problems, and thus to limit navy forces to a particular geographic area. Surprises, most notably the Soviet invasion of Afghanistan and the Iranian revolution, highlighted the value of naval flexibility.

As for shore-based naval aircraft, they are fundamentally limited by the distance they must fly to get to the battle, and also by their endurance once they appear. For example, in World War II it was common for long-range (land-based) allied maritime patrol aircraft to escort convoys. Each aircraft would fly out, up to about 750 miles (about five hours' flying time) for an eight-hour shift, keeping U-boats from approaching the convoy on the surface. The very long distance from base made it impossible for a second aircraft to join the battle much before it was due. In one particular case, in 1943, the bomber escorting a convoy used up all of its depth charges quite early in its mission, missing the target U-boat each time; it was then condemned to watch the U-boats, which soon realised it had run out of ammunition, attack the convoy. By way of contrast, a nearby escort carrier could have flown sortie after sortie, and it probably would not have run out of weapons during the convoy's run across the Atlantic.[8]

On the other hand, long-range aircraft are very effective strike weapons, because they are so mobile. Again, during World War II German torpedo bombers proved extremely effective against convoys running both to Russia and to Malta. Their bases were out of range of counterattack, and they could appear suddenly in overwhelming numbers. The key difference from the convoy example was that the air effort was transient; it did not have to be maintained continuously far from home. Ships seem much better at continous distant operation.

Note that a P-3 prosecuting a SOSUS contact corresponds, not to the allied patrol bomber of 1943, but rather to the German strike bomber. It is a means of reacting rapidly to a transient target, rather than a means of maintaining continuous protection of a moving seaborne force. Note, too, that the extremely close connection between a SOSUS prosecution sortie and the central source of intelligence makes the P-3 the closest US analog to classical Soviet tactical practice.

Carrier Battle Groups

For the US Navy, the carrier battle group is the most powerful single offensive asset. The notional peacetime carrier battle force consists of a carrier, a supporting ("station") underway replenishment ship, one or two missile cruisers, two or three missile destroyers, two or three ASW-oriented destroyers (*Spruance* class), and one to three fast nuclear submarines in direct support.[9] In wartime, carriers would generally work at least in pairs, and the ideal tactical unit would be a *battle force* built around three or four carriers, with other ships in proportion. It can also move at very high speed: at 25 knots, the formation can cover 600 nautical miles per day.

This force would be spread over a very wide ocean area, specifically to complicate detection, since an enemy might well find it difficult to recognise it as a single unified force. A typical modern two-carrier force might extend over an area of 56,000 square miles. If the force were imagined as centred at Washington, DC, its carriers would be located at Richmond, Virginia, and at Baltimore, Maryland, over 30 miles away in each case. Anti-aircraft ships would be over 100 miles away: at Philadelphia; Harrisburg; Clarksburg, West Virginia; Norfolk; Trenton; and Dover, Delaware. Combat air patrol stations would be even further out, at Pittsburgh and Raleigh, North Carolina, and enemy aircraft would be intercepted as far away as Albany, New York, over 300 miles from the centre of the battle group. Meanwhile the carriers would be able to strike as far away as Indianapolis and St Louis, about a thousand miles from the battle group.[10]

The current force level goal is 15 deployable carriers, sufficient (in wartime) to form at least three full battle forces and one lower-capability force. This figure is determined, not by estimated total wartime requirements at a prudent level of risk (which would lead to a much higher force level), but on what seems affordable, based partly on past experience of maintaining just such a force. In the past, the 15-carrier force level has been justified, too, on the basis of the need to sustain two forward-deployed fleets, each with at least two carriers: the Sixth Fleet in the Mediterranean, and the Seventh Fleet in the Western Pacific and in the Indian Ocean. The latter generally had three carriers, because its wartime mission included strikes both north and south within its very large operating area.

Experience has shown that it takes a total of three carriers to sustain one forward, allowing for time spent working up or returning from deployment, and refitting between deployments. Carriers working up in the Atlantic constitute the Second Fleet; those in the Pacific are the Third Fleet. In wartime, the Second Fleet would provide most of the NATO Strike Fleet for the Norwegian Sea. The Third Fleet would provide forces for early strikes in the North Pacific.

Each carrier operates the full spectrum of naval aircraft. The current standard carrier air wing consists of 24 F-14 long-range fighters and 24 F/A-18 fighter-bombers controlled by 4 E-2C airborne early warning aircraft; 10 long-range A-6 bombers supported by 4 KA-6D air-to-air refuellers and 4 EA-6B counter-measures aircraft; 10 S-3 ASW patrol aircraft and 6 SH-3 ASW helicopters complete the package. Carriers often embark EA-3 electronic reconnaissance aircraft, to provide passive over-the-horizon intelligence of enemy forces (such as anti-ship bombers). This is an extremely flexible mixture, because both the F/A-18 and, in future (but to a much lesser extent), the A-6 can "swing" between the air-to-air and air-to-ground roles. The F/A-18 was designed specifically for the "swing" concept. The new version of the A-6, the A-6F, will be able to carry long-range air-to-air missiles (AMRAAM, or AIM-120A), and therefore may be able to serve as a long-range picket.[11] Moreover, the actual mix of aircraft aboard a carrier can be varied to suit particular missions.

F-14s, each carrying four long-range Phoenix missiles, can be expected to occupy Combat Air Patrol stations between the carrier and any approaching air attack. The chief air threat, at least from the Soviets, is a mass of bombers, each bearing an air-to-surface missile which can home on the carrier. Typically the bombers launch together, and they do not launch until they can lock their weapons onto their target, presumably the carrier. Such tactics are dictated by the belief that it takes several weapons to sink or disable the carrier, and by fear that unless the weapons are locked on properly, they will tend to home on the wrong targets.

In theory, the F-14s should be located far enough out to destroy enemy bombers before the latter can hope to launch their weapons; a few years ago the typical distance was 150 nautical miles.[12] Given sufficient warning, fighters could fly out even further, towards an incoming raid. The Soviets understand such tactics, and can be expected to try to jam the system: by jamming the long-range radars (both aboard the ships and aboard the E-2s) which direct the fighters); by jamming the communications links which actually control the fighters; and by jamming the weapons the fighters carry. One reason the F-14 is so highly valued is that, because its own onboard radar is so powerful, it retains considerable effectiveness even if the longer-range radar data is not available to it.

Much depends on how well the threat axis, the direction from which attack is to be expected, can be predicted. Given sufficient prediction, E-2s can be stationed most efficiently, and F-14s can be stationed at maximum range, and maintained there by tankers. The Soviets understand this consideration, and can try to split up their raid to approach more or less simultaneously along several axes. However, at some more distant point there probably is a single threat axis, before the raid splits. If the F-14s and E-2s are far enough out, then, they can be concentrated. These considerations explain the potential importance of external sensors, such as land-based over-the-horizon radars, which can provide very early warning.

Once the raid materialises, fighters waiting on the flight deck can be launched to add to the defence. Their efficacy depends upon how much (and how specific) that warning can be.

Operationally, the major problem is to avoid "blue on blue" – friendly on friendly – engagements. In theory, if every aircraft can be tracked simultaneously, every one can be identified and the problem avoided. However, that is extremely difficult, particularly if the attacker jams many of the defending radars. For example, if the battle lasts any considerable time fighters will have to return to the carrier to refuel and rearm. They will have to pass through the fleet's close-in air defences, and somehow they will have to be distinguished from incoming attackers. Similarly, if the carrier force simultaneously strikes and defends itself, returning strikers will have to be distinguished from attackers. In World War II, the Japanese recognised this problem and sought to exploit it by following back returning raids. The counter was to assign radar picket ships and aircraft specifically as "Tomcats", to separate out the followers.

Fighters define an outer air battle zone, in which the incoming bombers are the targets. Further in is a missile zone, in which the surface ships of the battle force fire their own area defence weapons against incoming bomber-launched missiles. Depending upon missile performance and also upon the arrangement of the force, this might begin as much as a hundred miles out from the carrier. Each AAW ship can be characterised by the number of "channels," or simultaneous engagements, it can support. In the past, since AAW missiles were guided all the way from ship to target, the number of channels equalled the number of missile directors on a ship, typically two to four. The current Aegis and New Threat Upgrade systems are radically different from the earlier concept. Each missile is equipped with a command-programmable auto-pilot, which the ship can use to send it into an acquisition "basket" around the expected position of an incoming target. The missile director radar is needed only for the last few moments of missile flight. As a result, each ship can simultaneously direct several times as many missiles as it has directors.

The specialised missile ships fire "area" weapons; the targets have last-ditch weapons of their own: short-range missiles (Sea Sparrow and RAM); short-range automatic guns; and jammers and chaff launchers.

The offensive and defensive elements of the air wing interact. For example, the greater the offensive range of the attack and fighter escort aircraft, the less the chance that an enemy can locate and attack the carrier before she moves on. Similarly, speed is the basis of carrier ASW. A submarine trying to engage a fast target has two choices. It can lie in wait nearly dead ahead of the force, or it can rush in on the flanks. The S-3s patrol the lane ahead of the force, and should be able to detect and kill most submarines there. Surface combatants can pick up the noise made by submarines forced to run at high speed to rush the flanks, and carrier-borne helicopters patrol the area immediately around the ship.[13]

Although each carrier operates the full spectrum of aircraft, it is tactically convenient to specialise in operation. For example, one carrier might be the primary AAW unit, supplying and controlling fighters on combat air patrol. Another might be responsible for battle group ASW (S-3 operations), and a third for strikes. This functional division is attractive partly because the deck operating cycles associated with each warfare area are quite different. For example, combat air patrol requires constant cycling of small numbers of fighters, to maintain sufficient numbers on station far from the force. Strike warfare, however, often requires a carrier to arm and prepare a large number of aircraft for a concentrated attack, flying them off together and then recovering them together. ASW requires cycling, but at a slower pace than combat air patrol, because the aircraft have greater endurance and because (in the case of S-3s) they patrol at greater ranges, ahead of a force. In each warfare area, the other carriers would function as back-ups, and as sources of additional aircraft.

The two-carrier tactical unit is often predicated on the desire always to maintain a spare deck. In addition, it is much easier for two carriers to maintain continuous operations, each flying for 12 hours out of the 24. In wartime, fleet AAW (particularly the maintenance of combat air patrols) would impose the greatest operating burden, so that out of the four-carrier battle force, two carriers might be assigned to that task. ASW would also be a 24-hour task, but the operational tempo would be much lower. The three-carrier battle force, then, could, for example, maintain two-carrier fleet AAW but cut back on S-3 operations, as might be natural in an area with only a limited submarine threat, such as the Indian Ocean.

The carrier group is not fully self-sustaining: intense combat will soon exhaust the capacity of the accompanying "station" ship, a fast AOE or a slower AOR. In wartime, the station ships in turn would be replenished by underway replenishment groups (URGs) shuttling between forward bases and the battle groups. A typical URG might include a tanker (AO), one or more ammunition ships (AE), and a combat stores ship (AFS), escorted by a missile destroyer and three frigates. Current US plans call for 10 such groups.[14] They in turn would be supported by point-to-point ships, carrying fuel, weapons, and essential stores out to the forward bases.

These three levels of logistical support reflect three levels of sophistication. The "station ships" carry a combination of fuel, weapons, and stores, and are designed specially for very fast replenishment, since a ship being replenished cannot fight. The ships of the URGs are also designed for quick transfer at sea, but they are more specialised (although some tankers also carry limited amounts of ammunition). In each case, rapid replenishment requires that materiel be carried quickly to the upper deck, in quantities easy to transfer by line (or by helicopter), and that makes stowage aboard the underway replenishment ship relatively inefficient, in terms of weight per unit volume. Finally, the point-to-point ships are essentially civilian shipping, designed to carry materiel in quantity.

Surface Action Groups

The US Navy is unique, not only in maintaining a substantial full-deck carrier force, but also in maintaining surface action groups built around its battleships. The rationale is that, in peacetime, the Navy must be able to deal with numerous (and possibly simultaneous) surprises in the Third World. The carrier force is very limited; a battleship can provide naval force in a Third World crisis, relieving a carrier and thus perhaps making it easier to operate the carriers in more concentrated, hence tactically more effective, groups. In wartime surface action groups might support amphibious operations. They might also be used in areas of slightly lower threat than those near the Soviet Union, such as the Caribbean or the South China Sea.

In theory, a battleship, with her immense surface-to-surface firepower (16-inch guns plus missiles) would operate with one Aegis missile cruiser and three Aegis destroyers (DDG 51 class). The four Aegis systems would provide substantial anti-aircraft coverage. The ships carrying them would also provide a useful ASW screen. Tomahawk and Harpoon missiles aboard all five ships could deliver a useful strike against ship or land targets. Blimps or other air vehicles (such as RPVs) can provide over-the-horizon surveillance, both of the sea and of incoming aircraft.

Compared to the carrier battle group, what is missing is long-range coverage, which seems less important in the Third World than in the anti-Soviet scenario. For example, Aegis cannot kill Soviet anti-ship bombers delivering their missiles outside its range, although it may well be able to kill off the missiles themselves, and so save the force. The other missing element is sustained long-range strike firepower: missiles are relatively inefficient ways of delivering high explosives. A battleship-based surface action group might well be able to launch about 200 Tomahawks, carrying a total of about 100 tons of explosives. A single carrier's magazines accommodate about 20 times as much in bomb tonnage.

The 16-inch gun is a unique resource. Unlike an aircraft or a cruise missile, its shell is virtually impossible to counter. Moreover, unlike an aircraft, the shell is unmanned, and so does not present an enemy with the opportunity to capture pilots. The gun, moreover, can deliver shells at a very considerable rate, between one and two rounds per gun per minute, for shock effect. This attribute should be particularly valuable in an amphibious operation, as (given sufficient reconnaissance) the battleship should be able to destroy enemy ground forces massing for counterattack. A battleship carries about a thousand shells.

Against these virtues, range is limited to about 20 miles. Future sub-calibre shells may reach two or three times that range, carrying large numbers of bomblets or other submunitions. In their case effectiveness will be determined by the extent to which air spotting (for fire control) is available. The most likely solution is a light-weight remotely piloted vehicle carried by the battleship. The battleship *Iowa* tested such vehicles late in 1985.

The notional wartime surface action group does not include an underway replenishment ship, because, given its limited sustained long-range firepower, it would not be expected to sustain intense combat for very long. In peacetime, however, surface action groups built around the battleships will often be accompanied by station ships, because they must be able to sustain themselves to maintain US naval presence in crisis areas of the Third World, such as the Middle East.

ASW

The current US naval force structure includes escorts for seven military convoys (each with one missile destroyer and nine frigates) and for amphibious groups (a total of 14 missile destroyers and eight frigates).

Only the carriers are provided with organic long-range ASW aircraft. To the extent that it is valuable to provide such aircraft ahead of a moving force, at present they must be land-based P-3 Orions. One might, therefore, imagine a squadron of Orions assigned to each of the seven notional military convoys, to provide

continuous distant air coverage in relays. That in turn might limit
the efficacy of the convoy escort groups in areas far from US bases
– in surprise scenarios in the Third World, for example.[15]

The other major NATO navies are similarly organised, although
the details tend to be less public.[16] The typical tactical units are a
small carrier group built around a helicopter/VSTOL carrier, and
an ASW group consisting of frigates, often accompanied by a "station" ship. A British ASW support force consisting of an *Invincible*,
several missile destroyers, and several ASW frigates would exemplify the first. As for the second, the Dutch, for example, plan to
maintain two open-ocean escort groups, built around two elaborate command/control destroyers (the *Tromps*) and the "Standard" frigates, and one inshore group, built around the new "M"
class frigates. The two open-ocean groups would be supported by
the two *Poolster* class underway replenishment ships, which can
also support ASW helicopters of their own. Similarly, the Canadian Navy operates three underway-replenishment ships, and can,
in theory, operate three ASW groups (one in the Pacific).[17]

An ASW support group would have one of three roles. It could
support a formation at sea, detecting and destroying submarines
approaching or actually attacking it. For example, in wartime the
British ASW support group would provide distant ASW cover for
the NATO Strike Fleet. The same type of group would be able to
support a vital convoy, or an amphibious force in transit to its
objective, or an underway replenishment force. Second, the support group can patrol a choke point against submarines trying to
pass through. Third, it might occupy an open-ocean position, either
prosecuting long-range contacts or coming to the assistance of a
convoy under heavy attack. The first and last roles recall World
War II experience, when convoy was the primary ASW strategy
and it was soon discovered that escort groups which always
worked together were most efficient. The "station ships" had their
origin in the wartime allied use of tankers for the underway replenishment of convoy escorts; their successors can also supply
replacement weapons.[18]

The reach of the frigates of the group is limited by the range of
their sensors.[19] Water conditions limit sonars, which are (both

currently and almost certainly in future) the only effective submarine detectors, to three possible working modes: direct path, bottom-bounce, and convergence zone. Direct path is radar-like operation: the sonar continuously tracks its target. The extent to which a particular sonar can fully exploit water conditions depends upon its frequency (low frequency makes for long range), its power output, and the quality of its signal processing (to pick faint echoes out from the background noise). Current medium-frequency sonars, such as the British Type 2016, are limited by frequency; they are unlikely to be effective beyond about 8000 to 10,000 yards. Lower-frequency sonars, such as the US SQS-53, can sometimes reach out as far as 20,000 yards in the direct-path mode.

All sonar performance figures are subject to the vital *caveat* that they are subject to local conditions. For example, even the largest low-frequency sonars rarely achieve their full theoretical direct-path ranges, but on occasion they can substantially exceed it. An early postwar US medium-frequency sonar, SQS-4, was rated at a range of 5000 yards (which was its usual performance), but in a test under unusually favourable conditions it was able to track a target at 19,000 yards. Detailed sonar performance figures tend to refer to specific water and target conditions, and the figures usually published are nominal averages.

In deep water, as in the Atlantic, sound waves directed down from a ship are refracted around to bend back up, to meet the surface in a "convergence zone". The range to the convergence zone depends upon water conditions; in the Atlantic, the zone is about 35 miles (70,000) yards from a ship, and about 5 miles wide. In the Mediterranean, it might be 15 to 20 miles out and about 3 miles wide. It forms a circle around the ship, and additional zones are located at equal distances (in the Atlantic, at 70, 105, 140, etc. miles). To reach the convergence zone a sonar has to be able to operate at low frequency. The space between the direct-path zone, which may reach out to 20,000 yards, and the convergence zone, at 70,000, is blank; once a submarine has passed through the convergence zone it appears (to a ship) to vanish, at least until it reaches either the direct-path/bottom bounce zone or another (more distant) convergence zone.

The only intermediate mode of detection is bottom-bounce: sonar signals are directed to the bottom, and reflected from there onto the submarine. A typical bottom-bounce detection (depending on water depth) might be achieved at 40,000 yards. Bottom-bounce should provide the sort of detailed tracking available from the direct path, but like the convergence zone it applies only to a limited zone around a ship and is highly dependent on the composition of the sea bottom, the depth of the water, and other factors.

Similar considerations apply to a submarine, the most important difference being that a submarine can seek to operate at the depth at which her sonar is most effective, and can make use of changes of depth to track her target. The submarine may also be able to bounce her sonar signals off the surface.

From a tactical point of view, the most important point is that an ASW weapon, be it a homing torpedo or an atomic depth bomb, has only a finite effective or lethal volume. In the case of the torpedo, it would be the volume within which the weapon has to be if it is to home on, and catch, the target submarine before the latter can escape. Effectiveness depends, then, on placing the weapon close enough to the target. Convergence zone detection is nothing like precise enough for such placement, whereas direct path (and possibly bottom bounce) can be.

Low frequency means long wavelength, and, therefore, a large sonar. For example, the dome of the US SQS-53, the largest in current Western service, is about the size of a large personnel boat. Navies which expect to operate in relatively shallow water, such as the North Sea, tend to limit themselves to medium frequency, as lower frequency would buy them very little: there is no possibility of convergence zone operation. Finally, the popularity of the towed array can be traced in large part to its ability to operate at very low frequency (because it is so long), and hence to achieve convergence zone ranges. Existing towed arrays operate passively: they listen for submarine signals. By way of comparison, hull sonars tend to be designed for active operation (producing a signal which echoes off a submarine hull), although many of them can operate passively.

These considerations explain why and how frigates carry helicopters. Targets detected in the direct path zone can be attacked by a weapon directed by the ship: the US Navy uses a ballistic missile, Asroc. Many NATO navies use small helicopters, primarily the Lynx, instead. They are, effectively, manned and reusable missiles, since they carry no anti-submarine sensors of their own. Instead, they drop their torpedoes on command, as directed by the ship launching them. The advantage of a small helicopter is that it imposes only a relatively small burden on the launching ship; it can also be used to detect surface ships beyond the horizon, and so to support a long-range anti-ship missile, such as Harpoon or Exocet.

Any attack on a convergence-zone target demands much more. The area defined by the detecting sonar and by the width of the convergence zone must be searched and the submarine re-detected before it can be attacked. That is why US frigates with convergence-zone sonars carry helicopters equipped with sonobuoys. Thus a US LAMPS I helicopter drops its sonobuoys, relays their passive data back to its parent ship for analysis, and then attacks on command based on that analysis. Similarly, the new British Type 23 ("Duke" class) frigate, which is to be equipped with a towed array, is also to be equipped with the new large EH-101 helicopter, incorporating its own sonar and sonobuoys. In each case, the ship and her helicopter are part of a single tactical unit. On a larger scale, SOSUS defines an area of ocean in which a submarine is located; the P-3 prosecuting that contact is exactly analogous to the helicopter flying out to re-detect a towed array contact.

Some towed-array frigates are too small to operate helicopters. They must, therefore, operate within range of shore-based maritime patrol aircraft, which can prosecute their contacts, re-detecting and attacking.

The support group is limited in the area it can search, at best to within perhaps two or three convergence zones of its ships. Unless it has some integral maintenance facility, moreover, it may be limited in the extent to which its ships can maintain helicopters continuously airborne. For example, in principle the LAMPS I helicopters flown by several frigates could clear a lane ahead of the ships, sowing sonobuoys and then checking to see whether they detected submarines. However, the frigates do not carry sufficient fuel or spare parts to maintain such a screen; that would take something closer to a small aircraft carrier. By way of contrast, a carrier like the British *Invincible* can maintain a screen ahead of a moving force (in her case, of large Sea King helicopters deploying dipping sonars). She can also operate enough such helicopters to afford to detach one or more to investigate a distant contact, without fatally weakening the force as a whole.[20]

One final point is very important. The two most important current Western ASW weapons are guided torpedos with high-explosive warheads and unguided nuclear depth bombs. Given a general preference for non-nuclear warfare, the latter are clearly insurance against any risk that the torpedoes will fail in combat: that they will be too slow, or that they will not run deep enough, or that their warheads will not be lethal enough. In recent years it has been suggested that new Soviet submarines, both the deep-diving and very fast "Alfa" and the enormous missile-firing "Oscar" and "Typhoon," cannot be countered by the lightweight weapons carried by NATO surface ships and naval aircraft.[21] The usual conclusion is that successful wartime ASW will require the release of at least some nuclear weapons.

That seems extremely unlikely, given the general retreat from nuclear weapons in other military contexts. Moreover, because governments control their nuclear weapons so tightly, it is by no means certain that they will be released when needed. It seems much more likely that greater attention will be paid to improve weapon effectiveness. In this respect the success of a British Stingray lightweight torpedo against an anchored and submerged target late in 1985 was extremely encouraging. The US Navy appears to have its own reasons to assume that its torpedoes will be effective. For example, in 1986 it abandoned plans to provide a nuclear warhead for the new submarine stand-off (Sea Lance) missile. Instead, Sea Lance will carry a non-nuclear lightweight torpedo.

This is a very important development. As long as the Western navies *appear* to contemplate using nuclear weapons as insurance against the ineffectiveness of torpedo warheads (rather than, as on land, against the overall failure of a sustained conventional defence), then the Soviets may be encouraged to contemplate using their own naval nuclear weapons. Ironically, the question is so technical that few policy-makers have probably addressed it, at least until recently. Now the US Navy has taken the lead in making its conventional torpedoes so effective that nuclear ASW weapons can be foresworn.

The motive is more than political. Nuclear weapons, even nuclear depth charges, seem so destructive that many officers aboard surface ships and submarines fear that their craft will suffer from the weapons they launch at enemy submarines. The weapons may therefore literally be physically unusable. It may be that only aircraft can launch these weapons with anything approaching impunity.[22]

Amphibious Assault

Besides the carrier battle group or battle force, the major offensive arm of sea power is the amphibious assault group. It is not as well defined as the carrier group, but the principal types are the helicopter carrier (in US service, LHA or LHD or LPH), the well-deck ship (LPD or LSD, depending on the extent to which troops can be carried), and the beaching ship (LST). Men and materiel go ashore by a combination of helicopters and smaller beaching or amphibious craft, the helicopters providing tactical depth and a measure of tactical surprise. Because they can appear from a substantial distance, a defender cannot be sure of where the assault will occur until they actually land. For example, in 1985 the Royal Marines argued that they could not expect successfully to assault defended areas unless they could fly off at least 10 helicopters (carrying 300 men) for the first wave. The slower over-the-beach craft are needed to bring heavy equipment, such as tanks, ashore. As in the case of overseas transportation, weight still precludes easy air transportation.

Existing over-the-beach craft (except for US LSTs) are limited to about 10 to 15 knots, because they must have broad bow ramps

over which to unload their vehicles. As a result, they are quite
vulnerable to fire from the beach. This vulnerability is worst when
the craft actually beach to unload. Moreover, due to their limited
speed, they limit the amphibious group to a position close offshore,
where it may well be vulnerable to missile and even gun fire. Current US doctrine, then, is to provide much faster over the beach
craft in the form of air cushion vehicles (LCACs). The amphibious
group could remain over the horizon, out of the range of the
defenders, while LCACs and helicopters landed the initial assault
troops and their equipment.

Once the beach has been secured, further build-up can
presumably be supplied by commercial-type ships. Certainly even
the US Navy has nothing approaching the organic lifting capacity
required to sustain such a build-up.

All of this might seem superficially similar to what was done so
many times during World War II; indeed, some of the smaller craft
are virtually duplicates of their wartime predecessors. However,
the context has changed radically. Beginning in the late 1940s,
planners worried that the usual concentration of amphibious shipping would be an attractive nuclear target. Helicopters were seen
as a way of dispersing the amphibious assault fleet, and they
proved successful at Suez in 1956. After the nuclear threat had
faded, it was replaced by the threat of land-based anti-ship missiles, which seemed so deadly to thin-skinned amphibious ships.
Hence the current effort to keep the ships well offshore, relying on
the speed of the assault vehicles. The LCACs have the additional
virtue of being able to cross much more varied beaches than their
predecessors, so that their landing areas will be less predictable,
and of being able to discharge their cargo well inland: not for them
the terror of the surf line.

What is still missing is the massed gunfire support common in
World War II landings. The US Navy comes closest with the
16-inch guns on its battleships, but the sheer numbers of expendable surface warships are gone. Aircraft can substitute to some
extent, and ideally carriers would support any major landing.
The US Marines operate substantial numbers of Harrier VSTOL
fighter-bombers, which they expect to base ashore after landing.

However, these aircraft can share the flight decks, otherwise devoted to helicopters, of the big amphibious carriers.

Submarines

Submarines are very different from surface ships, because they are ill-adapted to operate in close concert either with each other or with other naval units. Their advantage of effective invisibility makes it virtually impossible for surface ships and aircraft to communicate freely with them. Although it is possible for one submarine to communicate with another (by sound signal), such communication is unpopular because it reveals the presence and, generally, the positions, of the submarines.

Schemes for submarine tactical communication tend, then, to be cumbersome at best. A submarine can receive very low frequency (VLF) radio signals at shallow depth, and extremely low frequency (ELF) at almost any depth. To receive higher-frequency signals (which carry more information per unit time), the submarine must place an antenna either at or above the surface. Typically submarines come up to receive radio signals at scheduled times. If the submarine is fitted to receive ELF signals (which carry very little information), they can be used to call her to come up to receive radio signals. Alternatively, a submarine operating close to surface ships could be called up by means of a sound signal, such as a coded sonar burst. Even then, the submarine commander probably would prefer not to send his own sonar signals; he would come up to receive a radio message. In any case, communication would be somewhat awkward, and at best it would entail some substantial delays. At this point only the United States (and probably the Soviet Union) operate ELF signalling systems, intended primarily to send emergency messages to strategic submarines.

Naval warfare often involves stealth, and submarines are its stealthiest manifestation. Submarine vs. submarine engagements tend to be ambushes, and submarine commanders may be loath to use their active sonars. They prefer to listen, plotting the direction to the sound generated by another submarine, and gradually building up sufficient data to engage. To the extent that submarine operation depends so heavily on sound reception, silencing is an important way of avoiding interference with that received sound, as well as a means of avoiding detection by the enemy.

Another important submarine characteristic is very limited volume. Typically a submarine of a given displacement has an internal or usable volume comparable to that of a surface ship of much less than half its displacement. For example, a large *Los Angeles* class submarine, displacing 6900 tons, probably has no more than the usable volume or deck space of a 3000-ton frigate. As a result, weapon capacity is very limited: probably no submarine in the world carries more than 30 torpedoes, and very few carry that many. Some do carry more weapons, in the form of missiles in vertical or near-vertical tubes, but such stowage is both specialised and limited. The result may be that, the greater the variety of weapons available to submarines, the fewer of any one type a submarine can carry. The problem is aggravated by the fact that a submarine cannot generally have her weapons replaced at sea. Departing on a lengthy peacetime patrol, she must carry weapons adapted to the wide variety of scenarios which may occur during that patrol.

Underwater speed and endurance are also important. In smooth water, surface ships can make speeds of over 30 knots, about 34 statute miles per hour. All but the largest are, however, limited by rough weather to substantially lower speeds, and hull sonar operation generally limits surface ships to about 20 to 25 knots. Thus a submarine capable of, say, 25 knots underwater can often escape from nominally faster surface ships.

However, the submarine may not be able to maintain that speed for very long. Nuclear submarines do have, in effect, indefinite endurance. The storage batteries of diesel-electric submarines are usually good for no more than an hour at full speed; underwater endurance may be several days at much lower "creep" speeds. For example, the Soviet Foxtrot class, which has been supplied to several Third World countries, is credited with a submerged endurance of 350 nautical miles at 2 knots (175 hours, or slightly over seven days); full underwater speed, good for an hour, is 15.5 knots. The battery in turn can be recharged by the diesels, but they require air, so they can run only when the submarine is in contact with the surface. The submarine needs high sustained speed to make the transit from its base to its patrol or operating area. Typically, the commander of a diesel-electric submarine will run submerged at very low speed, conserving his battery so that he has available a single long burst of high speed, for example to evade pursuit after an attack.[23]

Published submarine speeds tend to be somewhat deceptive. Typically all nuclear submarines are credited with a speed of "about 30 knots", where 25 is more common; 30 or 33 knots is very special indeed. It took considerable effort for the United States to build a submarine, the *Los Angeles*, fast enough to keep up with a carrier battle group.

Generally a nuclear submarine will have two speed ranges, a quiet "tactical" range and a much noisier range up to its maximum speed. The maximum tactical speed may be only a fraction of full speed, but it may also be the highest speed at which the submarine can usefully employ her passive hull sonar because of the combination of flow and machinery self-noise.

Even though a submarine may be undetectable (at useful ranges) at quiet speed, if that speed is very low the submarine may be almost useless unless its commander sometimes risks higher speed (noisy) operation. Under such circumstances detection range may be much greater, and the submarine may become quite vulnerable. This issue is particularly relevant to US submarines operating near Soviet bases. Although the newer Soviet craft (such as Akula and Sierra classes) are very quiet *at tactical speed* they may have to run at higher speeds in order to reach their distant patrol areas. Their commanders must trade off the need to reach those areas against the increased vulnerability involved. For example, US submarines carry long-range anti-submarine missiles, currently Subroc and, in future, Sea Lance. The submarines cannot possibly detect quiet targets at long range – but the missiles should tend to deter Soviet commanders from running at speed, and hence should reduce their effectiveness by reducing their time on distant stations.

Mine Warfare

One other tool of sea power deserves extended discussion: the naval mine. Mines tend to operate more as deterrents than as actual killers of large numbers of ships, as those confronting even small numbers of them tend to try to clear them away before passing through mined waters. They can be used by relatively primitive navies to deny limited areas to even the most powerful forces; the classic example is Wonsan Harbor, Korea, in 1950, in which North Korean sampans and junks laid a field of about 3000 mines and delayed a US amphibious operation by several weeks. Very small numbers of US air-laid mines sufficed to close Hanoi–Haiphong harbour in 1972. More recently, a small field laid by a Libyan cargo ship closed the Red Sea for about six weeks, while Allied mine-hunters sought to ensure that they had found all of what turned out to be fewer than 20 bottom mines.

The Soviets (and their Czarist predecessors) are known to be enthusiastic exponents of mine warfare. Although details of Soviet mines tend not to be published, the Soviet stockpile is quite large. Minelaying platforms include surface ships, submarines, and the large jet bombers of Soviet Naval Aviation. Given its dependence on sea communications, NATO has always maintained substantial mine countermeasures forces. Unfortunately, as mines have become more sophisticated, the cost of unit mine countermeasures capability has risen. The size of the NATO countermeasures fleet, moreover, has declined, as many of the craft built during the NATO mobilisation of the 1950s have not been replaced. Worse, it is no longer possible to imagine that large numbers of commercial fishing craft can be converted into emergency minehunters and mine sweepers, as mines have become more difficult to counter. Commercial craft are still useful, however, in limited mine counter-measures roles.

The weapons separate into three broad categories: bottom mines, moored mines (which float above anchors on the bottom), and rising mines. Bottom mines are limited to depths of about 80 feet, since their explosions must damage hulls passing well above them. Typical exploders include devices which measure the magnetism inherent in a metal hull, devices which detect the sound a ship makes, and even devices which detect the pressure change in the water due to the reduction in water depth directly under a ship. Bottom mines can be particularly effective because their non-contact explosion may break a ship in half.[24]

Moored mines float below the surface. They cannot use the pressure mechanism, but generally employ either contact or magnetic or acoustic exploders. Because of its limited lethal volume, a moored mine is unlikely to be effective against submarines, which may pass it at a wide variety of depths.

The rising mine solves this problem. It floats below the range of submarine depths, and fires a weapon (such as a torpedo) up towards any target it detects. The weapon is fast enough to hit even the most distant (shallowest) targets. At present the US CapTor (enCapsulated Torpedo) mine is the only publicly announced example.[25]

In the past, the depth of water in which mines could be laid was limited by the weight (hence the length) of the mooring cable: the floating mine had to have enough buoyancy to lift it. Maximum depth was probably less than about 1000 feet. However, the case of a rising mine can be quite far beneath the surface. That tends to extend mineable areas, and in particular to include some strategic straits.

There is an important *caveat*. Thus far, no mine has incorporated any device which would allow it to distinguish between friendly and enemy ships. Minefields, therefore, fall into two categories: those through which friendly ships may have to pass, and fields through which only enemy ships are likely to pass. In the first case, friendly ships can be provided with charts of clear paths through the field. That is practical only so long as the mines have very limited lethal radii. It would be extremely difficult, however, to define a safe path through a field of deep rising mines, because each mine could be expected to attack targets over a considerable distance. This problem in itself would presumably limit the attractiveness of rising mines in strategic straits. In the case of a pure anti-submarine mine such as CapTor, the mine might distinguish between submarines and surface ships (which would be unprofitable to attack with its type of homing torpedo), but that would be all.

From an offensive point of view, then, apart from special ASW applications, mines are most likely to be used in relatively shallow water, clearly defined as enemy. Deeper-water ASW mines are probably usable only in the event of a general war against the Soviets and their allies. They can have little application in most conceivable Third World contexts. Given such restrictions on their use, mines may be unattractive for the US Navy to stockpile and maintain in very large numbers in peacetime. The US Navy has found a partial solution in Quickstrike, a standard aircraft bomb converted into a mine by the insertion of a special exploder. For deeper water, specialised weapons are needed. They must displace conventional bombs aboard an aircraft carrier, or torpedoes aboard a submarine, and therefore may not be carried in peacetime – or at the outset of a war.

Mines are effective because they are difficult to counter. In the past, they could be swept by devices which would cut mooring cables, or deceive acoustic or magnetic mines into exploding prematurely. However, modern mines are often impossible to decoy; pressure mines, introduced in World War II, were the first in this category. They must therefore be hunted on the sea or harbour bottom: high-definition sonars show their shapes, and special disposal vehicles are sent down to destroy them one by one. At best this is tedious. At worst, in the case of a rising mine, it is almost impossible, since the mine can attack targets quite far away from its case. Mine-hunting necessarily sweeps out narrow paths, which may be irrelevant to a wide-area rising mine.[26]

Matters only become worse as the mineable depth increases. Moreover, as the sophistication of the mines increases, individual mine countermeasures craft become substantially more expensive. Worst of all, mine countermeasures craft are essentially irrelevant to the usual peacetime (non-central war) naval mission.

The forward maritime strategy imposes an additional mine countermeasures requirement on the US Navy. It must be able to project forces at high speed into areas (such as those near landing beaches) which may be mined. Mine countermeasures ships tend to be quite slow (which is a necessary consequence of their limited size), far too slow to accompany 30-knot battle groups or 20-knot amphibious groups. The United States therefore requires at least some portable mine countermeasures capability. That is a minesweeping (and, in future, mine-hunting) helicopter, which can operate from an amphibious carrier or even, in theory, from a large-deck carrier. This mobility was dramatically demonstrated in 1972, when US helicopters swept Hanoi-Haiphong, and in 1974, when they helped sweep the Suez Canal after the Yom Kippur War.

Helicopters are expensive, and they cannot carry anything approaching the weight or sophistication of equipment aboard a surface craft. However, they are unlikely to trigger mines in the fields they sweep. They are, therefore, valued not only for their portability but also because they can sweep ahead of the surface craft, clearing particularly sensitive mines intended to destroy the sweepers or hunters. They can, therefore, reduce losses of these relatively expensive and sophisticated craft. Sweeping helicopters are limited in that they cannot sweep deep mines, because they cannot tow or accommodate the long line required to reach substantial depths.

Mine countermeasures extend beyond the immediately threatened area. Mines (aboard their carriers) can be destroyed at source, or in transit. For example, Soviet submarines are the most likely means of mining US waters. To the extent that they are destroyed near the Soviet Union (i.e., at source), or in transit towards the United States, they cannot mine American waters.

To the extent that general purpose naval forces can forestall mine attacks on the United States, they reduce the requirement for special-purpose mine countermeasures craft. Attack at source or in transit, then, makes it easier for the United States to afford a balanced fleet; it maintains mine countermeasures craft to deal with Soviet mines which survive the assaults of the general-purpose forces. It is sometimes suggested that, understanding this strategy, the Soviets will cleverly lay "sleeping" mines in US ports in peacetime, activating them when war begins (US variations on this theme have also been proposed). Unfortunately, mechanisms subjected to long-term corrosion underwater tend not to be reliable. It would hardly suit the Soviets' purposes to announce immediately hostile intent either by prematurely sinking US ships or by having bottom mines wash ashore.

Are classical fleet tactics really viable in the face of extremely lethal modern anti-ship weapons? Modern ships certainly seem quite fragile, especially in comparison to their predecessors. Why were the battleships so much tougher? One reason is certainly that it was easier to protect against the weapons they faced, armour-piercing shells, than against modern weapons such as large shaped charges.

Since about 1920 dense weapons (guns) have gradually been replaced by lighter but more voluminous self-propelled weapons (aircraft, torpedoes, and guided missiles). The self-propelled weapons are more voluminous because they represent more of the total weapon system: in a gun, most of the weight, cost, and volume of the total system is invested in a permanent structure in the ship. By way of contrast, a torpedo launcher may weigh much less than the weapon it fires. Self-propelled weapons impose "low over-head", a low minimum cost on the ship designer. In very small numbers, they can be carried by relatively small craft, although those numbers may not provide much tactical effectiveness.

Self-propelled weapons are usually associated with increased battle range, because so often they are also self-guided. For example, in World War II carriers could engage at hundreds of miles because the pilots of their aircraft, given crude initial headings, could locate and strike their targets. Naval guns could attack only at 10 or 20 miles, not merely because of the limitations of ballistics (a ship could not easily have accommodated a 100 mile gun), but, as importantly, because targets could not be located nor guns aimed accurately enough at greater ranges.

Greater range typically places a greater burden on sensors, many of which must be external to the ship itself. In a modern air battle, for example, carrier-based fighters might be directed by early warning aircraft rather than by the carrier herself, partly because the battle may occur well beyond the carrier's radar horizon.

Battleships were "weight-critical": they might have considerable free internal space, but they needed every bit of buoyancy to support all those guns and all that armour. By way of contrast, modern warships are "volume-critical": their weapons and electronics do not weigh very much (compared to the total weight of the ships), but they take up every bit of available volume (which is why modern warships often seem so boxy).[27] The larger vital volume involved was more difficult to armour, since the weight of protection (for a given thickness) is proportional to the surface area it must cover.

The first warships to be affected by this new reality were aircraft carriers, whose hangars proved so difficult to protect. The outstanding exception was the British armoured-hangar carrier. In this case a moderate degree of armoured (passive) protection was purchased by restricting total hangar volume, which, given British practice, meant severely limiting the total number of aircraft. The British choice was to eliminate fighters (which were considered ineffective at the time the ships were designed) in favour of strike aircraft.[28] The US Navy rejected this choice, and the evolution of American carrier tactics is a nice illustration of the gradual shift towards active defence.

Before about 1939, Americans assumed that it was literally impossible to protect carriers, or at least to protect their flight decks (i.e., their offensive firepower) from air attack. The US Navy therefore emphasised scouting, so that it could get in the first attack. For example, of the four squadrons aboard American carriers, one consisted of scouts; two more of strike aircraft (torpedo and dive bombers). Only one could be considered defensive (fighters), and even it was probably designed primarily to help the strike force get through enemy defences. One might describe this policy as an attempt to achieve sea control (in this case, maritime air superiority) through "attack at source", the problem being to find the source in time.

In 1939, however, it was found that aerial scouts could give some early warning of enemy attackers, and therefore that some defence was feasible. The number of fighter squadrons per carrier was doubled, to two.

Although the aerial-scout idea was promising, it was radar which made carrier air defence truly effective. By 1944 radar-controlled fighters were dominant. At the Battle of the Philippine Sea, the Japanese succeeded in locating the American carriers before themselves being detected, a failure which would have been fatal four years (or even two years) earlier. This time, however, the result was the destruction of the Japanese air striking force, at very little cost to the defenders.

This was not the end of the story. Success at the Philippine Sea depended on a fighter control organisation, in which radar data was filtered in Combat Information Centres (CICs) aboard the carriers. These centres in turn could not handle many distinct targets simultaneously. Note that, although the Japanese sent in numerous aircraft, they came in groups, to attack particular ships, because the probability that any one aircraft would sink a ship was quite small. Thus the total number of radar targets, and the total number of interceptions the CICs had to arrange, was fairly limited.

The *Kamikazes* appeared a few months later. Because a *Kamikaze* was intended to crash into a ship, rather than merely drop a bomb or torpedo, it had a fair chance of killing or at least disabling its target. There was no longer a need to mass attackers, and the Japanese soon learned that they could disperse to saturate the CICs. The US Navy, in turn, was forced back to "attack at source", sending out large numbers of fighter-bombers to hit, and thus to disable, Kamikaze airfields. It did not of course abandon the active defence of the fleet, but that active defence no longer sufficed in itself.

Meanwhile a new threat, the bomber-launched guided missile, appeared. Like the *Kamikaze*, it had a high killing probability, and therefore it could be effective on a one-shot basis. The Germans introduced such weapons in 1943, and it was assumed that the Soviets, having captured German technology, would soon follow suit.[29] The *technological* reply was a combination of automated CICs (to overcome saturation) and better long-range anti-aircraft weapons. The *tactical* reply was a return to the theme of "attack at source", which was a major postwar carrier strike mission. There was no expectation that attack at source would eliminate the entire Soviet naval air threat, but rather that success would depend upon a combination of fleet air defence and attack at source, just as in 1945, against the Kamikazes.

Further developments in fleet anti-aircraft weapons opened up a new possibility. The Aegis system is designed specifically to deal with saturation missile attacks, i.e., with missiles after the bombers have already launched them. Note that the continued survival of the carrier force is only a means to an end, the end in this case being to maintain a flexible sea-based striking power. The combination of Aegis and carrier-based fighters offered something more, a means to expand the objective to gaining maritime air superiority.

Only the fighters could reasonably hope to intercept the missile-bearing bombers. If they were the only very effective anti-aircraft elements of the fleet, they would have to try to destroy any missiles the bombers launched, and the bombers themselves could survive the engagement by launching early, to distract the fighters. If, however, there was an effective back-up system, the fighters could concentrate on the bombers, and thus end the problem. The fleet would act both as bait and trap: as bait, because the Soviets would feel compelled to destroy so important a threat, and trap, because their most effective anti-carrier weapon, the missile-firing bomber, could be destroyed by the combination.

Some illustrative figures may be useful. The Soviets tend to operate their anti-ship bombers in regiments of about 20 aircraft each, and each Backfire carries one or two missiles. A regiment, then, may carry as many as 40 weapons for its attack. One might imagine a carrier battle force consisting of four carriers, each with 20 operational F-14 fighters. Of all these fighters (out of a total of 96 F-14s, 80 of them assumed operational), 30 might be airborne simultaneously, and each would carry four to six long-range missiles (Phoenix) and a cannon. There may also be eight anti-aircraft ships, four of which might be equipped with Aegis. Actual figures are classified, but one might imagine that each of the Aegis ships can handle ten targets simultaneously. Pre-Aegis ships can handle between two and four targets simultaneously. The entire force is equipped with data links which make it relatively easy for targets to be assigned to specific ships, so that there is little overlap.

None of these weapons is perfect. However, it seems reasonable to imagine that each fighter can destroy two bombers with missiles (i.e., at long range, before they can drop their weapons) and one more with the cannon, as they retire. If that is true, then the fighters can wipe out three Soviet regiments before they can fire, and another regiment and a half afterwards. In a four-regiment (80-bomber) attack, then, none of the bombers will survive, but they will have launched up to 40 missiles before their death. The fleet will still have to survive that attack.

Like the Phoenixes launched by the F-14s, the Soviet missiles are not perfect. If they are assigned the relatively high reliability of 75%, 30 of them will actually attempt to attack the battle force. The missile ships, however, will be able to deal simultaneously with between 48 and 56 incoming missiles, and the odds of a successful hit are slim indeed. Moreover, missiles surviving Aegis would also have to survive a variety of closer-in weapons and jammers. Again, it is not clear how well any single system would do, but the sheer number of systems should eliminate all the leakers. Finally, the carriers themselves should be able to absorb some substantial damage before being put out of action.

This returns the fleet to much the position at the Battle of the Philippine Sea, in which it could reasonably accept the possibility of air attack in expectation of destroying the attacking force in the air.

All of this depends, of course, on effective airborne early warning, effective estimation of the direction of attack (the threat axis) for good placement of the fighters, and on effective coordination of defensive forces, so that they do not all concentrate on some of the attackers while the others penetrate successfully. Both the US Navy and the Soviets are aware of this point. For example, in the early to mid 1950s the Sixth Fleet conducted a series of full scale Air Defense Exercises. At first a surprising number of attackers managed to penetrate all the way to the carriers without even having been detected. It turned out that better tactics (such as better placement of early warning aircraft) and, even more importantly, better training of controlling staffs (in combat information centres) could solve the problem. From the Soviet point of view, the key to success would be denial of information and information exchange, through radar countermeasures, deception, and jamming, including jamming of communications circuits.

More generally, modern volume-critical ships, then, have had to shift largely from reliance on passive (armour) defence to active AAW, by destroying incoming attackers. Active AAW in turn is often a collaborative effort within a fleet. Layered AAW does have a better chance than a single ship of destroying an incoming missile. By way of contrast, the efficacy of armour is very much a single-ship issue.[30] Thus the shift from passive to active AAW, which is largely a consequence of the shift from weight- to volume-critical ships, also motivates a shift from the classical idea of the capital ship – the ship which can only be sunk by another capital ship – to what amounts to a capital *fleet* of mutually supportive ships and aircraft, a cooperative organism.

This is not to suggest that modern warships lack all passive protection. The larger a ship, the more weight it can devote to a limited degree of armour. For example, in the mid-1970s the US Navy designed a 17,000 ton "strike cruiser". Compared to the existing 12,000 ton nuclear-powered cruiser, it had some additional command and control facilities but, more importantly, it had significant armour protection for such vital spaces as computer rooms. However, its protection was pathetic compared to that of a World War II cruiser of similar tonnage, because even the few protected spaces had so great a surface area.

Moreover, sheer size still provides protection. Most weapons damage a ship over a given, and quite limited, area. Much therefore depends on how large that area is compared to the total size of the ship. If the ship is large enough, it may be possible to duplicate vital functions far enough apart that a single hit cannot disable the ship. For example, large warships such as carriers often have their engine rooms well separated. Moving vital equipment in from the skin of the ship will also provide a degree of protection.[31]

Sheer size also reduces the relative cost of active self-defence. It has other virtues: flexibility over the life of a ship (in modification), and better seakeeping, which is particularly important in the kind of northern waters the maritime strategy emphasises. Moreover, ship size in itself need not be expensive. What is expensive is the additional equipment which a larger ship can accommodate. Whether that equipment is bought or foregone is an issue of self-discipline, not basic design policy.

Even a relatively small ship can be designed to survive considerable damage, as the US frigate *Stark* demonstrated after she had been hit by two Exocet missiles in May 1987. One of the warheads exploded; the other did not. Because both weapons had been fired from short range, their motors still contained large quantities of fuel, and they continued to burn after striking, feeding fires aboard the ship. One hit near the ship's missile magazine, and the explosion and consequent hot metal fragments might have been expected to destroy the magazine and, therefore, the forward part of the ship.

In this case the important elements of protection included the splinter armour wrapped around the missile magazine, the internal bulkheads which helped contain the damage, and the combination of automatic halon sprays and refractory material which helped the crew fight the fire. It was also very important that the crew had available to it fire-fighting pumps far enough from the damaged part of the ship to survive the initial damage. Most of all, the ship survived because her well-trained crew could take advantage of her design in order to save their ship.

Men are still a principal element of sea power. Technology has not quite taken over.

Notes
1. This is an ideal. It also reflects the evolution of major navies, for which mutually supporting fleets came long before reliable long-haul communications. Moreover, the capacity of long-haul radio was very limited until quite recently. However, US administrations blessed with high-capacity communications have tried to exert detailed control of fleet operations several echelons of command down the line. For example, during the 1973 crisis Henry Kissinger is said to have issued rudder orders to ships of the Sixth Fleet. The *Mayaguez* incident was largely managed out of the White House crisis room, in some cases with ludicrous results. A carrier, the *Constellation*,

approaching the scene was told to "orbit at 35,000 feet" because someone in the crisis room thought she was an EC-121, an aircraft also called Constellation. The failure of the US naval air raid on the Bekaa Valley is generally attributed to excessive detailed control exerted by command echelons above the formation (the battle group) actually involved. The tendency to tight control from above is usually blamed on the modern fear (which this writer would heavily discount) that minor errors by commanders on the scene can cause a nuclear holocaust.

2. Patrick Beesley has described this arrangement in detail in his *Room 40*. The British failed fully to exploit their sources (in effect, the first real-time "national technical means of intelligence") because they did not develop a suitable operational intelligence staff. They solved this problem in World War II, often with spectacularly successful results, as Beesley relates in his *Very Special Intelligence*.

3. The location of SOSUS stations is classified. However, the chronology of SOSUS shows that it was developed at a time when the key scenario in US thinking was an all-out Atlantic or Atlantic and Pacific war, and SOSUS installation would require the acquiescence of the country in or near whose waters the arrays were laid. This condition certainly does not apply in the Indian Ocean. Similarly, one might guess that SOSUS is not emplaced in the South Atlantic or in the South China Sea.

4. The classic anti-aircraft IFF problem is avoiding "blue on blue," i.e. friendly v. friendly engagements when the fleet is both striking an enemy surface target *and* defending itself against air attack. Returning strike aircraft must be distinguished from incoming enemies, who may try to join them turning strikes in order to penetrate unobserved. If operations are protracted, friendly fighters may have to return from their distant stations to be refuelled and rearmed; they, too, must be distinguished from attackers trying to sneak in. Aircraft are generally fitted with special transmitters (transponders) which send out identifying codes when they are interrogated, but aircraft returning from a strike may have had their transponders damaged, and enemy aircraft may try to simulate friendly transmissions. In the past, too, anti-aircraft gunners have often been trigger-happy, particularly when friendly fighters have chased attackers into zones theoretically limited to surface anti-aircraft fire.

5. One might contrast the logistics of air attack. To make a momentary appearance over the Falklands, a Vulcan bomber had to be refuelled several times, and its refuellers also had to be refuelled; it took a total of 18 tankers per sortie. This is quite aside from the question of whether a single transient sortie was militarily worthwhile.

6. The British had already abandoned fixed-wing ASW aircraft in favour of helicopters, which could operate from relatively small

ships. Indeed, they had designed an "escort cruiser" to accompany future carriers, relieving them of the need to waste scarce deck space on ASW helicopters. Note that, to the extent that long-range ASW remains a valuable element of fleet operations, that already made the British dependent on fixed bases. In any case, limiting fleet air ASW to helicopters left only long-range fighters, radar aircraft, and strike aircraft aboard the big-deck carrier. If air defence was split between land-based aircraft and ship-based missiles, the large carrier could be eliminated altogether: it could be (and was) argued that ship-based missiles could take over the strike role, although in fact their effective range was quite limited compared to that of strike aircraft. Moreover, the tonnage of deliverable explosive would be much reduced.

7. In theory, shore-based fighters (or fighters aboard the US carriers the British fleet supported) would deal with Soviet long-range bombers, which were the only important air-to-surface threat in the scenario. Harriers were placed aboard the British VSTOL carriers for a very different reason. In the open ocean, the Soviets could pose the threat of long-range anti-ship missile attack, which (until very recently) required the assistance of Bear D targeting aircraft. Harriers could certainly deal with Bears operating at high altitude and at relatively low speed. Similarly, the British could argue that, to be effective, open-ocean submarine operations required intelligence support, in the form of "snooping" aircraft (such as Bears) – which, again, the Harriers could reasonably be expected to counter.

8. See Rowher, *Critical Convoy Battles*, pp. 144–5.

9. Given the difficulties of direct communication with the submarines, it might be more realistic to think of them as operating well ahead of the battle group or battle force. Note that only a single underway replenishment ship might suffice to support a pair of carriers operating together. The US Navy now posesses only four very fast (26 knot) ships of this type, and the presence of slower ones (20 knot) would presumably inhibit battle group operations.

10. This particular example is taken from Navy briefing charts included in Secretary John F Lehman's testimony to the Seapower and Strategic and Critical Materials Subcommittee of the House Armed Services Committee, June 24, 1985.

11. A modified wing was introduced in 1987: the specialist refuellers are eliminated, and the F-14 and F/A-18 levels reduced to 20 aircraft each, to double the A-6 (long-range attack) force to 20, and to add an additional EA-6B and an additional E-2C, for a total of five of each. Other experimental wings had been tried a few years earlier. For example, the *John F Kennedy* operated 14 F-14s, 28 A-6s, 5 EA-6Bs, 10 S-3s, 5 E-2Cs, and 6 SH-3H helicopters. As of 1987, plans called for 11 of the 14 active air wings to be of the new type, together with both

reserve air wings. Of existing carriers, only the two oldest, *Midway* and *Coral Sea*, cannot operate the F-14, and therefore are equipped with 48 F/A-18s.

12. This figure was used in the standard aircraft charts issued by the US Naval Air Systems Command, from the mid-1950s on.

13. The flank attack was not really a major problem before the appearance of nuclear submarines, as diesel submarines cannot sustain high speeds for more than about an hour, without exhausting their batteries. A nuclear submarine does have the option of trailing a carrier group, which may find it difficult to search the noisy area aft. That was the threat presented by Soviet "Charlie" class missile submarines. It in turn led to US interest in the "direct support" of carriers by friendly nuclear submarines, which could themselves trail the "Charlies". They could also use their superior acoustics to search ahead of a force. The tactic is limited by inherently poor communication between submarine and ships or aircraft, and some have suggested that, given the excellent performance of shipboard towed arrays, submarines are better used in more distant operations ("associated support"). Until the early 1970s, the US Navy operated its long-range ASW aircraft aboard specialised ASW carriers, designated CVS, which were converted World War II-built attack carriers. It was never possible to replace them, and instead existing attack or strike carriers were modified to operate ASW aircraft alongside their fighters and attack bombers. The concept of operating carriers together in larger numbers, so that temporary operational specialisation is possible, is a partial reversion to the CVS idea. The difference is that the designated ASW carrier still has her full attack and fighter complement on board, and that the designation can shift rapidly, from ship to ship: the carrier is still a general-purpose warship.

14. Force components and breakdowns are taken from the annual surface ship force requirements reports to Congress, in which surface combatant warships are listed in the categories given here. They are not organised into those groups in peacetime.

15. The new large amphibious ship (LHD) is designed for alternative employment in "sea control", i.e., as a low-capability aircraft carrier using Sea Harrier fighters and helicopters for ASW. It cannot operate the existing S-3 long-range carrier ASW aircraft, but presumably will be able to operate the SV-22 tilt-rotor aircraft now under development. Current (1987) plans call for a total of five through FY91.

16. The British pledge to maintain a force of about 50 (formerly 70) active destroyers and frigates has never, for example, been predicated on any precise breakdown of the tactical use of these ships. It is almost certainly an affordability figure, analogous to the US force goal of 100 attack submarines. Realistic wartime requirements far exceed the 50

or 70-frigate figure, but it is unrealistic to attempt to meet them. At the time of the Nott White Paper (1981) a variety of estimates of wartime British force dispositions did appear in print, but they were clearly unofficial. See the Swartz "Addendum", pp 33–41 for examples of NATO operational concepts.

17. Critics will argue that the current state of the Canadian Navy would not permit such operation, but there are four destroyers and 16 frigates, with six more frigates under construction. Many of the current ships badly need refits, and the force structure implied by the existence of the refuellers probably dates from the 1960s.

18. Underway replenishment in the Pacific was by separate tankers, ammunition, and store ships which met the fast carriers, but which did not steam with them. The Germans were responsible for the concept of the "one stop" replenishment ship, but their ships did not accompany the units they supported.

19. This is a very simplified discussion; actual performance, for a given sonar, depends critically on local water conditions and depth. For example, there are acoustic layers which can trap sound signals. In the Atlantic, the surface layer is several hundred feet deep; a submarine lying beneath it is very nearly hidden from surface ships. In the Mediterranean in summer, the corresponding layer may be only 50 feet deep, and ships find their hull-mounted sonars useless. That is why the French and Italian navies use variable-depth sonars, which they can tow beneath the surface layer. Similarly, linear passive arrays are generally towed well beneath the surface layer, to enjoy acoustic conditions similar to those experienced by a submarine.

20. *Invincible* has other virtues as well. She provides important command and control (e.g., intelligence analysis) for the force as a whole, and can probably extend the endurance of the force by refuelling her escorts. She might be seen as one end of a spectrum of carrier/ underway replenishment ships; most NATO underway replenishment ships can support at least one helicopter. Published descriptions of the new British AORs indicate that they will be able to support a few helicopters and will incorporate some limited command/control capability. Compared to *Invincible*, they will lack a long flight deck (which is useful even to helicopters) and thus the ability to fly off Harrier jet fighters.

21. A heavy submarine torpedo, such as the US Mark 48, weighs about 3500 pounds; it is 21 inches in diameter and 230 inches long. The warhead weighs several hundred pounds (more precise figures are classified). By way of comparison, the current US lightweight service torpedo (which many NATO navies also use), the Mark 46, weighs 568 pounds and is 12.75 inches in diameter and 102 inches long. Its warhead weighs less than 100 pounds. The new Mark 50 lightweight

torpedo will weigh about 800 pounds. These figures were taken from N Friedman, *US Naval Weapons* (Annapolis: US Naval Institute, 1983).

Lightweight torpedoes form the main non-nuclear armament of NATO ASW aircraft, including ship-launched helicopters; they are fired by surface ships, both from short-range torpedo tubes and via stand-off missiles such as Asroc, Ikara, and the French Malafon (although the latter carries a rather heavier weapon). They will be carried by future submarine stand-off weapons such as the new US Sea Lance, and Mark 46 currently forms the payload of the CapTor deep-water ASW mine. Of all these systems, only some of the aircraft and Asroc have nuclear alternatives.

22. Some observers have suggested that, even though doctrine may favour the exclusive use of conventional weapons, commanders *in extremis* may fire nuclear weapons to save themselves. This is unlikely. Nuclear weapons, both anti-submarine and anti-aircraft, have unpleasant side effects (respectively, shock damage to the launching platform and possibly devastating damage to electronics), which are worse the shorter the range. A commander would generally not even consider himself *in extremis* until his attacker had closed to very short range, quite possibly to a range shorter than the minimum at which a nuclear weapon could not be used without commiting suicide. Nuclear weapons seem most attractive for long-range *offensive* use, which is a very different proposition.

23. "Foxtrot" figures are taken from A D Baker III and J L Couhat, eds., *Combat Fleets of the World 1986/87* (Annapolis: US Naval Institute).

24. The sphere of gas produced by the explosion bounces off the keel of the ship, causing it to flex and ultimately to break. Modern "under the keel" torpedoes employ a similar killing mechanism.

25. The Soviets almost certainly have rising mines of their own; the British Armed Deep Team Sweep (ADATS) would appear to be a means of attacking their mooring cables.

26. For a more extended discussion of issues in mine warfare, see G K Hartmann, *Weapons That Wait* (Annapolis: US Naval Institute, 1979).

27. It took some time for this change to be understood. The first US missile destroyer, the *Charles F Adams*, was designed like one of its weight-critical forebears. As a result, it was extremely, even uncomfortably, tight. Modernisation was difficult at best, and the high cost entailed by that tightness explains why only three out of 23 ships in the class were ever modernised.

28. The choice turned on technological projection. Carrier-based fighters were ineffective when the British ships were designed, in 1936, because there was no way to provide them with sufficient early warning, or to vector them into the paths of oncoming raiders. A few years

later radar and the associated combat information centre (action information organisation, in British parlance) could do just that, and the sacrifices entailed in providing an armoured hangar seemed much less acceptable. For example, the last British fleet carrier design of World War II, the *Malta*, had a virtually unarmoured (US-style) hangar. The US adoption of a limited degree of flight deck armour can be explained more on structural than on protection grounds.

29. The Germans sank the Italian battleship *Roma* and severely damaged the British *Warspite* at Salerno. This experience inspired the US and British navies to begin work on anti-aircraft guided missiles (to kill the bomber before it could launch the missile), which became Terrier, Talos, and Seaslug.

30. Except in that more hits will be made on a single ship alone than on a ship among many other ships under attack.

31. These statements require some qualification. Underwater weapons often cause shock damage which extends over a very large area; the most extreme form is whipping, in which an explosion under a ship's keel may cause the entire ship to flex and even to break. Even then, however, larger size gives scope for protective construction.

5. The Strategy of Sea Power

The US Maritime Strategy is one of a wider class of naval strategies designed to achieve and to exploit sea control. In the case of the Maritime Strategy, sea control is to be seized primarily by early offensive action. This seizure in turn should release offensive naval forces for operations directly affecting the associated battle on land. The offensive orientation of the strategy should shape the future US fleet and perhaps by allied fleets as well.

This strategy is by no means the only approach to sea control, although, as will be argued below, it is forced upon the United States by a variety of boundary conditions. Indeed, the contrast between the Maritime Strategy and what many perceive as more traditional approaches to sea control explains why the strategy has been so controversial.[1]

The special features of the Maritime Strategy can probably best be appreciated in the wider context of the strategies which major navies have followed in the past.

Basic Naval Roles

Major navies exist for two basic purposes: to contest the use of the sea (offensively or defensively), and to attack targets ashore.[2] Typically the goal of free use of the sea (while denying it to an enemy) is termed *sea control*. The alternative, to deny free use of the sea to an enemy, perhaps without being able to use the sea freely, is termed *sea denial*; clearly, total sea denial is one of several ways of assuring sea control. Generally neither goal can be completely achieved; the victim of sea control can always slip a few ships out to sea. On balance, however, a navy which achieves sea control, or command of the sea, can be sure of passing most of the shipping it protects wherever it wishes, within the area it controls, and of excluding most enemy shipping.

The existence of submarines tends to blur these distinctions, as it is possible for a navy to achieve control of the *surface* of the sea – in the sense of being able to use the surface freely, and being able to deny its enemy free use – without being able to prevent its enemy from operating submarines fairly freely. That would be the case with strategic missile submarines, which would be able to avoid detection, but which also would not contest the free use of the surface of the sea by enemy warships. They would be reasonably safe, given the limited ranges at which the surface ships could expect to detect them.

Thus sea control often (but not always) really means securing a reasonable degree of safety for surface ships, perhaps without actually denying the sea to enemy submarines.

Finally, the land or deep attack role is usually termed *power projection*. Naval presence, the primary peacetime use of navies to influence events abroad, is effective to the extent that it carries the threat, more or less direct, of projecting power. In fact it is not always clear that power projection is distinct from sea control or sea denial, because one means of attaining sea control is to destroy the enemy's fleet in its bases or in its home waters. In that case, power projection and sea control might be considered two aspects of the same strategy.

That is the current US position, sometimes described as a doctrine of *maritime superiority*. This might be considered parallel to "air superiority", a doctrine in which what amounts to air control is achieved by destroying the enemy air force either on the ground or near its bases, i.e., by projecting air power into the enemy's base structure.[3]

On the other hand, amphibious forces are clearly designed to project power ashore to affect operations on land.[4] Similarly, one can usefully describe a submarine on deterrent patrol as presenting the threat of power projection. However, given maritime superiority as a goal, one might ask whether the usual distinction between sea control and power projection is really useful, or whether it does not amount to an implicit strategic choice.

To the extent that a nation requires either overseas trade or coastal shipping in order to carry on a war, sea control exercised against her amounts to strangulation, so that power projection ashore may be a very secondary issue. On the other hand, to the extent that a nation is autarkic, or at the worst can rely on land lines of communication, the only effective offensive use of sea power against her is power projection ashore.

The two world wars present examples of both cases. In World War I, the Royal Navy successfully blockaded Germany. Although Germany could meet many of her requirements by using resources within the area of Europe she controlled, she needed just enough from overseas for the blockade to prove painful. The hardships it entailed caused civil unrest, and some would suggest that the German Army itself was affected.[5] In World War II, Germany conquered so much of Europe that she could operate autarkically, although she did try to operate a few blockade-runners, e.g. to bring rubber and other strategic materials home from the Far East. It seems clear that, on balance, the British blockade accomplished little. The main direct offensive impact of naval forces on the war in Europe was projection of power ashore, in the form of the great invasions.

On the other hand, in both wars the allies required sea communications for their survival, and sea denial, as exercised by the Germans, was an effective threat. Like the allies, Japan required sea communications in order to survive, let alone fight. By mid-1945 Japanese industry had very nearly collapsed due to the loss of those communications, although it is clear in retrospect that the Japanese Army was quite capable of bitterly contesting the invasion planned for that fall.

After 1945, the primary military threat faced by the United States was a Soviet invasion of Western Europe. It appeared that the situation of the Soviet Union in some future war would most closely resemble that of Germany in World War II: an autarkic power, not particularly dependent on sea lanes, and capable of threatening the existence of the Western Alliance by threatening to cut its vital sea lanes. Blockade, the classic naval strategy of the past, no longer seemed relevant. As in World War II, sea control was essential if the allies were to survive very long militarily, but in itself sea control could not defeat the autarkic Soviets, because it could not threaten their source of economic or military power. For naval power to cause them to abandon the war would require some form of power projection, some direct intervention on land. This is still very much the case: the Soviet Union is still an autarkic power, although it makes extensive use of the Southern Sea Route from the Black Sea through the Suez Canal and the Indian Ocean to the Far East. The Soviets are also increasingly using the Northern Sea Route (in summer) which, unlike the Southern, would be difficult to block. Finally, the Soviets do depend on their large fishing fleet for a significant proportion of their food, at least in peacetime.

The Soviet Union does have overseas dependencies, like Cuba and Vietnam, which require sea communications in order to survive as military powers. However, it seems unlikely that the prospect of losing those dependencies would make much difference to a Soviet Union bent on offensive action in Europe.

US military forces were implicitly divided up into those used to sustain land combat on the European continent (armies, tactical air forces, and the naval forces required to guarantee their sea communications) and forces capable of striking directly at the Soviets (sea and air power projection forces). As in the purely naval case, peacetime presence (or deterrence) amounts to the threat of wartime power projection. In the case of the post-1945 period, such power projection has come to mean the threat of nuclear attack. One might see US (or, indeed, Western) military development since World War II, then, largely as a conflict between forces designed for sustained land combat on the continent and forces designed to threaten the Soviet Union directly, so as to induce her to abandon either combat or the threat of combat. There is also an important additional theme: forces required to fight (or to threaten to fight) in the Third World.

Very generally, again, it would seem that the land forces on the continent (including those which may be shipped from North America) are important in inverse proportion to the plausibility of the nuclear (power projection) threat. The more plausible the threat, the less likely that the Soviets will actually call its bluff and invade Europe, and therefore that land forces (and sea control) will matter. The less plausible the nuclear threat, the better the possibility that the Soviets will invade, and that land forces on the continent will be engaged. One might see the period up to about 1955 as one of Western nuclear dominance, and hence of the dominance of power projection forces. After 1955, the Soviets built up sufficient long-range nuclear forces to threaten North America, and nuclear power projection became less and less plausible. On the other hand, the sheer cost of building up the necessary nuclear forces sapped Soviet conventional land forces, so that it was not necessary for NATO to build up the land (or protracted-war forces). From about 1965 on, however, the Soviets were able to rebuild their tactical forces. It became more and more obvious that the threat of nuclear attack could deter another power from mounting a nuclear attack, but that a Soviet land invasion of Western Europe was again possible.

NATO was never willing to build up what it saw as sufficient land forces to meet the projected Soviet non-nuclear threat. On the other hand, it also could not afford to depend on a nuclear threat to prevent even the slightest Soviet land attack, since that would invite devastating nuclear retaliation; it would hardly be plausible. NATO's current strategy, adopted in 1967, is "flexible response". NATO would field sufficient land forces to deal with a limited Soviet attack. However, it would continue to rely on the threat of nuclear escalation, i.e. ultimately of an unacceptable degree of projection, to keep the Soviets from making the large-scale invasion which its forces could not expect to stop. As Soviet nuclear forces have been built up, this policy has become less and less credible, although the Soviets certainly have not yet shown great willingness to call NATO's bluff.[6]

NATO nuclear credibility has been particularly controversial in the United States, which has pressed for more powerful land forces to raise the threshold at which NATO would have to choose between nuclear use and surrender. The lower the resistance of the NATO army, the earlier the point at which this choice must be made and, it is argued, the better the chance that NATO leaders

1. *Above:* The battle group of associated ships and aircraft is the most powerful basic tool of Western sea power. The *Midway* battle group is shown. Besides the carrier herself, it includes two anti-aircraft ships, a missile cruiser (top) and a missile destroyer (just below the carrier); two ASW ships, a frigate (at the extreme left) and a destroyer (at bottom); and two underway replenishment ships (trailing: a tanker and a specialised AOR). This photograph was taken in 1981, and the battle group was clearly under strength. It was also much more closely bunched than normal practice dictates.

2. *Below:* The McDonnell Douglas F/A-18 Hornet symbolises the flexibility of carrier aircraft. It is designed to carry both air-to-air and ground attack weapons, so that a carrier can swing from one role to the other without changing her aircraft.

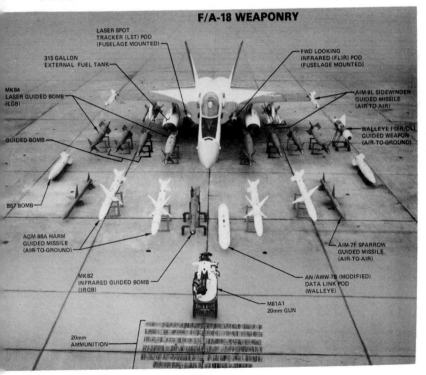

F/A-18 WEAPONRY

LASER SPOT TRACKER (LST) POD (FUSELAGE MOUNTED)

315 GALLON EXTERNAL FUEL TANK

FWD LOOKING INFRARED (FLIR) POD (FUSELAGE MOUNTED)

MK84 LASER GUIDED BOMB (LGB)

AIM-9L SIDEWINDER GUIDED MISSILE (AIR-TO-AIR)

WALLEYE I (ER/DL) GUIDED WEAPON (AIR-TO-GROUND)

GUIDED BOMB

B57 BOMB

AGM-88A HARM GUIDED MISSILE (AIR-TO-GROUND)

AIM-7F SPARROW GUIDED MISSILE (AIR-TO-AIR)

MK82 INFRARED GUIDED BOMB (IRGB)

AN/AWW-7B (MODIFIED) DATA LINK POD (WALLEYE)

M61A1 20mm GUN

20mm AMMUNITION

3. *Left:* Sustained battle force operations require not only combatant ships but also support. Here the carrier *Constellation* fuels from the *Sacramento*, a fast replenishment ship (AOE) built specifically to shuttle ammunition and fuel to the Nato Striking Fleet.

4. *Below:* Successful battle force operations require early warning, which is achieved by a combination of ship-borne and airborne radars. Just to the right of the island of the carrier *Independence* can be seen the "flying saucer" radomes of two Grumman E-2C Hawkeye radar aircraft, which would normally patrol in the direction of an expected attack. The Hawkeyes can also provide the carrier with full radar data, so that she can shut down her own radars and thus elude many forms of electronic surveillance.

5. *Inset:* The forward strategy changes the import of new technology. Here the missile cruiser *Bunker Hill* fires two anti-aircraft missiles (RIM-66Cs) in quick succession from her forward vertical launcher; note the two smoke trails. The launcher was originally developed to fire anti-aircraft missiles faster. However, it can also fire heavy surface-to-surface weapons (Tomahawks), and thus it restores long-range striking power to the surface fleet.

6. *Below:* In a non-nuclear age, individual missiles cannot damage vast targets. They can, however, destroy important individual targets. Here a Tomahawk missile launched by a submerged submarine over 400 miles away flies above a bomber (an old RA-5C) in a simulated Soviet-type revetment. Moments later, it exploded, destroying the bomber. The Soviet anti-ship bomber force cannot, therefore, be safe unless the Soviet Navy can keep US submarines many hundreds of miles from its airfields.

7. *Inset:* The archer and his arrow: a Soviet Badger anti-ship bomber with an AS-6 missile underwing. This aircraft can carry another missile under its other wing; alternatively the recess in its belly can accommodate a single weapon. Large missile size buys supersonic performance and a massive warhead. Soviet Backfire bombers carry similar anti-ship missiles. One objective of the Maritime Strategy is to destroy the Soviet anti-shipping bomber force so that it cannot dispute control of the seas.

7A. *Above:* Archer killer: an F-14 Tomcat long-range fighter aboard the carrier *Nimitz*. To the extent that Aegis and other shipboard systems can kill missiles launched by Soviet bombers which survive the initial air battle, the Tomcats can concentrate on attacking bombers alone. Their job is to destroy the Soviet Naval Air Force, to win the decisive battle against what amounts to the Soviet battle fleet.

8. *Below:* Soviet submarines are another major missile threat. This Echo II class submarine was designed primarily to attack carriers using long-range SS-N-3 cruise missiles, the launchers for three of which are visible here (by the big holes cut for missile exhaust during launch). The submarine fires at targets it cannot detect, using a data link to missiles in flight (which look down at the target) and also to a Bear D radar aircraft. Because the data links require it to remain surfaced, the system as a whole is vulnerable during much of the period of flight of the missile. A later replacement, the Oscar class submarine with the SS-N-19 missile, need not surface; the submarine receives all her data prior to firing. In wartime, this type of submarine would almost certainly be assigned to anti-carrier rather than to anti-submarine work.

9. *Above:* A Bear D displays its big surface search radar (in the bulge below the belly). The radar, which an Echo II uses for targeting, is as much part of the Echo/SS-N-3 weapon system as the missile or the submarine. British light aircraft carriers were assigned Sea Harrier fighters specifically to destroy Bears and thus to break up SS-N-3 missile attacks. SS-N-3 is also carried by eight Soviet surface ships.

10. *Below:* The Soviets designed their newer strategic submarines specifically so that they could operate from bastions, and they built a navy to defend those areas. This is a Yankee class strategic submarine modified to carry 12 SS-N-17 long-range ballistic missiles.

11. *Top:* The US Navy has also sought longer missile range in its submarines, but for a very different purpose: to extend the patrol areas of its craft, so that they are less vulnerable. In Maritime Strategy terms, such extension increases the effort the Soviets must expend to deal with the US force, and so reduces the Soviet ability to wage war against shipping in the open sea. A Trident missile is shown being loaded aboard USS *Ohio*.

12. *Above:* The war in the bastions would be fought primarily by US submarines; USS *Olympia* is shown. The tube running down her side houses her towed array. Later ships of this class have Tomahawk launching tubes forward.

13. *Below:* In ASW, long range means low frequency, which means long wavelength and great size. This dome, the largest in current Western service, houses an SQS-26 sonar. More recent US warships are fitted with a later version of the same set, SQS-53. The shipyard workers give some idea of the scale. In US submarines, a comparable sonar fills the entire bow.

14. *Right:* Long ASW detection ranges require something more than a ship and a ship-launched weapon. The prosecuting helicopter becomes an integral part of the total system. Here the frigate *Whipple* is accompanied by her LAMPS I helicopter. The pipe-like antenna at the top of her mast is the data link by means of which the helicopter feeds her sonobuoy data to the ship for processing. The range of the system is limited by the range of that link.

15. *Centre right:* An aircraft can find submerged submarines only by dropping an underwater sensor, a sonobuoy. Sonobuoy size in turn is limited because a searching aircraft must lay substantial fields, and complexity (hence cost) must be limited because hundreds of thousands must be expended annually. Here a standard-size sonobuoy is loaded into the ejector rack of a P-3 Orion patrol aircraft.

16. *Below right:* Just as helicopters are needed to prosecute contacts made by long-range (shipboard) tactical sonars, aircraft are needed to prosecute very long range contacts made by strategic sensors such as SOSUS. This is a P-3, the standard US ASW patrol aircraft. It was developed from the Electra airliner, and in recent years there has been some concern that in a future war it may have to operate in areas contested by Soviet fighters, perhaps flown from Soviet carriers.

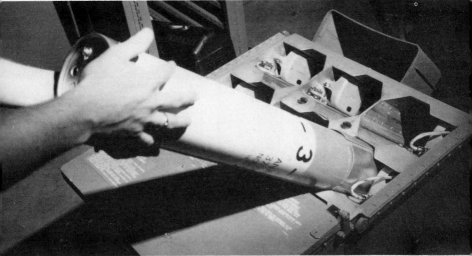

18. *Left:* Modern ships look as they do in large part because modern weapons are so large. This Standard Extended Range anti-aircraft missile has just been loaded into its magazine aboard the destroyer *Mahan*; the men nearby give some indication of the scale. The missile is stowed without the large fins required to stabilise its booster, to reduce the space it occupies. Just before it is fired, the fins are attached manually. This type of operation is not practical for a fully automated launcher such as the current Mark 26 or the vertical system now entering service, and an alternative (fin-less) booster design, to achieve long range, has been developed.

17. *Left:* ASW may be the last refuge of Western naval nuclear weapons. It is not always clear, however, that the damage will be one-sided. Here the destroyer *Agerholm* has just fired a nuclear Asroc missile, in its only full test. Many surface officers have suggested that the shock effects of so powerful an underwater explosion would quite possibly disable or even sink their own ships.

19. *Below:* Marine amphibious forces complement carrier striking groups. The small helicopter carrier *Iwo Jima* is shown, with troop-carrying CH-46 helicopters forward, small UH-1s at her deck edge, and big CH-53s aft. The CH-53 airframe has been adapted for minesweeping, and this type of ship can support a helicopter mine countermeasures operation.

20. *Bottom:* Helicopters cannot lift really heavy equipment, such as large tanks, which must go by water, and, at least at present, must ride over the beach by way of a craft with beaching capability. Two are shown: an LST, a fast ship with transoceanic range which can beach (lowering a ramp by means of the "horns" forward), and an LCU (LCU 1641 is shown), which must be transported in the floodable "well deck" of a larger ship. This LCU is loaded from the auxiliary (aft) ramp of LST 1179. All such beaching craft are relatively slow, because their bows must be broad and flat (to accommodate ramps), and thus are vulnerable to shore fire. The new air cushion craft should be less vulnerable, because it is much faster, and because it can unload well inland, and thus can bypass the killing zone at the surf line.

21. *Above:* The recommissioned battleships can help relieve the pressure on carriers, and they will also support opposed amphibious landings. USS *New Jersey*, the first to be recommissioned, is shown. The large crane allows her to refuel escort ships in heavy weather, and so to extend the range of the force she heads.

22. *Below:* Modern naval weapons can be extremely destructive. As here, a torpedo exploding under a ship's keel can snap her in half. Ships can be designed to survive this kind of damage, but the main hope for existing ones is probably some type of anti-torpedo weapon. The old 14,000 ton US light cruiser *Wilkes-Barre* is shown. Properly designed, using recent ideas, a much smaller ship could have survived this type of attack.

23. *Above:* A carrier cannot accommodate very many attack aircraft, but she does have very large magazines. As long as her attack aircraft can strike relatively unscathed, they can shuttle back and forth to deliver those weapons. In Libya in 1986 the Navy demonstrated its ability to neutralise Soviet-style air defences. EA-6B Prowlers like this one shown aboard the *Nimitz* contributed heavily to that success.

24. *Below:* The US Maritime Strategy requires substantial allied contributions. Soviet strategy also envisages the use of allies, which may use Soviet-supplied weapons to help close important sea lanes. Many client states received Komar-class missile boats like the one shown here. Styx (SS-N-2) missiles fired by an Egyptian Komar in 1967 sank the Israeli destroyer *Eilat*, the first known victim of a ship-to-ship missile. Three years before, the threat of such boats had kept US Mediterranean amphibious forces from remaining for very long in any one place during a Cyprus crisis.

25. *Above:* Surface ships are the most visible, and probably the least important, element of Soviet naval power. An effective strategy helps maintain that evaluation, so that money is spent on killing the most serious – rather than the most impressive – threats. This is the largest current Soviet surface ship, the VSTOL carrier *Kiev*. A larger carrier should enter service early in the next decade. It is by no means clear whether the Soviets will be able to afford many more.

26. *Below:* Naval aircraft aboard the carrier *America* prepare for the raid on Libya, 15 April 1986. The attack demonstrated the reach of US maritime power. Because the carrier aircraft were able to penetrate Libya's Soviet-supplied air defences with impunity, the attacks served a wider purpose, to emphasise the vulnerability of many other, similarly supplied, Third World states. The aircraft illustrated are two F-14 fighters, an A-7 attack bomber, and, in the background, an EA-6B Prowler radar-countermeasures aircraft.

27. *Above:* Soviet reliance on bastions is an important motivating force in the US maritime strategy. This Typhoon class strategic submarine was designed for operation from within protected waters; from them, it can fire its long-range ballistic missiles against targets in North America. Although not very slow, it can hardly be agile enough to deal with a determined attack submarine opponent. Instead, it must rely on a combination of silencing and the protection of other submarines, surface ships, and ASW aircraft.

28. *Below:* Inertia is the besetting problem of the Soviet system. This new Delta IV class strategic submarine is a case in point. Its basic hull and, almost certainly, many of its basic systems duplicate those of the first modern Soviet strategic submarine, the Yankee, which first appeared two decades ago. The principal change is in the missiles carried, in the tall hump so visible aft of the sail. The doors visible on the ramped portion of the hump probably conceal a towed communications buoy. The function of the pipe atop the fin, visible on the right, is not certain, but it may well house a towed wire antenna. As with their US counterparts, reliable communication with strategic submarines is extremely important to the Soviets.

29. *Above:* The need to maintain peacetime presence is an important "boundary condition" on the design of the US fleet. Conditions on the uncertain edge between peace and limited war often do not quite match those of a full war, as the USS *Stark* incident shows. A neutral ship on station, even in a war zone, cannot lightly fire her weapons when aircraft approach. In wartime, however, she can fire upon detecting them. In the case of the *Stark*, moreover, it appears that she had been overflown so many times without consequences, that the final, fatal, approach was dismissed as routine. In this case what mattered was that the damage could be contained. The basic design of the *Stark* was sturdy enough to limit the damage, and to present the well-trained crew with sufficient resources to save their ship. Such ruggedness is often largely a function of the sheer size of the ship. The ship is shown after her fires had been put out and sufficient firefighting water pumped out to restore her full stability. The damage due to one Exocet missile is visible as plating torn from her hull, and as plating distorted on the front of her superstructure, due presumably to the heat of the fire. Damage from a second missile, farther aft, is not visible.

would be so terrified of the effects of Soviet nuclear attack that they would prefer surrender.

It is in this context that the current US naval programme has been questioned. Critics have suggested that money invested in costly power projection units, such as carrier battle forces, might better be invested in land forces in Europe, which in turn might help deter the Soviets from some future adventure by raising the nuclear threshold.[7]

Implicit in this criticism is the assumption that the projection forces cannot be expected significantly to affect the course of a land campaign in Europe. Sea control forces (distinguished from projection forces) are still valued, because they may be needed to sustain a land campaign in Europe. The critics' assumption is that, to be effective in the land campaign, naval power projection would entail such huge risks that it would not be practicable, since the price of power projection might be sustained sea control. Alternatively, one might associate risky forms of power projection, such as landings on or behind the flanks of an advancing Soviet army, with a margin or surplus of sea power over that required to sustain sea control. The critics would argue that funds required to support any such margin can better be invested in ground forces.

The critics assume a static relationship between sea control and surplus naval force. The US Maritime Strategy operates on a very different assumption: that sea control can be seized by early offensive operations, after which the requirements of sea control will fall drastically. Thus, after the earliest stages of a war, most of the navy (assuming it is properly configured) will become available for power projection. However, given the offensive approach to sea control, this portion of the overall naval force cannot be dispensed with, whatever one's view of the utility of naval power projection in a major war, *because exactly this force is required to seize and guarantee sea control in the first place.*

Naval power projection attacks would necessarily be mounted on the tactical or strategic flanks of the Soviet advance. A typical tactical flanking attack might be an amphibious assault to retake Jutland (Denmark) after the Soviet line of advance had swept past. Strategic flanking attacks might be exemplified by amphibious or air attacks on Soviet territory far from the Central Front, e.g. Leningrad, or the Crimea, or Petropavlovsk. In each case, large naval forces would have to approach concentrations of Soviet tactical air power and coast defence craft, and they might well have to accept expensive losses.

The critics ask whether such losses can ever be worth their results. After all, the Soviets are well aware of the principle of concentration on the strategic objective, and that they would never, therefore, be foolish enough to divert forces to their flanks. The situation is somewhat more complicated, however. A tactical flanking assault would threaten the lines of communication to the advancing Soviet Army, and it would have to be dealt with. It is notoriously difficult for armies to turn to face flanking attacks, and a timely attack could reduce the pressure on NATO armies under attack. Of course, whether this could be done would depend very much on the timetable of the war.

Strategic flanks are another matter. Clearly the Soviets would not be able to divert large ground forces from a continuing offensive to deal with distant threats, even to their own soil. They could, after all, expect to deal with those problems after they had reached their main objective. However, the viable threat of such assaults would certainly affect prewar Soviet dispositions, and it would reduce the concentration the Soviets might hope to effect. That would be particularly important in the event the Soviets did not fully mobilise, e.g. to achieve surprise or to avoid some internal problem.[8]

Certainly dispositions designed to deal with any one attack on the seaward flank would not seriously disrupt Soviet plans. However, there are no fixed roads in the sea. The Soviets must deal with a very wide variety of possible seaborne attacks. It is much easier for a fleet at sea to shift from one possible assault area to another than for troops and their supporting structure (including aircraft) ashore to be redeployed. Thus even relatively small seaborne forces may, by their varied threats, tie down substantial ground and tactical air forces. For example, the same ships can threaten both the Black Sea and the Kola Peninsula, shifting from one to the other within about ten days. It would take much longer to move masses of men and materiel over the corresponding land routes within the Soviet Union. In the Far East, the same Seventh Fleet threatens both Kamchatka in the north (with its concentration of strategic submarines) and the sensitive area near the Chinese frontier in the south. Moreover, because troops have to be concentrated on the central front, it will be difficult for the Soviets to concentrate enough troops on each peripheral front to prevent amphibious forces from gaining at least some ground.

The case most frequently cited is the Far East, where the implicit US threat certainly ties down substantial defensive forces. It probably prevents the Soviets from massing sufficient forces to attack Japan, thus helping to guarantee the wartime supply of vital manufactured products to this country. Moreover, the presence of large mobile US forces helps reassure China, and thus indirectly to keep very large Soviet army and air forces tied down on the Chinese border.

Some other implicit assumptions also deserve mention here. First, it is not altogether clear that the scenario of a Soviet *blitzkrieg* is appropriate. Even the most optimistic Soviet leader would have to reckon with the (albeit unlikely) possibility that NATO really would react to an invasion by firing nuclear weapons, and therefore that an invasion of Western Europe might prove unprofitable. It seems more likely, then, that any European war would develop out of some unforeseen contingency (such as an uprising in Eastern Europe), in which both sides gradually fed forces into the conflict. NATO has a massive mobilisation potential, and might well be able to sustain a stalemate somewhere in Germany.[9] Perhaps, then, the outcome of the war would be determined more by ultimate mobilisation capacity than by the strength of standing NATO ground and tactical air forces (bought, perhaps, at the expense of naval power projection forces).

Second, it seems quite likely that the massive urbanisation of Western Europe would present any invading Soviet army with substantial obstacles, and therefore that it would be difficult for NATO to be defeated very quickly. One might conclude that the NATO deficiency on land has been somewhat overstated, and that desperate expedients like the sacrifice of naval forces may not quite be justified.

Third, in the event of a major European war, it is by no means clear that NATO (or, for that matter, Warsaw Pact) air forces on the ground at the outset would survive for very long, given the sheer scale of striking power against fixed installations enjoyed by both sides. Similarly, it seems likely that a very large proportion of the air forces on both sides would fall victim to IFF (identification friend or foe) failures, so that few organised air units would remain after the first few days.[10]

In that case surviving naval air arms might contribute a disproportionate fraction of total NATO tactical air power – if they were available, i.e., if they had already carried out their main purely naval mission of seizing sea control without themselves being ground down to nothing.

It is, then, by no means clear that *any* European war would quickly end in a Soviet victory at the English Channel. Stalemate would make the possibility of turning the only available tactical flank, on the sea, extremely valuable. The situation might then resemble that in 1914–18, when the British twice contemplated large amphibious assaults on the flanks. In 1914–15, Admiral Sir John Fisher planned an attack on the Baltic, to relieve pressure on the Russian army by threatening Berlin and other German urban centres directly. The scheme had to be rejected as too risky. Again, in 1917–18, the British planned an attack on the Flanders coast, with the dual objectives of forcing the German Army to fall back and destroying U-boat bases. Once more, the attack had to be cancelled as too risky. It is by no means clear that these proposed attacks would have been effective, as existing technology would not have moved troops ashore and then inland very fast; but the strategic possibilities were certainly well appreciated.

In each case, risk was assessed in terms of the possible loss of sea control through the loss of valuable capital ships and thus of the British margin over the German fleet. Thus the destruction of the German fleet in harbour would have been a prerequisite for the exercise of British sea power on the German-controlled coast.[11]

The Allies did make several attacks on the *strategic* flanks of the Central Powers. In 1915 the British, ANZACs, and the French landed at Gallipoli, abandoning the attempt when the cost, in sea control, seemed too high. Later allied control of the Mediterranean permitted operations based on Salonika, and also the assaults on the Ottoman Empire through Mesopotamia and then through Palestine. Allied control of the Mediterranean also supported the Italian front against Austria, which also might be seen as a strategic flanking operation.

Renewed interest in the amphibious aspect of a major war represents a reversion to World War II concepts; after about 1948 the US Navy tended to equate power projection with air strikes. The reason was that concentrations of amphibious shipping made extremely attractive nuclear targets. More recently, many have assumed that modern anti-ship missiles, fired from shore, would make short work of amphibious ships constrained to anchor in fixed positions. However, with the appearance of fast shuttle craft such as the new US air cushion landing craft (LCAC), the large valuable amphibious ships need no longer remain very close to shore.[12] Moreover, it was assumed (perhaps incorrectly) that it would never be possible to concentrate enough troops at such an invasion to overcome the masses of Soviet troops which would always be available.[13]

Particularly as the US nuclear arsenal grew, power projection in major war came to be equated with nuclear attack from the sea, by carrier aircraft and by missiles. Although the navy might not be able to deliver enormous tonnages, it would be able to deliver attacks from anywhere along the Eurasian periphery. Thus it would be difficult for the Soviets to emplace fixed defences against naval attacks.

Within the NATO context, the US Navy argued that, at least along the flanks of the alliance, carriers represented the most powerful available concentrations of tactical airpower, and that their intervention might help the NATO land forces to stop Soviet attacks. This argument might be extended: naval strike forces constitute a useful strategic depth for NATO. The Soviets might expect to destroy a large fraction of the fixed airbases, and thus of NATO tactical aircraft, in the first hours of a conflict, but they could not expect to kill carriers well offshore. At the least, the attacks on air bases closer to the NATO-Warsaw Pact border would have to alert the carrier battle groups.

If, now, nuclear weapons seem less than likely to be used, and if

European stalemate is more likely than *blitzkrieg*, then the naval power projection of the past may seem more appropriate. That will not make projection much less risky, but it will make it more valuable.

Not all navies are (or have been) designed for both sea control/ sea denial and power projection; indeed before the advent of aircraft carriers it was not possible for navies to attack targets well inland. On the other hand, even navies not designed to carry out such attacks may prove flexible enough to mount them. The British experience in the Falklands is a prime example. The Royal Navy had been redesigned almost exclusively for sea control, which generally meant protecting ships in the North Atlantic (including the NATO Strike Fleet) from Soviet submarines. Yet, thanks largely to its retention of carriers (albeit for sea control), it was able to project power ashore in the Falklands, attacking Argentine army positions by a combination of bombing and naval gunfire.

The Search Problem as the Basis of Tactics

The key to naval strategy is the vastness of the ocean, in which ships can so easily hide. Submarines live by stealth, but even specific surface ships are difficult to find and to identify. As a result, naval tactics are largely dominated by the need to locate enemy ships, or to hide from enemy locators.

To deny an enemy the free use of the sea requires first some reliable means of locating his ships, and then a means of destroying or immobilising them. The two are interrelated, since different means of attack require different degrees of precision in target location. For example, a shell must be aimed at a precise point in space, since it generally cannot correct for aiming errors, and since its destructive area is quite limited. A modern anti-ship missile, however, can search for its target over an area of several square miles.

Anti-submarine warfare illustrates the basic alternatives in naval strategy. NATO ASW strategy is actually a combination of sea denial, convoy, and attack at (or near) source. The relative emphasis on each element depends on a combination of available resources and the level of Soviet submarine technology.

Submarines are so difficult to locate that the location problem is broken down into detection (which places a possible submarine somewhere within the battle area), classification (the decision that what has been found really is a submarine, on which it is worth while to expend weapons), localisation (bringing the submarine within the lethal volume defined by the weapon), and actual homing, which brings the weapon to the submarine. Failure at any one stage negates the whole attack.

NATO maintains long-range submarine detectors such as SOSUS. They can hear submarines at very long (oceanic) ranges, but at such distances location cannot be very precise. Typically a maritime patrol aircraft (such as a P-3 or a Nimrod) is sent out to search the area, probably several thousand square miles in size, defined by the long-range contact – to classify and to localise the possible target. Contact is likely to be intermittent, and time elapses between the original detection and the arrival of the aircraft. During that time, the submarine (if ever there was one – anti-submarine warfare is plagued by false detections) may leave the search area; the longer the elapsed time and the higher the submarine speed, the better the chance that it has left. Similarly, the aircraft cannot search several hundred square miles instantly. Protraction of search time, too, gives the submarine a chance to escape.[14]

Once the aircraft has a good estimate of submarine location, it can attack, using a homing torpedo which begins yet another search, this time over a much shorter range. The torpedo cannot actually detect the submarine outside (at most) a few thousand yards, so the torpedo must be dropped very close to the target.

Only after all of the other hurdles have been passed can the torpedo actually explode against the submarine – which it may or may not kill.

A simple calculation will illustrate this point. Long-range detection is clearly difficult; otherwise submarines would not be worth building. Then one might imagine that the probability, per day, that a submarine is detected by SOSUS or similar systems is quite low, say 5%.[15] One might also imagine that it is much easier for the patrol plane to find a submarine sufficiently precisely within the area defined by SOSUS, say 60%. Then one might imagine that the actual chance of a homing torpedo hitting a submarine is about 50%.[16] Each aircraft carries six torpedoes, so that, if it does locate the submarine well enough, it has an excellent chance – in this very simple model, 98.4%.[17] However, the net probability that the combination of SOSUS and the aircraft connects with the submarine is only about 3%, so the probability that the submarine will be sunk is something less than 3%, which seems rather disappointing.

However, the submarine is likely to remain on station for several weeks, say for 50 days. Each day (assuming that SOSUS remains intact) it must face that 3% chance of being killed. Over 50 days, its net chance of being killed is about 78%. A system which might be quite ineffective in a very short, sharp war becomes devastating over the course of a protracted conflict, provided that it itself is not attrited. The combination of SOSUS and the patrol plane is devastating because it applies every day, whether the submarine is exerting itself to attack shipping or not.

The value of the exercise depends upon other factors. During that 50 days on station, the submarine is sinking ships. What scale of losses can the West afford, while the Soviet submarine force is being ground down? That depends on the need for cargoes landed every day in Europe, and on the sheer size of the Western merchant fleets – which have been declining rather sharply of late. How long is the war itself likely to last? If it is assumed that the war will be over within a week or so, due to the threat of nuclear escalation, then 50 days of ASW seems irrelevant.

The SOSUS/P-3 combination is clearly designed to achieve sea denial *and not necessarily sea control*, because it does not *in itself* protect the likely targets of the submarines, the ships crossing the Atlantic to deliver cargoes to Europe. It is easy to imagine an alternative system designed more to protect the ships than to destroy the submarines, in which ASW firepower is concentrated together with the likely targets: convoy.

Say, for example, that a submarine attacking a convoy suffers a 50% chance of loss if it approaches close enough to be sure of sinking one ship. The probability of loss is high partly because the submarine reveals itself by attacking. One might, then, assume proportionately higher changes of loss (75 and 87.5%, respectively) if it exposes itself long enough to sink two or three ships. Many submarine commanders will therefore prefer to avoid coming close enough to attack effectively. A few, however, will take the risk. They will be killed off relatively quickly, since the chance of dying in a convoy battle will be quite high. As a result, very few merchant ships will be sunk – but many submarines will survive.

In this case the analysis is much more complicated, as so much depends on the aggressiveness of the submarine commanders. In the case of SOSUS, the rate of ship sinkings is initially high; it falls off steadily over time as submarines are killed. In the case of convoy, the rate is initially limited because only a small proportion of submarine commanders care to risk destruction by the co-located ASW forces. Much then depends upon just how risky such attacks are found to be. If the odds are really bad, the submarine force is soon neutralised, as the aggressive officers do not survive more than one or two convoy battles. However, it may be that the odds are grossly overstated – that they are, for example, 5% for the first ship, and only a little more after that. In that case the less aggressive commanders initially neutralised by their estimates of the odds will decide to enter the battle, and the effective size of the anti-shipping force will increase drastically.

The distinction is not total, because SOSUS does detect submarines by the sounds they make. The faster the submarine, the louder its sound. It can therefore be argued that the average Soviet commander may try to avoid high speed running, to reduce the chance of detection. Effectively immobilised, he may find it much more difficult to carry out attacks, since on average the targets will not cross his path.

World War II illustrates both cases of convoy warfare. Most of the German U-boat "aces" were killed relatively early in the war, and productivity per U-boat fell off dramatically. When the odds really became bad, after mid-1943, the U-boats had to be withdrawn, even though relatively few had been sunk. On the other hand US submariners in the Pacific discovered that the odds of being killed by Japanese convoy escorts were extremely low. By 1944, they saw convoys as concentrations of targets, not potential danger zones.

Because it focuses on the ships to be protected, convoy is clearly a *sea control* measure, an alternative to trying to deny the sea to enemy anti-shipping forces.

Convoy also made it more difficult for the anti-shipping forces to find targets. The concentration of the targets leaves most of the ocean empty. In World War I, the Germans had no means of locating merchant ships in the open ocean; they spread their U-boats in hopes of coming upon ships spread out along the major trade routes. Sightings, and therefore attacks, declined very sharply when most of the ocean was emptied. Moreover, even if it came upon a convoy, a U-boat could attack only a few targets at a time. Most of the ships in any substantial convoy would therefore necessarily escape.

Concentration, moreover, makes control possible. In both world wars, the Allies were able to ascertain approximate U-boat positions, largely by code-breaking and radio direction-finding (D/F). Convoys or individual important ships could, therefore, be routed away from such danger areas. Such simple evasion saved enormous numbers of ships in both world wars. Diesel-electric submarines are not particularly mobile, so information on their approximate location remains valid for some considerable time.

The two strategies place very different requirements on a navy. Successful convoying requires enough escorts to make the attack on any one convoy extremely dangerous. The number of convoys (and therefore the number of escorts) depends, not on the scale of the enemy threat, but rather on the number of ships to be protected. Early NATO convoy studies suggested that about 600 escorts would be required for the North Atlantic, on the basis of eight to 12 escorts per convoy. Such figures were achievable only because of the sheer size of wartime escort-building programmes. However, as ASW technology advanced, the wartime escorts had to be discarded: they could not accommodate the new weapons and sensors.

The scale of sea-denial forces need only be sufficient to

prosecute the expected number of daily contacts. In the case of SOSUS, for example, one might imagine that the Soviets could operate only about a dozen attack submarines in the Atlantic, a mixture of old (noisier) nuclear submarines and newer, quieter diesels; the best nuclear submarines would be retained in home waters to protect ballistic missile craft. On average, then, there might be no more than one contact a day (more if the SOSUS detection rate against noisy nuclear submarines were substantially higher than 5% per day). No single base could support SOSUS prosecutions over the entire North Atlantic, and one might want to support a prosecution from each of several bases, but clearly the numbers of aircraft involved would not be very large.

On the other hand, SOSUS depends for its efficacy on sounds the submarines make. If they are sufficiently silenced, its 5% per day probability of detection might vanish altogether in many ocean areas: its few big detectors may be reduced to a range of hundreds or even tens of miles. That seems to be the case at present, as the newest Soviet submarines are extremely quiet (Sierra and Akula classes). In that case it may become impossible to maintain open-ocean coverage, and NATO may be forced back to a dense array of short-range detectors covering some specific area. That appears to be the character of the new Fixed Distributed System. The mathematics of the system would change radically, because the dense array would have to be concentrated athwart the route the submarine would take into or out of its operational area. One might, for example, suppose that the dense array would detect a transiting submarine 50% of the time, and that (as in the SOSUS case) a P-3 would manage to kill about 60% of the submarines it is sent to hunt (although the number might fall because the aircraft would find it more difficult to re-detect a quiet submarine). Then the net chance of killing a submarine would be 30% per passage through the array, and a submarine would pass through twice per patrol, for a net loss rate of about 51%.

This is not quite comparable to the loss rate in SOSUS, because once the submarine has passed through the array, it suffers no other major threats. Moreover, knowing that the array is finite – and that the forces monitoring it are finite – the Soviets could choose to rush it. They would sacrifice a few submarines, in the knowledge that the monitoring forces are limited in their attack capacity. In that case the effective loss rate in the array might be substantially less than 30%.

Yet another possibility is to deal with the enemy force at or near its bases, where it is concentrated. The classic version is a close blockade (to keep the enemy from coming out) supplemented, perhaps, by attacks on enemy ships in harbour or on the bases themselves. Sustained blockade, however, carries with it the cost of maintaining the blockading forces, which may suffer losses either to enemy action or to the hazards of the sea. A modern variation, "attack at source", seeks to solve the problem as quickly as possible, by a massive attack on the enemy forces in or near their bases. Applied to submarines, this is the ASW version of maritime superiority.

Compared to convoy, this type of strategy requires less numerous, though quite different, forces. Really close blockade almost certainly requires submarines, since only they can live for very long in nominally enemy-controlled waters. They in turn suffer from the usual limitations on submarine communications, so that it is difficult at best to coordinate adjacent submarines within the blockade. That in turn limits blockade efficiency, as submarines must be spaced far enough apart not to detect and engage each other, yet close enough to have a reasonable chance of detecting their targets, reliable sonar ranges being quite short. Individual submarines may also be limited in their ability to deal with several targets at the same time. Given the limited detection range of individual submarines, US and NATO planners of the late 1940s and early 1950s expected to use several hundred submarines to seal off Soviet submarine bases.

Efficiency requires that the blockaders be so close together that detection of an escaper is almost certain. If the blockade is relatively inefficient, it becomes an attrition strategy comparable to that already discussed under the head of SOSUS. However, it has an interesting twist. The enemy may find the presence of the blockaders intolerable, and he may therefore devote considerable forces to dealing with them. If those forces must be subtracted from the anti-ship submarines the blockaders are trying to kill off, then the effect of the blockaders' mere presence may be to keep a large fraction of the enemy sea denial force at home.

The main limitation on close blockade or attack at or near source is that it must occur in areas the enemy can defend. Therefore it merges into a variation, blockage of choke points located between the enemy base and the open ocean, yet beyond easy range of enemy defensive forces.

NATO was formed at a time of crisis in ASW. In World War II, the allies had enjoyed something roughly equivalent to SOSUS in that German U-boats could be located at long range by a combination of code-breaking (to predict their positions) and radio direction-finding (D/F: the submarines themselves had to report to their own command centre in France). Given these locations, aircraft could be sent out to attack them. However, it seemed most unlikely that the wartime technical miracles of code-breaking and radio direction-finding would be repeated against the Soviets, who after all had captured many of the wartime German naval officers and records. As a result, for a time after the war, the allied navies had to rely in part on "flaming data". Ships sunk by submarine were expected to send out distress signals, and the areas around those sinking could be searched by aircraft. This desperate pass explains just how miraculous the advent of SOSUS must have seemed.

Nor did convoy seem terribly attractive. The Soviets had captured German U-boat technology which seemed sufficient to overcome existing escorts. It was assumed that the Soviets would soon mass-produce the new U-boats and their weapons. Countervailing escort technology was developed in time, but it forced up the cost of the escorts, and so ultimately made it impossible for NATO to field them in sufficient numbers. Again, the impossibility of maintaining convoy escorts made the SOSUS-based strategy extremely attractive. However, SOSUS itself is vulnerable to the drastic improvements in Soviet submarine technology recently reported.

SOSUS did not enter service until the late 1950s.

Thus, for the first few years of its existence, NATO's naval commanders emphasised "attack at source". It was conceived as a form of blockade: submarines had to begin and end their patrols at their bases, in the latter case not only for repairs but merely to replenish their weapons. Attackers at or near the bases could, therefore, expect to encounter numerous submarines. Much clearly depended upon how dangerous those base areas might be. Submarines, which could hope to live in the face of Soviet defensive measures, were the obvious choice for "attack at source".

This was not a new idea. In World War I, frustrated by ASW failures, the British built special submarines for forward operations. They also tried to seal the U-boat base at Zeebrugge, in 1918. The British tried to operate ASW submarines close to German U-boat bases during World War II but, as ASW improved, they had to draw back due to heavy losses. Similarly, about 1950 the US Navy planned to operate ASW submarines close to Soviet submarine bases. About a decade later, US doctrine called instead for submarines to operate in choke points further from Soviet naval bases.[18]

The key question in the blockade or "attack at source" approach is just how determined the enemy is to move his submarines out onto the sea lanes for anti-shipping warfare. If most of the submarines begin the war in home waters, and remain there for a substantial period after the war breaks out, the combination of barriers and forward blockade may destroy a large percentage of the force before it can do any harm at all. If, however, the submarine force is dispersed *before* the war begins, then it will do considerable damage before attrition begins.

This has been a very controversial issue. Knowing how effective "attack at source" could be, NATO naval strategists of the 1950s and 1960s assumed that the Soviets would begin a war by surging their submarines out into the North Atlantic for an anti-shipping campaign. Some went so far as to view SOSUS more as a means of providing war warning (by detecting the pre-war surge) than as a means of killing off the Soviet submarine force once war had begun. More recently, and certainly since the late 1970s, the perception has grown that the Soviet fleet will, at least at first, concentrate on directly protecting the homeland (and the valuable strategic missile submarine force) against allied naval forces. Only after a time would significant numbers of Soviet submarines and naval aircraft be assigned to anti-shipping duties.[19]

This possibility opens up another approach to neutralising Soviet anti-shipping forces: to tie them down by giving them something less harmful (or more hazardous) upon which to concentrate, capitalising on the different national priorities of the two nations involved. In the case of the US Maritime Strategy, Soviet strategic submarines, which the Soviets evidently consider a valuable national asset, are deliberately threatened largely to force the Soviets to mount an intense ASW campaign in their home waters – employing their own submarines, which otherwise might mount an anti-shipping campaign on the North Atlantic.[20]

The problem of the strategic submarine (SSBN) illuminates the distinction between sea denial and sea control, to the extent that the latter amounts to protection of free use of the sea. Because Soviet SSBNs do not threaten allied shipping as such, sea control measures which protect shipping, or which discourage submarines from attacking ships at sea, are largely irrelevant to them. The only relevant countervailing strategy would be sea denial: to make the sea dangerous for these craft. That in turn implies prosecution by sea denial measures: either by hunting down the submarines one by one, using a long-range detector; or by blockading their bases and transit areas.[21]

Conversely, if it is assumed that SSBNs are so quiet (or are so well operated) that they cannot be detected at long range, and if their operational security is such that it is virtually impossible to pick them up at their bases, then one can argue that they are effectively invulnerable: applied to them, sea denial is *not a feasible strategy*. That has been the Western position. It appears that the Soviets feel otherwise, and that at the least they hope to trail Western SSBNs. Assuming that the Western evaluation is correct, this Soviet expectation should tie down a fair number of Soviet nuclear attack submarines which otherwise would present a considerable threat to Western sea control. The prospect is a kind of mirror image of the concept of directly attacking Soviet SSBN operating areas as outlined in the current US Maritime Strategy.[22]

The broad strategic ideas outlined here are applicable to the other major areas of naval warfare affecting sea control: anti-air warfare (AAW) and anti-ship warfare (ASUW).

In the case of AAW, most Soviet naval aircraft are land-based bombers equipped with long-range anti-ship missiles such as AS-4 and AS-6. They are designed to exercise sea denial in the areas contiguous to the Soviet Union, to destroy NATO aircraft carriers and amphibious ships approaching Soviet waters. However, if they are not required for this mission, they have an enormous open-ocean ship-killing potential, because no existing NATO surface ship (other than a carrier equipped with long-range fighters) can expect to kill such bombers before they launch their stand-off missiles.[23]

The long range detection/kill option is not really open, because, even though the aircraft are not difficult to detect, killers (long-range fighters) cannot possibly always be available. Evasion is difficult because the bombers are so much faster than surface ships. It is, however, conceivable that a surface force could evade, leaving decoys in the area the bombers expect to attack, and perhaps arranging for an aerial counterattack.[24]

That leaves three options: forcing the bombers to concentrate on something other than sea denial, or directly protecting their targets, or killing them at source. US maritime strategists have proposed a mixture of the first and last. By threatening "attack at source" by their attack aircraft, US carriers force the bombers, which might otherwise be extremely effective anti-shipping weapons, to concentrate instead on dealing with them. The fighters aboard the carriers in turn should be able to destroy the bombers in the air, eliminating the threat they represent. The carrier battle forces, then, act as both bait and trap.

The alternative·is to accept that the bombers can come out at will, and to emphasise short-range defensive missiles and electronic countermeasures, to mitigate their effect. This was how the British sought to counter Exocet-firing Argentine aircraft in the Falklands. Since the bombers can shuttle back and forth to pick up new missiles, this strategy may exhaust the defence. At the least, it demands much more of terminal defences.

Strategy and the Structure of Navies

The reader should not imagine that a naval staff typically assembles a menu of possible strategies, and then makes an explicit choice. The broad possibilities are limited, and each has been tried so often that they are implicitly understood. Resources generally do not permit any navy to follow many of them at the same time, so that a review of different navies over time seems to show that one or another of the basic choices usually predominates, and that the state of naval technology exerts the chief influence.[25]

The primary choice, between sea control and sea denial, is determined by national strategy rather than by technology. NATO cannot sustain a war *unless* its associated navies maintain a considerable degree of sea control, because sea lanes are important as internal lines of communication within the NATO alliance. On the other hand, NATO might seek to maintain sea control in several quite different ways: by so arming escorts that Soviet attempts at sea denial (i.e., interdiction of sea lanes) would generally fail; or by blocking Soviet access to the open sea, i.e., to the sea lanes (using choke points); or by attacking the Soviet fleet "at source", i.e., at its bases; or by forcing the Soviets into a decisive engagement with a superior NATO fleet.

For its part, the Soviet Union is a largely autarkic empire, for which sea lanes of communication (such as the Southern Sea Route) may be convenient, but are hardly essential. On the other hand, the Soviets do take the threat of seaborne attack into account, so they must attempt to deny the sea approaches to the Soviet Union to the Western navies. Sea denial in the open ocean presents them with important wartime opportunities when fighting an alliance held together by sea lanes.

The Concentrated Fleet

One other broad strategic concept seems important: the battle fleet, the concentration of naval power. At present the Western navies tend to operate in concentrated formations; Soviet tactics emphasise dispersion. Concentration makes for mutal support in

defence as well as in offence, since nearby ships can cover each
other. Dispersion almost necessarily means that each ship must
defend itself, although concentration in attack is still possible,
given long-range missiles and reliable long-haul communications.

The precise meanings of concentration and dispersion depend
on technology, and in particular on the range of defensive weapons
and sensors. During the 1950s, for example, the US Navy emphasised the development of longer-range defensive weapons because
it expected to operate its ships in more dispersed (but still mutually
supportive) formations. The fear was that an entire closely concentrated formation might be destroyed by a single nuclear weapon.[26]
On the other hand, the closer the ships, the greater the overlap
between their defensive systems. For example, about 1960 the US
Navy began to install large sonars (SQS-23) aboard some of its
carriers and cruisers, where formerly sonars had been fitted only
to destroyers. The fear was that, given the limited range of the
escorting destroyers' sonars and the new open formations, submarines would be able to slip between them. Sonars aboard the carriers and cruisers would be able to locate these "leakers", and
the new long-range ASW weapons would destroy them. This particular idea proved impractical for the carriers, but the basic concept
is still valid: the less concentrated the fleet, the more important it is
to spread defensive firepower among the units of the fleet.

The battle fleet is the most extreme concentration of naval
power, a concentration of power so threatening to any enemy that
it must be destroyed before he can begin to consider operations
against the vital sea lanes, not to mention any attempt to operate
against the land mass of the United States. The fleet is, further,
conceived as so powerful that the enemy's necessary attempt to
destroy it will in turn entail the destruction or neutralisation of his
own naval forces. If the main fleet is properly designed, then, an
enemy can choose only between remaining at home (as a "fleet in
being") and coming out to fight a losing battle.

Once it has fought the decisive battle, the fleet can carry out its
original, perhaps non-naval, threat. For example, it may attack
enemy land forces. Similarly, because it is designed to present a
threat to the land, the fleet is well suited to project power into the

third world, because nothing short of a great-power fleet can possibly destroy it. The current US Maritime Strategy is an *application* of this idea, but the basic concept has been implicit in US naval thinking since 1889.

These abstract principles explain not only the current US Maritime Strategy, but also classical US and British naval practice. At present the closest existing approach to a classical battle fleet is the US carrier battle force.

There is no law of nature stating that such a fleet can do what is required of it. However, one can very reasonably conclude that the existence of a viable battle fleet is a precondition for the US maritime strategy, and, to the extent that the strategy in turn is virtually determined by a variety of boundary conditions, that the technology and tactics required for a viable fleet are a precondition for effective Western sea control. Recent exercises and current and projected technical developments seem, moreover, to show that the fleet concept is workable in the face of Soviet tactics and equipment.

It seems reasonable to equate concentration to a belief that sea control is a workable goal, that formations of surface ships (including non-combatants) can survive. Total dispersal would seem to imply an expectation that individual ships cannot survive for very long, and that operating several ships together merely provides an attacker with more targets and hence with an opportunity to do more damage per strike.

Some Western writers have described a variation on this theme, a kind of "naval guerilla warfare", in which units, normally dispersed, concentrate to carry out a strike, then disperse before the concentration can itself be attacked. Unfortunately such tactics, while possibly quite effective in sea denial, seem inappropriate to sea control, because they do not lead to any kind of guarantee of the safety of shipping. They do not, for example, provide any means of dealing with an enemy sea denial force which is not itself concentrated, and so which does not offer a worthwhile strike target. Sea control, not the survival of Western warships, is fundamental to the Western position.[27]

The other argument against concentration is that the sea is very broad, and that some versions of sea control require that defensive power be spread out to match dispersed attackers. For example, there is a practical upper limit to the size of an individual convoy, and command and control limits the number of escorts per group. As a result, convoy escort groups, which themselves are (in effect) small concentrated fleets, must be multiplied to cover large numbers of merchant ships.

The battle fleet concept transcends the particular types of ships now in service. It continues classical American (and, for that matter, British) naval strategy from the era of battleships. Because it reflects fundamental national requirements, it will presumably continue into whatever future we can imagine. Note that concentrated fleets are generally associated with the strategy of command of the sea, since the success of the basic strategy implies that large ships, and concentrations of such ships, can operate freely at sea. However, sea control is not always associated with a concentrated-fleet strategy.

In the case of the Maritime Strategy, the fleet has three related parts: a massed carrier battle force, a forward-area submarine force, and an amphibious/Marine force. The carrier battle group presents an unacceptable threat of direct attacks against Soviet land targets. The submarines directly threaten the most valuable Soviet naval asset, the ballistic missile submarine. In addition, their cruise missiles threaten Soviet land targets. For example, one might imagine the use of non-nuclear submarine-launched Tomahawks to suppress Soviet air defences so as to permit the carrier group to make repeated attacks. The amphibious units directly threaten Soviet territory.

To counter the carriers, the Soviets must launch their own anti-ship bombers, which are perhaps their most potent anti-shipping weapon. The carrier battle group is uniquely well equipped to destroy those bombers in the air. Submarines which might otherwise attack shipping in the open ocean must first attempt to destroy the carriers, and the battle group can become a killing ground for them. As for the US submarines, the Soviets must tie down large numbers of their own attack submarines to counter them. Thus their presence tends to neutralise a major Soviet anti-ship force.

Some historical cases show how a main fleet supports sea control on an oceanic scale. In World War I, the Royal Navy concentrated its power in the Grand Fleet, which was based at Scapa Flow. Had there been no corresponding German battle fleet, the Grand Fleet could have been used to support amphibious operations, out-flanking the German position on land. This consideration helps to explain why the German High Seas Fleet was maintained almost entirely as a "fleet in being". For their part, the Germans always hoped that they could upset the balance of naval power by falling upon a portion of the Grand Fleet, and thus achieving local superiority. However, the net effect of maintaining the High Seas Fleet was to limit the surplus of naval resources available for sea denial, in the form of surface raiders and submarines. Moreover, because the Germans could not easily send out surface warships, the allies could escort convoys (and carry out other ASW operations) with very lightly armed craft.

Thus the Grand Fleet served (i) to prevent the Germans from projecting their power into England, by invasion; (ii) to enforce expenditures upon the Germans, and so limit their sea denial potential; and (iii) to cover the ASW escorts, which otherwise would necessarily have been larger and more expensive craft. To the extent that ASW success depended on the number of escorts, this economic argument seems extremely important.

In World War II, the British Home Fleet served a similar purpose. It neutralised the German battleships, and so made it possible for ASW escorts to function in the Atlantic. Conversely, when the Home Fleet was *not* able to cover a convoy route against German capital ships, the escorts could not function effectively. Convoy PQ-17 was the worst case of this kind. Because it appeared that the battleship *Tirpitz* was coming out to attack the convoy, the Admiralty ordered it dispersed (to reduce the number of ships the battleship could sweep up). Without escorts, the convoy was virtually wiped out by U-boats and aircraft.

Finally, there is the case of Task Force 38/58[28], the US Fast Carrier Task Force, and in many ways the prototype of a key element of the modern maritime strategy. The fast carriers could hit both land and sea targets, and they supported the two major Pacific amphibious assaults of 1944, Saipan and Leyte Gulf. In each case, the amphibious attack forced the Japanese to expose their own fleet to counterattack. The task force, then, provided both bait and trap. It won sea control at the Philippine Sea in June 1944 by destroying the Japanese naval air arm sent out to attack it. At Leyte four months later, the US fleet drew out what was left of the Japanese battle fleet, and again inflicted crippling damage. Through 1943 the Japanese had carefully maintained what amounted to a fleet in being.

The current argument, then, would be that basic US national strategy, which is a forward strategy, depends on the viability of the main fleet. Without a viable concentrated fleet, an enemy can easily concentrate enough power to defeat in detail any more disperse defence of the sea lanes, without fearing that he is uncovering some vital interest of his own.

Critiques of the Battle Fleet Concept

Critics of the current US fleet doctrine have argued that the idea of a fleet built around capital ships is fundamentally flawed, that it is too expensive to build a fleet designed specifically to fight and survive a decisive battle. They have argued instead for a stealthy fleet, difficult to detect and to attack. This ignores the natural stealthiness of naval forces. Even a 97,000-ton aircraft carrier is quite small against the vastness of, say, the Norwegian Sea.

The intentionally stealthy fleet could survive a war (if in fact it can be made stealthy enough), but it is not clear that it can win the central prize, sea control. Stealth would presumably make it easy for the fleet to attack shore targets, and thus perhaps to gain sea control by destroying enemy ships and aircraft in home waters. It is not, however, clear how it could overcome the inherent dispersion of Soviet submarines, and the possible dispersion of their aircraft. Moreover, however stealthy the ships of the fleet, the merchant ships carrying essential material are anything but stealthy. They must still be defended.

There are, moreover, technical problems. Small stealthy ships cannot accommodate many large weapons, and it is not clear that precise guidance can always make up for the limited weapon size required. It seems unlikely that large ships can be made particularly stealthy.

The critics cannot, after all, know precisely where technology is going. A fairer characterisation might be that they doubt whether the current defensive technology will be sufficient to deal with predictable Soviet developments. However, one might look at the question rather differently. The United States is almost forced to follow something like a battle fleet strategy, from quite general strategic considerations. Technology is by no means necessarily an independent force. Rather, technologists can be encouraged to develop answers to particular questions – if the questions are intelligently posed.

Of course technology does not develop entirely in response to particular operational requirements, and of course some requirements may be impossible to meet. However, existing technology is extremely rich, and remarkably capable. It seems more reasonable to seek technological *and tactical* solutions to the problems posed by an attractive overall strategy than to abandon the strategy on the ground that existing technology has not altogether solved those problems.

Thus it might be most appropriate to consider the battle fleet strategy as laying requirements *to be fulfilled*, determining (in a very general way) a type of defensive/offensive technology which is needed. In the past, in the US Navy, this kind of thinking led to the development of the fleet air defence fighters and their control organisation, which proved so successful in the Pacific. Note that the battle fleet had to change: in 1944 the carriers, not the battleships, were central. But the underlying strategy, of a concentrated fleet, did not change.

Another major argument is that the fleet is irrelevant to the major Western naval mission, securing sea control. By "sea control" critics of the Maritime Strategy mean anti-submarine warfare, on the assumption that the only important Soviet threat to free Western use of the sea is the attack submarine (attacking merchant shipping), and that a classical fleet is unable to deal with submarines which it cannot detect, at least at long range. The counter-argument is that the fleet will tend to attract those submarines not tied down by the forward submarine offensive, and that it will be the most effective available concentration of anti-submarine firepower. Submarines concentrated against the fleet, moreover, will not be attacking vital shipping.

This concept invites comparison with the Japanese use of submarines in World War II. The Japanese had a large modern submarine fleet, which they used almost exclusively for a combination of strategic scouting and attacks on major US warships. They achieved some impressive initial successes against US carriers and against one battleship, but did not interfere with the relatively vulnerable sea lines of communication across the Pacific, which supported the allied position in, for example, New Guinea. For the modern case, the question would be how to evaluate the US carriers in comparison to the shipping, since carriers offered up to submarine attack might well take some damage (and the submarines would certainly take some losses). The situation is complicated by the relatively small number of US carriers (although in 1942 the United States had even fewer) and by the relatively long time required to replace them (which is much longer than in 1942).[29]

If effective sea control requires units which cannot efficiently form part of a classical fleet, then, given finite national resources, investment in that kind of fleet detracts from sea control.

It is also argued that a concentrated fleet can do little to neutralise widely dispersed sea denial forces. That is quite true; the question is whether the Soviets, sensing the approach of war, would disperse their forces. That in turn depends upon the motives behind Soviet naval operations. If the Soviets are concerned, as many believe, primarily with defence of the homeland, then they are unlikely to disperse their defensive forces.

If, however, the Soviets take sea denial very seriously, then the pre-war surge is likely, and at least at first it can be very effective. German surface raiders in the two world wars provide an interesting historical example. In each case, the Germans had a few ships at sea at the outbreak of war, when the British surface blockade was imposed. It was extremely difficult to break any more out, but the ships already at sea took a very long time to hunt down, and did disproportionate damage. Had the Germans had more time to prepare, and had they therefore been able to deploy more raiders, the damage would presumably have been far worse, simply because it is so difficult to find an individual ship in the open sea.[30]

The particular main fleet strategy adopted by the United States has been criticised in another, broader, way. To the extent that the US fleet has to present a credible threat in order to force the Soviets to accept a decisive battle, it may be asked whether that threat will be so credible as to lead to early nuclear escalation. This applies both to the submarine threat to Soviet ballistic missile submarines and to the carrier threat to Soviet naval air bases.

The counter-argument is that neither side is particularly anxious to escalate. By their "bastion" doctrine, the Soviets have shown that they *expect* attacks by Western naval forces; they do not expect to rely on some vague threat of escalation. After all, they have shown in many other ways that they would much rather avoid nuclear use, depending on the sheer mass of their conventional forces to achieve results. More generally, it seems unlikely that *either* side would consider the war at sea so vital as to be worth the risk of escalation to disastrous damage on land. There is too much evidence that political authorities on both sides believe that virtually any use of nuclear weapons would soon lead to widespread central use.

Notes
1. The Maritime Strategy *does* correspond closely to the kind of strategy the US Navy developed both before and immediately after World War II. It differs significantly from the convoy-oriented sea control strategy practised by the Royal Navy during and after World War II. One reason why is that the Royal Navy was generally debarred from "attack at source", since attacks against land targets were the jealously-guarded prerogative of the Royal Air Force. The US Navy operated under no such restriction, and the Royal Navy used its participation with the US Navy in the NATO Strike Fleet to justify the retention of minimal land attack air forces after World War II. See N Friedman, *The Postwar Naval Revolution* (Annapolis: US Naval Institute and London: Conway Maritime Press, 1987).
2. It is important to distinguish such oceanic missions from coastal

defence, the object of which is to prevent an enemy from attacking from the sea, either by bombardment (which can include air attack) or by actually landing troops. The NATO Baltic navies (of West Germany and Denmark), for example, are designed primarily to prevent the Soviets from landing behind the seaward flank of the NATO armies. They are, therefore, primarily sea denial navies. It is, however, also possible to see the West German Navy as a forward defence ASW and anti-surface ship navy, preventing the Soviet Baltic Fleet from approaching the Danish Straits. The German Navy also contributes to NATO ASW strength for the North Sea.

3. These ideas are not new. For example, in their wars against the French and the Spanish during the eighteenth and early nineteenth centuries, the British habitually sought sea control, which they maintained through a combination of blockade and direct attacks on enemy ports (such as "cutting-out expeditions").

    Thus a purist might suggest that an amphibious raid on an enemy naval base contributed primarily to sea control rather than to some larger land strategy. Even that is not entirely clear, because it might be argued that the threat to the naval base would force the enemy to concentrate land forces to defend it, and thus might weaken his land forces elsewhere.

4. However, the seizure of an island or choke point may be desirable primarily for its effect on the war at sea, and thus may be considered primarily a matter of sea control.

5. During the great spring 1918 offensive, German troops, who had been deprived of foodstuffs and even of quality uniforms and shoes by the blockade, stopped to loot the British units they overran. The consequent delays contributed to their ultimate defeat. One might argue further that the sense of desperation which surrounded the offensive was largely due to the clearly foreseeable decline in German economic fortunes, which again might be traced to the blockade.

6. It might be argued that Mikhail Gorbachev's attempt to secure nuclear disarmament in Western Europe comes very close to calling the NATO bluff.

7. John Mearsheimer has developed a theory of "conventional deterrence" parallel to nuclear deterrence, arguing that the Soviets tend to calculate their chances of success (in terms of a scientifically defined "correlation of forces") and that the West can field land forces powerful enough to deny the Soviets a high probability of success in the type of war with which they feel most comfortable, a *blitzkrieg*. However, there is little evidence that past aggressors have worked on such fine calculations, nor does it seem likely that Western intelligence agencies could be very sure of the details of the Soviet calculation. It seems more reasonable to assume that nuclear

deterrence rests on much stronger foundations, namely on the feeling, shared by most statesmen, that nuclear war would have unforeseeable, and probably fatal, consequences, rather than that it takes X warheads of Y accuracy/yield to defeat country Z. Certainly the present author never encountered convincing calculations of the latter type in well over a decade of strategic work for various US official agencies.

8. The Soviets are generally credited with a very strong interest in strategic deception, and with the capacity to achieve the necessary coordination, in peace as in war. There is abundant evidence that wishful thinking can make such deception effective. For example, in 1973 the United States government, which did not want to imagine that another Middle East war was possible, dissuaded the Israelis from concluding that the Egyptians would attack, reinforcing factors which in themselves caused the Israelis to want not to imagine that an attack was imminent. In the past, the Soviets have often benefited both from deceptions intended to make them seem more aggressive or more powerful (as in Stalin's postwar operations) and from deceptions intended to mask their aggressive intent (as in the period just before they crushed Hungary in 1956). The closed nature of Soviet society helps make deception effective. It seems likely, moreover, that excessive Western belief in the efficacy of technical intelligence devices (principally satellites) makes the West vulnerable to carefully planned deception. In recent years, for example, there have been claims that the Soviets were able to manipulate US estimates of the accuracy of their long-range missiles.

9. This was the outcome projected by Brigadier John Hackett in *The Third World War*.

10. In the early 1980s, it was commonly suggested that IFF errors would kill about 40% of the aircraft returning from a major strike. There is no reason to imagine that the Warsaw Pact is much more expert at IFF; indeed, it is probably somewhat less effective, given its more centralised command structure (which should be less tolerant of errors at low levels). Given a loss rate (to enemy fire) of only 10%, that means that half of the NATO strike air arm would be destroyed during each major attack. Airfield destruction would add to the carnage.

11. The British were badly affected by the naval losses suffered in their strategic flanking attack at Gallipoli, in 1915. Their sea control did support a strategic flanking attack from Salonika, in 1918, which contributed heavily to the collapse of Austria-Hungary, Turkey, and Bulgaria and hence to that of Germany herself. Because the land base of operations, Salonika, was already in allied hands, the question of risking valuable ships did not arise. However, the need to supply Salonika did strain total allied naval and merchant ship resources at

a time when they were already badly affected by the U-boat campaign.

12. Under some circumstances this issue is moot. In the case of D-Day, there were almost no big, valuable amphibious ships, because many of the shuttle craft came directly from England – and no coast defence gun or missile could sink that. Fast air-cushion craft would have made this kind of operation even easier, because they could have crossed the Channel in an hour or two, just as commercial Hovercraft (technologically their close relatives) do at present. The distinction between the small number of major amphibious ships, which are worthwhile targets, and the numerous shuttle craft actually carrying troops and materiel ashore, which generally cannot be sunk in sufficient numbers to stop the attack, is important.

13. Pre-1941 versions of the US ORANGE plan concentrated on a combination of blockade and bombing to cause Japan to surrender, because clearly the United States could never mobilise enough troops to invade; US planners thought otherwise in 1945. It does seem arguable that the Soviets would use nuclear weapons rather than tolerate an invasion *of their own territory*, but that certainly would not exclude descents from the sea into the rear of a Soviet army entrenched in Central Europe. Nor is it entirely clear that the Soviets see the threat of nuclear weapons as a useful counter to *any* non-nuclear threat. The ORANGE assumptions are set out in the Navy WPL series of publications, describing the ORANGE plan, which are held by the US Naval Operational Archives in the Washington Navy Yard. See also the forthcoming history of ORANGE by Edward Miller (US Naval Institute, 1988).

14. The patrol aircraft lays a pattern of listening sonobuoys, and monitors the sounds they receive. It processes these signals to decide whether a submarine is present, where it is likely to be, and how fast it is moving. The quieter the submarine, the longer the search will take – in effect, the shorter the range per buoy. Submarine speed limits the amount of time the boat is likely to spend in the area defined by the initial contact, and so limits available processing time.

15. Presumably SOSUS does not provide uniform coverage over the entire North Atlantic. The Walker spy ring probably provided the Soviets with indications of its limitations, by providing what amounted to the US plot of estimated Soviet submarine positions in the Atlantic. The effect would be to provide Soviet submarine commanders with a map of possible sanctuaries. It would then be particularly important for NATO to route shipping through areas of SOSUS coverage, so as to minimise the value of such sanctuaries. This situation is further complicated by the existence of US mobile surveillance ships (T-AGOS), which in effect move the geographic coverage of the overall system,

filling in gaps in the coverage of the fixed arrays.

16. These are *illustrative* numbers, to give a feeling for the situation; they are not to be taken literally.

17. In reality, the aircraft would drop two torpedoes; the submarine would evade, and the aircraft would have to try to redetect (reacquire) it, for a lower net kill probability.

18. This was not due primarily to the increasing threat of Soviet inshore ASW. Rather, as US submarine sonar improved, it became possible for individual submarines to detect targets over much greater distances, and so for a small number to enforce a wide barrier, e.g., across a choke point several hundred miles across. Given the high cost of individual nuclear submarines, close blockade (which required substantial numbers around each port and each inlet) made little sense. This was opposite to British World War I surface blockade practice, which was motivated by the need to fall back without any real hope of increasing detection range.

19. After a time, the Soviets would surely begin (indeed, be forced) to realise the anti-shipping potential of their naval forces. Thus, their prewar orientation is most unlikely to solve the sea control problem.

20. This turns out not to be a new idea. In 1956, the Committee on Undersea Warfare of the US National Academy of Sciences carried out a special study of the implications of nuclear power for submarines, Project Nobska. One of the conclusions was that the United States should deploy ballistic missiles aboard submarines near the Soviet Union largely as a way of forcing the Soviets to focus on ASW rather than on submarines for anti-shipping warfare. More recently, some have seen submarine-launched cruise missiles (Tomahawk) in much the same light, as a means of concentrating attention on an immediate threat.

21. Trail by an attack submarine, the time-honoured nightmare of ballistic submariners, is an extension of blockade, in that the trailer picks up the SSBN either at its base or while it passes a choke point. Trail is essential in either case because it is carried out in peacetime: the trailer is not permitted to shoot to kill when the SSBN appears.

22. The numbers involved can be quite significant. In theory, the Soviets would want to assign more than one attack submarine to each SSBN. To keep even one attack submarine continuously at sea (over a long period) probably requires a total of about three, or perhaps about 100 in all to deal with about 30 operational Western SSBNs. In 1987 the Soviets possess fewer than 50 modern high-performance nuclear attack submarines. Even so, there is no indication that the Soviets will easily abandon their hope of shifting the wartime strategic balance. Note that the origin of the first modern Soviet nuclear attack submarine, Victor I, is sometimes ascribed to a requirement to escort Soviet

Yankee class SSBNs, presumably to protect them against US trailers. In theory, a US anti-SSBN campaign would require substantially fewer attack submarines, since the Soviet SSBN operating area is constrained to "bastions".

23. However, even in the absence of a carrier, the Soviets must often close to *confirm* the identity of targets. Their independent sensors cannot effectively identify or discriminate between targets, which they see merely as blips on radar scopes. The technology required to positively identify ships on radars is only beginning to appear in the West: inverse synthetic aperture radar (ISAR), which uses the motion of the radar target itself to generate what amounts to a high-definition radar.

24. Soviet practice is to preplan the flight, on the basis of intelligence data. The bombers do not actually search for the target, because excessive use of their radars would open them to detection and counterattack. Thus they can be expected to fly (at fairly low level, to avoid radar detection) almost straight to the expected target area, popping up, turning on their fire control radars, and shooting as soon as they can identify the target within the target fleet. This type of tactic ought to make them somewhat vulnerable to decoying.

25. See Swartz, "Addendum", pp. 55–57.

26. Ships were expected to operate out of sight of each other. One consequence was a revival of high-frequency (HF) radio, which had been replaced by very- and ultra-high frequency (VHF/UHF), both of them effectively limited to the line of sight. HF, which can extend over very long distances, in turn presented the Soviets with D/F opportunities. Modern satellite communications can eliminate this particular problem.

27. There is one important exception: Western submarines *would* execute a form of naval guerrilla warfare, and this phrase is often used in connection with a US submarine offensive. In the case of operations near Soviet bases, a major goal of the guerrilla war is to hold down Soviet forces, just as guerrillas in land warfare tend to hold down conventional land forces.

28. The designation was changed back and forth as command switched between Admiral Spruance and Admiral Halsey; the idea was that one staff would carry out an attack while the other planned the next.

29. The larger question is how the United States Navy can deal with the prospect of serious wartime losses. The United States began World War II with seven fleet carriers. During 1942 it lost four; another (*Saratoga*) was severely damaged, and another (*Ranger*) was considered too small and too slow to be used in the major maritime theatre, the Pacific. The only new carriers immediately available were converted tankers, freighters, and light cruisers, only the latter

being suitable for fast fleet operations. One saving grace was that contemporary aircraft could operate, albeit inefficiently, from such extemporised craft. Moreover, the industrial mobilisation begun in 1940 produced full fleet carriers from the end of 1942 onwards. At least as importantly, the battles which sank the US carriers also destroyed the Japanese carrier force. Unlike the US force, it could not easily be reconstituted, because the Japanese lacked the necessary industrial base. It is not clear how well the current US industrial base would do in a similar crisis. The problem has not really been studied in recent years because of the concentration on short wars, but it deserves reconsideration now, as protracted warfare becomes more conceivable. Incidentally, it is by no means clear that the Soviets could easily reconstitute their own losses: their non-military industrial base, which would have to provide the means of national mobilisation, is relatively weak.

30. Individual surface raiders were more effective hunters than individual submarines because they could spot targets over a greater area (or, for that matter, evade hunters further away). They were, however, far more vulnerable to detection (and destruction) by air, and they were much more expensive than submarines. Imminent technological solutions to the larger problem of finding individual ships at sea have been promised for many years, but they have never materialised.

6. The Soviet Style of Naval Warfare

The Soviet Navy differs fundamentally from most Western navies in its style of operation and therefore in its equipment. The style reflects both its origins as a coastal defence force and the nature of Soviet, as opposed to Western, society. Soviet operational priorities, at least as they are observed in peacetime, also differ from those of Western navies, just as the position of the Soviet Navy within the Soviet military establishment differs radically from those of Western navies. All of these differences carry important implications for Western naval strategy.

It is also important to keep in mind two political dimensions of the Soviet Navy. First, the central planning system tends to impose a considerable inertia. It is very difficult for any Soviet government to make radical changes in a continuing plan, if only because such changes tend to ripple through the entire economy. Planning involves not only the output of a single factory or group of factories, but also the raw materials and subcomponents they use, and the transportation among them. A project typically involves a series of centrally determined obligations by factories and other industrial enterprises, obligations which should cause the intended product, be it a car or a cruiser, to materialise at the desired time. The Soviet system is unique in that what would, in the West, be subcontractors have *no mutual obligations*, only obligations to the single central planning agency. They therefore enjoy little or no flexibility with which to meet surprises in the production process. This type of centralisation, with its emphasis on perfect planning and on avoiding surprises, parallels Soviet tactical practice; as one might expect, both mirror the same social and political system. Detailed central planning would be difficult enough without any disruptions,

but nature always provides surprises. Further man-made disruptions (in the form of changes demanded from above) are therefore
extremely unpopular among the planners, who hold considerable
political power. Moreover, to the (considerable) extent that factory
management jobs represent political patronage by the ruling
Communist Party, those managers can exert political pressure to
annul changes, such as major programme cancellations or
redesigns, which cause them difficulties. This inertia explains the
great continuity in Soviet warship, aircraft, and armoured vehicle
design, a continuity that often seems to cost combat capability.[1]

Industrial inertia has one other important consequence.
Because changes in production rates (to reflect changed circumstances) are difficult at best, those rates are much more likely to
reflect plant capacity than force structure. As a result, the Soviets
generally produce substantial surpluses of some kinds of equipment, which becomes available to their client states at very low
prices. From a US point of view that is a considerable complication,
since it raises the capability of what may become independent
Third World states; Libya is a good example. On the other hand,
the Soviets have to maintain a monopoly on many kinds of production within their bloc. For example, none of the satellite countries
builds submarines. Whatever their own needs, then, the Soviets
must maintain production of some systems to replace those sold
earlier to their own clients. They cannot afford to send them out of
the bloc for replacement.[2]

Thus it would appear the Khrushchev showed particular cour-
age when he cancelled the 1956–60 plan in mid-stride and substi-
tuted a seven-year plan (1959–65). One might even suspect that the
ripples caused by this and by other major initiatives helped expel
Khrushchev from office, and that his heirs, particularly Leonid
Brezhnev, therefore followed a much more cautious course.
Mikhail Gorbachev has sometimes been compared to Khrushchev,
in his willingness to make drastic changes to achieve economic
efficiency, even at a considerable political cost. One of his major
problems is that efficiency requires decentralisation and thus
some loss of power to the central planners and, by extension, to the
Party apparatus as a whole.

Second, Soviet military and naval doctrine is subject to drastic changes imposed by the national leadership, so that sometimes the term "mission obsolescence" seems more appropriate than "bloc obsolescence".

Khrushchev is the prime example. From 1955 on, he pressed for greater and greater concentration on nuclear forces at the expense of conventional ones, partly to cut manpower requirements and costs. He lacked manpower because of the demographic "echoes" of the purges of the 1930s, and he needed money to develop what he saw as the decisive new technologies of missiles and nuclear weapons themselves. As a result, formations were drastically cut and many officers forcibly retired.[3] The production of such conventional weapons as fighter-bombers and tanks was curtailed, although such production could not be altogether stopped, due to the demands of industrial inertia.

The services were extremely unhappy, and their anger seems to have been a factor in Khrushchev's dismissal in October 1964.[4] His successor, Leonid Brezhnev, seems to have followed a pattern of giving the services roughly what they wanted, and of bringing back the sorts of manpower-intensive conventional forces Khrushchev hated. For their part, the services were able to argue that Khrushchev's minimum deterrence or all-nuclear policy had done little good in the Cuban confrontation. In this sense Cuba had the effect, for the Soviets, that Korea had for the United States: it demonstrated the limit of nuclear coercion.

The Soviets certainly did not abandon strategic nuclear weapons after Khrushchev's fall: they built up a force the United States could not hope to destroy in a first strike. The effect of this development was to deprive the United States of any real hope of limiting damage to itself in a nuclear exchange. For the Soviets, the ultimate significance of these weapons was that they could prevent the United States and her allies from effectively threatening the Soviets with nuclear weapons, and thus from negating Soviet non-nuclear forces. At the very worst, a NATO armed only with conventional weapons could never hope to defeat the vast Soviet Union, with her buffer of satellite states. At the best, the sheer weight of Soviet non-nuclear forces could hope to overrun NATO Europe.

The initial goal in the reconstruction of Soviet ground forces was to secure the Warsaw Pact against what the Soviets saw as a significant NATO ground threat. That was probably achieved (in their eyes) by the late 1960s, although reportedly they were still nervous of NATO ground forces during their invasion of Czechoslovakia in 1968. Modernisation since about 1970 has been directed largely towards achieving a capability to invade NATO Europe without having to invoke nuclear weapons.

Ideally, of course, the Soviets could hope to use their own strategic nuclear forces to destroy the United States, but that seems to have been a much more distant possibility.[5] The size of the funds which went into rebuilding tactical non-nuclear forces suggests that the Soviet military (and its political masters) discounted apocalyptic concepts of strategic nuclear warfare. As in the West, they never altogether rejected the real possibility of tactical nuclear warfare, although in recent years the Soviets have apparently come to see an entirely non-nuclear conflict as a real, and probably most likely, possibility.

Their view of the significance of this possibility differs radically from that held in the West. Western military doctrine generally separates nuclear from non-nuclear weapons. If nuclear use is deterred, then it is pointless, for example, to expend efforts early in a war to destroy enemy nuclear weapons which are unlikely ever to be used. The Soviets, however, see the threat of nuclear escalation as an important consideration at all stages of a war. They therefore consider it essential to deprive their enemy of his tactical nuclear weapons; Western nuclear weapons and their platforms would be important early targets. Indeed, they would tend to attract Soviet attackers and thus perhaps even to reduce the weight of Soviet attack on Western non-nuclear systems. For example, the Soviets would concentrate naval forces against NATO SSBNs, quite possibly to the benefit of Western shipping and Western surface forces.[6]

In theory, once all Western nuclear systems had been destroyed, the mere existence of Soviet nuclear weapons would be sufficiently coercive as to end the war on favourable terms, even if Soviet non-nuclear forces had suffered badly. In Soviet terms, elimination of many Western nuclear weapons would decisively tip the "correlation of forces" in their direction. In fact, given the existence of highly survivable systems such as sea-based ballistic and cruise missiles and long-range weapons in North America, it is unlikely that the Soviets would be able to achieve such results in any limited non-nuclear attack.

Nor can the Soviets assume success in these measures. They must still provide against the possibility that their threats may fail, and that they may be unable to pre-empt a Western attack. They therefore take what they consider to be prudent steps to limit damage. These measures have included particular attempts to protect (and decentralise) the Soviet leadership, particularly after the United States began to show interest in anti-leadership targeting. However, it is important to see these measures in perspective, as prudent insurance against the possibility that the Soviet nuclear threat will fail, rather than as an enthusiastic acceptance of the requirements of nuclear war-fighting.

A stable Soviet nuclear doctrine explains a changing attitude towards strategic defence. Until about 1965, any Soviet leader had to assume that hostilities would begin with a crushing US or NATO nuclear strike. Strategic defences would help the Soviet Union survive to keep fighting. Once the Soviets had shifted to a theory of nuclear deterrence, however, they had to fear that superior US technology would reduce the threat value of their own nuclear forces, and so would make it easier for a permanently hostile West to contemplate nuclear attack. They therefore had to welcome the ABM Treaty, particularly since their own ballistic missile defense programme showed little promise of success. Since then, ballistic missile technology has stabilised; defensive technology once again shows promise. The Soviet objective has not changed; to neutralise the threat of US strategic weapons. The means may be changing, since the Soviets can choose between continuing their threat (by neutralising any US strategic defence through political assault) or by erecting their own strategic defensive system, or by some mix of the two.

The Soviets assume a degree of mirror-imaging on the part of their enemies. That in turn explains their efforts to protect their own strategic weapons, e.g. aboard ballistic missile submarines, from expected *non-nuclear* attack. These efforts in turn help make the bait-and-trap concepts inherent in the current US Maritime Strategy attractive. US nuclear-capable naval forces (such as SSBNs, attack submarines armed with Tomahawks, and carrier battle forces) are bait the Soviets cannot refuse, even in the non-nuclear phase of a conflict (which may be the entire conflict). Similarly, the Soviets cannot afford to uncover their own nuclear-capable naval forces. Abstract Soviet doctrine has real military consequences.

The Evolution of Naval Roles

The Navy's coast defence role came first, before World War II. Much of modern Soviet naval development consists of its extension well out to sea, to counter modern Western naval strike forces; carriers and missile-carrying submarines.[7] Basic features of the coast defence philosophy remain, and they are a fundamental limit on Soviet naval flexibility. Moreover, the Soviet Navy retains large short-range coast-defence forces, consisting of small fast attack craft (armed with torpedoes and missiles) and coast-defence guns and missiles. They absorb a significant, though declining, fraction of its overall budget.[8]

The other major naval role is the support of land operations. That originally meant little more than shore bombardment and landing troops behind the seaward flanks of enemy positions. However, in the mid-1950s, this naval bombardment role expanded to include long-range nuclear attack; the strategic missiles are now, in the 1980s, considered part of the long-range artillery at the disposal of the Soviet General Staff. This artillery in turn must be protected, and that protection mission partly explains the creation of the current "bastions". The tactical style orginally developed for coastal defense can still be seen both in the complementary army support role, and in the defence of the bastions.

Most importantly, note that the bastion and extended coastal roles are effectively forms of army cooperation; the Soviet Army is the basis of the Soviet military machine.[9] Moreover, they are really associated with only a single scenario, the case of a major NATO-Warsaw Pact war. It appears that, as the Soviets have reached what they see as sufficiently powerful forces to deal with their main scenario, they have come to investigate others. Moreover, their own doctrine, which posits that the threat of nuclear weapons will probably deter the West from attacking, must also make them wonder whether their own main scenario is so very likely. Too, given the rather difficult postwar history of the Soviet Navy, it would be natural for its leaders to seek some independent role. These considerations would explain Admiral Gorshkov's vision of the Soviet Navy as the protector of "state interests abroad" in peacetime.[10]

About 1981, Soviet naval writers pressed for recognition of a Soviet "naval science" distinct from the existing "military science", and reportedly the navy proposed the creation of a separate "oceanic TVD" under naval control. Although couched in the usual opaque Marxist language, the first proposal would have certified a distinct naval role and naval identity. It was vociferously rejected. Moreover, there is some evidence that the Soviet establishment as a whole began to react to the high cost of the new Soviet ocean fleet. In 1982, there were reports that the new Minister of Defence, Dmitri Ustinov, wanted the naval programme curtailed and, symbolically, Admiral Gorshkov removed. That was impossible as long as Leonid Brezhnev remained in power, but as soon as he was replaced by Andropov, reports of the demise of the Soviet building programme surfaced. To the extent that Chernenko represented a continuity in Brezhnev's practices, Andropov's death saved the naval programme, at least through the 1981–1985 Plan. However, Gorshkov was dismissed not too long after Andropov's protége, Mikhail Gorbachev, consolidated his own power.[11]

It may be well here to observe that, while the nature and capabilities of Soviet warships and naval weapons are relatively difficult to change over time, it is certainly imaginable that those ships and weapons would be used in ways radically different from those to be described here. Indeed, the current US image of Soviet wartime naval operations is quite different from that common in, say, the early 1970s. It can only be suggested that the picture now used is substantially more sophisticated than earlier ones, and therefore that it explains earlier events in a more satisfactory way. In a larger sense, the issue of Soviet naval strategy and tactics is the old one of intentions vs. capabilities. To meet the full range of *capabilities* of the Soviet fleet would take far more resources than to meet the flesh-and-blood Soviet fleet actually observed at sea. The Soviets are well aware of their own shortcomings, but they seem so deeply ingrained as to be extremely difficult to eradicate.

Soviet Tactical Style

The Soviets appear to have developed their style of tactics from the coast defence tactics of the post-Revolutionary period. At this time Soviet industry could hardly hope to build substantial warships, nor could an impoverished Soviet Union maintain even many of the existing Czarist warships in full commission. Even so, surviving Czarist officers, now in Soviet service, argued that the country had to build up a conventional fleet. Younger officers argued otherwise; they proposed a new (and, more importantly, less expensive) kind of naval strategy. Such claims fell on particularly receptive ears. Not only were the resources for conventional naval development lacking, but official Soviet propaganda, both internal and external, proclaimed that new strategies somehow reflecting the new Marxist-Leninist ideology were inherently superior.[12]

The key to the new naval science was to abandon any pretense at sea control, i.e., at conventional or Mahanian ideas. The Soviet Union would not try to maintain a sea-going main fleet capable of threatening other main fleets in their home waters or on the open sea, because even if it could manufacture the ships of such a fleet, it could not afford the trained manpower a fleet would require.[13] Certainly the Soviet Army required the bulk of available military resources. Not only is the Soviet Union a land power sharing land frontiers with many potential enemies, but traditionally the army has been by far the dominant service. For example, for a time after World War II there was no independent Soviet navy at all. Even now, when the navy is constituted as a separate service, army control is guaranteed. All of the Soviet services come under a single unified General Staff, which in fact functions as an army staff.[14]

Instead of sea control, the younger Soviet officers concentrated on sea denial in the approaches to the Soviet Union. Enemy naval forces were to be countered by a combination of the relatively inexpensive forces at their disposal; small submarines, motor torpedo boats, land-based naval aircraft, and coast artillery. If all these resources could be coordinated, then, even though individually relatively weak, they could have a considerable cumulative effect on any attacker approaching the Soviet coast, and might well be able to destroy him. Note that, unlike a classical fleet, the new naval force was essentially shore-based, rushing out to sea only when an invader approached. Coordination of this shore-based force in turn required centralised control of the entire battle, generally from a position ashore.

This tactical style had considerable appeal. First, it embodied the strong Soviet preference for cooperative or collective over individual efforts, as the essence of Socialism. In the post-Revolutionary period, it was much more important for initiatives to be consistent with existing ideology than to be particularly practical, as the ideologues had taken over.

Second, the new ideas differed sufficiently from conventional naval doctrine to be describable as the fruit of Marxism-Leninism freshly applied to existing problems.[15] This argument would have helped advocates of a new "Soviet school" of naval warfare to triumph over their older and more conventional forebears: the Soviet military establisment of the 1920s and early 1930s was particularly open to radically new ideas.

Third, central control was far preferable politically to the sort of independence traditionally associated with naval forces, in the form of the usual captain's prerogative. This was particularly important for a post-revolutionary state which still had to depend heavily on specialists, such as senior naval officers, who had spent much of their careers under the old regime. Moreover, from the Revolution on, the Communist Party always feared a military coup. The greater the degree of centralisation, the easier to impose political control on the key military commander, and the easier to forestall trouble.

Central control had another important political aspect. The Soviet government profoundly distrusts its servants, and failure may carry the charge that the problem is sabotage ("wrecking"). The purges of the interwar period taught the average Soviet officer that there was only one usable counter: that he had gone "by the book", or followed his orders, and hence was not responsible; that failure had occurred because of factors beyond his control. Centralised control is then welcome because it reduces individual responsibility, which is not prized in a profoundly pessimistic society.[16]

Finally, the new tactics made the best of Soviet industrial limitations, indeed allowed the Soviet Union to avoid the worst maritime consquences of those limitations.

The central commander, generally located ashore, was the key to the new tactics. He alone could command his dispersed units to attack. That ensured coordination, at least in theory, since the separate arms making the attack would not have to coordinate among themselves. Similarly, all sources of information as to the location and nature of an approaching enemy force were supplied directly to him.

Emphasis on central command and control mirrors an extremely important feature of Soviet life, the extreme centralisation of political power. Soviet citizens are discouraged from showing initiative in their civil lives; it is much better to follow the rules and avoid risks. That civil education makes it difficult for the Soviet military to embody very much initiative at low levels. Both in the army and in the navy, therefore, tactics are designed for maximum central control and a maximum degree of central decision-making.[17] Another way to look at this situation would be to suggest that, in an army-oriented country, it was natural for the navy to reflect the army's style of operation: stereotyped tactics rather than individualism.

The high degree of centralisation means that the dispersed units which actually carry out the attack need not, indeed probably usually do not, communicate with each other in any great detail. The burden of successful coordination falls on the central commander. That includes the burden of avoiding identification (IFF) errors (friendly forces attacking other friendly forces). The IFF problem is inherent in the situation, as long as the attacking forces are widely dispersed; navigational errors are too easy to make. It is obviated if the target is radically different from the attacker, as for example if the target is a surface ship and the attacker is a submarine, or if the target is a large surface ship and the attacker is a small fast missile boat. However, as the battle moves further out to sea, identification can become more difficult, particularly if the prospective target is aware of the potential of confusion.

Missile weapons were a second key feature of the new tactics, since they could be launched from the inexpensive platforms available to the post-Revolutionary navy. Even these platforms (such as motor torpedo boats and naval bombers) were far from inexpensive in Soviet terms. Tactics therefore emphasised attacks at maximum range, to avoid losses. Greater range in turn permitted the attackers to disperse, so that counterattack became more difficult. Admiral Gorshkov, for example, wrote approvingly of the way in which widely dispersed units could achieve tactical concentration by using long-range anti-ship missiles.

Thus, where Western navies practice physical concentration, the Soviets concentrate their command and control resources. The implication would be that, whereas it might not be profitable to strike at the widely dispersed units of a Soviet attack group, it might be extremely profitable to strike at the central commander. That might not be possible on a physical basis, since it might be politically impossible to destroy a command bunker deep in the Soviet Union. However, the central commander probably is quite vulnerable to deception. His intelligence and command channels may not be immune to jamming or to other forms of disruption. The Soviets are well aware of this vulnerability; it explains the degree to which they have provided redundant command circuits, far beyond those available to Western navies.[18]

Centrally-controlled dispersed tactics are associated with another important trait of the Soviet military: a heavy emphasis on operational research, i.e., on the mathematical approach to warfare as a guide to tactics. Dispersed attacks are justified by calculations showing that, if enough weapons are fired in the appropriate patterns, hits are ensured, even at considerable ranges. Masses of such calculations are published by Soviet military presses, and many of them have been translated into Western languages. Many Westerners find such extensive scholarly work (by serving officers) impressive evidence of the professionalism of the Soviet Navy (and, incidentally, of its sister services). However, one can inject a note of scepticism: there is every evidence that the Soviet Union is an extremely pessimistic society, that few of its citizens really believe that its equipment will function as designed. Military officers are placed in a particularly difficult position. How can they explain failure? How can they deal with the contradiction between a cruel reality and the political expectations they must acknowledge? The elaborate operations research is one way out of the trap. It provides a "book solution" to most problems. As long as the individual officer follows the "book", he is individually blameless. If he takes risks and wins, he may be decorated – but he will not be forgiven for failure in the event he does not follow the preordained procedures.

The "book" has a larger significance. The Soviets like to say that their system is superior because it is "scientific". That claim extends to warfare: the Soviets claim that, unlike their Western counterparts, they operate according to scientific, i.e., mathematical, principles. Hence the fascination with operations analysis. Hence, too, the immunity of an officer who fails even though he follows the practice laid down as a result of that analysis. After all, if the analysis (the "science") is discredited, that in turn might discredit the entire idea that science (read, the Party's doctrine) suffices, with extremely unfortunate political results. Too, the validity of "scientific analysis" well accords with planning and control from above. Should "science" not suffice to predict what an enemy will do, and what a Soviet commander ought to do? Reportedly it is standard Soviet practice to game out (probably in fairly static form) alternative attack plans – to justify choices by "science".

The concept of the "correlation of forces" is probably the ultimate example of this kind of analysis. The Soviets have developed mathematical means of evaluating the balance of forces at all

levels of conflict, from the unit to the strategic. This technique
differs from those in vogue in the West not only in the seriousness
with which it is taken, but also in that (at least at the higher levels)
it attempts to take into account such apparently non-military factors
as economic efficiency and civil moral. However, the Soviets see
struggle between their "socialist camp" and the "capitalist camp"
as the normal state of affairs. It follows that what the West sees as
peacetime the Soviets see more as lower-level conflict, and that
virtually no factor can be discounted from the balance of power.

A strike against a carrier battle group in the Norwegian Sea
might be typical of Soviet naval tactical practice. In wartime, the
Soviet Northern Fleet may have at sea submarines armed with
torpedoes and with anti-ship cruise missiles, as well as surface
ships armed with anti-ship cruise missiles. They will also have
strike bombers armed with anti-ship missiles. There are also
detection and location assets, radio direction-finders on land and
naval reconnaissance bombers, such as Bears and Blinders, feeding the central naval command, helping it to maintain an accurate
plot of enemy and friendly movements.

The carriers would first be detected by interception of their own
radio emissions; such passive initial detection location is typical of
Soviet practice. It automatically picks likely targets out of the
general mass of ships at sea. Radio direction finders reporting to
the central command would determine their approximate location
by triangulation.[19]

The central command would order reconnaissance bombers
flown out to the estimated carrier position, to confirm the existence of the target, and to track it precisely enough to mount an
attack. Meanwhile the command would alert the available anti-
carrier forces and move them into striking position. The central
commander would be entirely responsible for their movements,
and thus for assuring no interference, and even for timing the
strike itself.

In particular, he would have to make sure that the incoming
bombers did not accidentally attack Soviet surface ships, by precisely defining expected target location for them. Similarly, he
would have to make sure that the missile submarines, firing,

perhaps, well over the horizon, would not attack the wrong targets. In each case, coordination would be achieved by orders from above. Different elements of the force would not, indeed might be unable to, communicate with each other.

It would, moreover, be important for each element of the attack force to limit its own search for the target, since search in turn would require radar emissions, which might alert the target to the impending attack, and might even trigger a counterattack. For example, the bombers would need to know just when to pop up (hence to open themselves to detection by enemy radar) and turn on their own radars, so as to locate the target. They would have to lock their missiles onto the target before launch, so they would have to be able to see it on their radars. Avoiding warning would require that they not turn on those radars until the very last minute, i.e. that the location information provided by the central command be precise indeed.[20]

This massive attack is required, first, to saturate target defences. Given that degree of saturation, the Soviets will have calculated the number of weapons which must actually hit the target in order to destroy or disable it. Soviet practice seems not to count mutual interference as a possible mode of failure in such attacks.

Much the same style applies to other tactics. In ASW, for example, all tactics begin with an approximate submarine location supplied by the central commander. The ASW units close in on the suspected position, attempting to shrink any uncertainty sufficiently to permit an overwhelming attack, in this case to overcome any evasion by the target.

The Evolution of Force Structure

The other major theme of interwar Soviet naval tactical development was "attack at source", in the form of special mine/torpedo regiments of heavy bombers assigned specifically to attack enemy fleets in port, before they could approach Soviet home waters. These aircraft could also be assigned to formation attacks on enemy warships approaching the Soviet Union, and so were well fitted to the sea denial strategy. Most were used against land targets during World War II; naval bombers were the first Soviet aircraft to bomb Berlin in 1941.

Postwar, the mine/torpedo regiments ultimately became the modern naval missile bomber force, and attack at source was largely abandoned. However, the Soviets probably can deliver mines by air. The major NATO ports are undefended, and aerial mining would be an effective way of shutting down the trans-Atlantic or trans-Channel supply lines. At present, although anti-ship missile attack is the first priority, mining is a major mission.

In the late 1930s, Stalin seemed to abandon the small combatant or coastal defence school of naval strategy, as he began to build an impressive high seas fleet. Cruisers and large destroyers were built in some numbers, and battleships and battlecruisers laid down. However, it is by no means clear that this fleet reflected some shift in basic naval policy. Rather, it seems to have been conceived as a necessary trapping of great power status, built up alongside the more functional coastal defence force. It may be significant that the Five Year Plan of main fleet construction (1937–42) coincided with massive naval purges, part of the larger purge of the Soviet military establishment. It is as though Stalin built his fleet (and, incidentally, much of his army materiel) to threaten foreign powers so that they would not take advantage of the real weakness caused by the purges. This particular fleet programme was interrupted by the war; in 1940, construction of large warships was suspended and the resources involved (such as armour production) shifted to the army, in view of the imminent threat presented by Germany. Stalin revived his naval programme, in virtually its prewar (hence quite outdated) form almost immediately after the war, using scarce resources to rebuild the shattered naval industries of Leningrad and Nikolaev.

The most important difference between postwar and prewar programmes seems to have been a much larger submarine component in the former. Even before the war, the Soviet submarine fleet was the largest in the world, and the Soviets depended on small submarines (the M-class) to defend their Far Eastern provinces against Japan. Postwar, in 1948 a Soviet admiral is said to have announced a force goal of 1200 submarines by 1960. Before Stalin died and the programme was drastically curtailed, about 300 new submarines had been delivered, including three new classes significant for Western naval strategy: the large Zulu, the smaller but numerous (total production was 236 in the Soviet Union) Whiskey, and the small closed-cycle Quebec.[21]

Stalin's plan to build a vast number of submarines seemed to fit the worst fear of postwar Western planners, a continuation of the wartime U-boat campaign (the Battle of the Atlantic) with the Soviets using late-war German technology, which late-war Allied technology had not quite matched. However, in retrospect it seems that Stalin's navy saw the Whiskeys primarily as advanced coast defence pickets. They did not have the endurance for extensive open-ocean war patrols, given the very considerable distance between bases in the north and the likely convoy areas in the Central Atlantic. It appears, then, in retrospect that the Soviets considered only their bigger Zulus suitable for open-ocean combat. Thus one might argue that the bulk of the large submarine force Stalin actually built can best be associated with the coast defence mission, rather than with the grandiose high-seas fleet.[22]

The big-ship fleet is significant for the current Soviet navy because many important officers like Admiral Gorshkov, nominally the architect of the later growth of the Soviet Navy, grew up in its shadow, with the knowledge that the Soviet Union could certainly afford to build a seagoing fleet. It was, however, very clearly an artificial creation. Construction of the largest units was cancelled soon after Stalin's death; they consumed far too many scarce resources. Some of the cruisers, and most of the destroyers, were completed, presumably in part to minimise industrial dislocation. Although the destroyers were conceived as part of seagoing squadrons, they can also be considered the last Soviet coast-defence warships, unable to keep the sea in the face of determined air attack. All later major Soviet naval units had their own anti-aircraft missiles.[23]

To Soviet naval officers like Gorshkov, mass cancellation must have carried undertones of the terrifying purges of the 1930s, as indeed Khrushchev's later transformation of the Soviet Army (under the banner of the "Revolution in Military Affairs") seems to have done. Surely it was symbolic of the abandonment of the large ships that Admiral Kuznetzov, who had been identified with the 1937–42 programme, and who had been reinstated postwar by Stalin, was dismissed in 1955. He was replaced by Admiral Gorshkov, who Khrushchev appointed specifically to make drastic cuts.

This was a time of radical change in Soviet military thinking. Stalin focused largely on Eurasian issues, although he did authorise the design and construction of special bombers capable of reaching the United States from the Soviet Union. Khrushchev, his successor, was fascinated by the possibilities of nuclear weapons. He argued that, whereas no conventionally-armed enemy could hope to conquer a nation as large as the Soviet Union, nuclear weapons could destroy the state – or, for that matter, the enemy. These decisive weapons could be delivered over transcontinental ranges. It followed that any Soviet victory in a future European war would be illusory, if it did not include the destruction or neutralisation of the overseas nuclear power, the United States. The United States could clearly deliver nuclear weapons to Soviet soil; the Soviets urgently needed some counterweight.

No existing programme could provide one. Stalin's bomber project had produced an ineffective jet bomber (the Myasischev Bison), and the longer-range turboprop Bear was still some years from effective service. The new Soviet ballistic missile programme had yet to provide a very long-range weapon.

The navy, however, could bring weapons to American shores, in the form of submarine-borne nuclear torpedoes and then cruise and ballistic missiles. Khrushchev is said to have announced, sometime in the late 1950s, that he had no interest in any submarine not armed with nuclear missiles. The building programme was transformed, and in a few years the Soviets built two series of cruise and ballistic missile submarines: diesel-powered Julietts and Golfs based on the Zulu powerplant (and, probably, other equipment) and nuclear Echoes and Hotels based on the November powerplant. The weapons were the SS-N-3 cruise missile (using inertial guidance) and the SS-N-4 ballistic missile.

There was a parallel anti-ship missile technology, which dated back to Stalin's time. Because it generally required that the missile be guided throughout its flight, it was initially limited to bombers (as the successor to their torpedoes) and to surface ships.[24]

In 1957, just as the naval strategic submarine programme was accelerating, the Soviets successfully tested a land-based inter-continental ballistic missile, the massive SS-6. By 1959, a land-based Strategic Rocket Force (SRF) had been formed to operate the land-based missiles. As an offshoot of army artillery, it vastly outranked the navy, and the naval strategic programme was can-celled (although ships under construction were completed).

The navy was permitted to extend the coast-defence perimeter outward, nominally on the theory that it was essential to deal with aircraft carriers before they could approach their launch lines.[25] The existing strategic weapons were literally redefined as anti-carrier weapons. For example, Soviet naval journals mentioned the use of cumbersome submarine-fired ballistic missiles against moving carrier formations. The SS-N-3 cruise missile acquired a homing device. Perhaps even more importantly, the new longer-range mission justified the construction of new cruisers, to keep the sea in the areas from which anti-carrier attacks were to be mounted. Finally, the Soviet Navy was given sole control of anti-ship bombers, surrendering its base defence fighters to the national air defence force, the PVO-Strany.

These shifts explain the new surface ships of the early 1960s, the Kynda and Kresta classes, products of Khrushchev's seven-year plan (1959–65). The navy seems to have hoped for something even more impressive, a big missile cruiser (which would have been escorted by a big helicopter carrier), but the cruiser was far too rich for Khrushchev's blood. The carrier survived as an ASW cruiser (*Moskva*, 1968).

Khrushchev's sins against the Soviet status quo were many, and he was deposed in October 1964. With him went the monopoly status of the SRF; the navy was permitted back into the strategic equation with the new Yankee class submarine and a 1200-mile ballistic missile, SS-N-6. It would have to approach the US coast to

fire, which manoeuvre the Soviets considered extremely dangerous, given the effectiveness of systems such as SOSUS. The navy
developed the idea of retaining its SSBNs as a strategic reserve,
the SRF making (and suffering) the initial attacks. Ultimately Yan-
kees would be surged out across the Atlantic, either for decisive
attacks or as decisive bargaining chips. Until then, they would be
held back in carefully protected sanctuaries or bastions. This bastion idea in turn motivated the development of special limited sea
control or ASW barrier ships: Kresta II and Krivak.[26] Such ships
could also deny the sea approaches of the Soviet Union to US
SSBNs; the primary example is probably Kara, which seems to
have been designed specifically for operation in the Mediterranean and in the Pacific.[27]

The next step was obvious. In the mid-1970s the Soviets began to
deploy submarine missiles with such long range that they could hit
the United States from within the sanctuaries: SS-N-8, aboard the
Delta class. Now it was more important than ever to guard the
sanctuaries, because the Deltas were long-range weapons on a par
with those of the SRF itself. They might even be easier to protect,
since they could not be hit by enemy ballistic missiles. The Delta
programme appears to have been paired with that which produced
the big VSTOL carriers of the Kiev class. It might be described
as the long-term programme of which Yankee was the interim product, since both must have begun in the first post-Khrushchev plan,
1966–1970.

The Non-Nuclear War Role

From the Soviet Navy's point of view, all of these programmes were
fundamentally flawed, in that their rationale was tied to nuclear
warfare. Through the 1970s, it became increasingly clear that
central war between the two superpowers was extremely unlikely.
In Soviet eyes, that did not mean that the basic competition was
over, but rather that attention had to shift to the revolution-
engendering conditions of the Third World. Admiral Gorshkov
seems to have seen this trend as a valuable opportunity. In the
mid-1970s, he began to argue that, by virtue of its ability to operate

abroad, the Soviet fleet could support "state interests" in the Third World, i.e., could protect Soviet proxies in their "wars of national liberation". He claimed, for example, that the presence of Soviet warships off Angola in 1974 had prompted a United States Congress wary of conflict to cut off aid to the anti-Soviet Angolan UNITA forces. The rather greater political impact of the recent conflict in Vietnam seems to have escaped his attention. Note that new aid to UNITA was part of the programme of the Reagan Administration which rejected the political consequences of the Vietnam War.

It now appears that the Soviet nuclear powered cruisers of the *Kirov* class reflect the Admiral's success. They are ideal for Third World operations, because they require no cruising fuel and hence no investment in underway replenishment.[28] Moreover, they are armed with a high-capacity anti-aircraft system, SA-N-6, which might give them a reasonable chance of survival in the face of serious air attack. However, they lack the kind of offensive fire-power required for true power projection. They may, then, be intended primarily to prevent Western naval formations from intervening in the Third World. Alternatively, the power-projection punch may be provided by the Soviet aircraft carriers now under construction. One might, for example, see such *Kirov* systems as the nuclear powerplant as prototypes of those in the carriers, just as the US nuclear cruiser *Long Beach* carried the prototype of the powerplant used in the carrier *Enterprise*. It is even possible that the cruisers were built first because the rate of powerplant output was limited, and only one or two ships could be built at the same time.

The other major new development in the Soviet surface fleet is three new classes: *Sovremennyy*, *Udaloy*, and *Slava*. *Sovremennyy* might be considered an anti-ship successor to Kresta II, with the same powerplant and with a new air defense missile. Udaloy might be considered a substantially larger Krivak successor. Together, they might be considered a means of extending a pro-SSBN barrier substantially further south than their predecessors, where they might expect to encounter NATO surface ships.

Slava is a *Kara production* successor, but with anti-ship rather than anti-submarine weapons, and with the same long-range high-capacity anti-aircraft system (SA-N-6) as the *Kirov*. It might be considered primarily an anti-carrier weapon, to survive under intense air attack in the Mediterranean and in the Pacific, replacing the earlier *Kynda*, as the latter is retired to such second-line areas as the Baltic.

All of these ships might be seen as expressions of a new willingness to contemplate protracted non-nuclear combat: they carry considerably more missiles than their predecessors. They are also probably much more expensive.

The Soviet Submarine Force

The surface ships may indicate the line of Soviet reasoning. Submarines remain its most prominent combat element. The Soviets operate large numbers of strategic submarines and nuclear and diesel attack submarines. Numbers are somewhat distorted by the inclusion in current orders of battle of numerous older craft, which would probably have only very limited utility in war. The older nuclear submarines, for example, are quite noisy and probably would not survive very long, at least against unbloodied allied forces. They may be on the point of being discarded, or they may be retained for use after allied ASW forces have been drawn down.

Modern Soviet nuclear submarine construction can be dated from the introduction of the Victor class attack submarine, the Charlie class short-range missile submarine, and the Yankee class strategic submarine in 1967–68. All shared common powerplant components. Charlie was not too successful, as it proved too slow to keep up with its prospective targets, but Victor developed through two modified versions. Yankee was fitted with new missiles to become Delta, and in 1987 it is still being built. Apart from a few prototypes and the Typhoon and Oscar class missile submarines, these ships constitute the modern Soviet nuclear submarine force; about 45 Victors (of which only the 21 Victor III are considered particularly quiet), 17 Charlies, and about 70 Yankee/Delta, some of the earlier units of which have been converted to other duties, including torpedo attack. Note the large proportion of the modern nuclear force devoted to strategic attack. The torpedo submarine force has never really recovered (in terms of numbers) from the post-Stalin cuts.

Older nuclear submarines include about 25 Echo II class stand-off missile attack submarines, which might be effective despite their noisiness, due to the range of their SS-N-3 and -12 weapons. The three Oscars are their successors. As of 1986, of the newest types, there were only prototypes of the Mike, Sierra, and Akula class attack submarines, with a few further units under construction. Six deep-diving titanium Alfas are probably only of limited value.

Of the large Soviet nuclear attack submarine force, then, only about 20 to 25 (Victor III and later) are currently at or beyond the capabilities of Western ASW. Only a very few (Sierras and Akulas) are so quiet that the big Western passive systems cannot easily detect them at long range when they are running at quiet speed. They constitute the current ASW silencing crisis, because the fear is that they will multiply significantly over the next few Five Year Plans. Such super-submarines would be able to evade not only SOSUS but also any passive barrier set up in the choke points. However, because of their superior silencing, they would probably be assigned to SSBN protection, and so might well not participate in early anti-ship operations.

It is somewhat difficult to define modern diesel boats. The bulk of the force, the 50 Foxtrots, are improved versions of the early postwar Zulu, and the 19 Tangos which followed are improved Foxtrots. They are all efficient submarines, but they lack any kind of spectacular performance. Many unclassified lists still carry large numbers (often 50 to 70) Whiskeys, but these submarines are well over 30 years old, and they cannot be considered particularly effective.

It would seem to follow that the effective strength of the Soviet offensive submarine fleet is declining. That is the natural consequence of bloc obsolescence; the Soviets have been building, but at nothing like the rates they achieved under Stalin, or even under Khrushchev. Moreover, many of their submarines are strategic craft which do not directly affect the issue of a non-nuclear war at sea. Big strategic submarines and very quiet attack submarines are quite expensive, and probably also fairly difficult to build. They are also probably quite difficult to maintain, partly because of their double-hulled construction, and partly because of the complexity of machinery required for effective silencing.[29]

The rate of attack submarine construction may fall further if Gorbachev, like Khrushchev before him, finds it necessary to cut his military procurement budget in order to finance industrial modernisation. If Gorbachev also cuts his standing conventional forces, he will have to rely more heavily on his nuclear deterrent, which would probably mean that Soviet submarine construction would tend more towards strategic than towards torpedo submarines.

All of this is not meant to denigrate the Soviet submarine force, only to place it in perspective. Out of about 320 to 350 submarines, about 120, just over a third, are reasonably modern attack types, and about another 70 perform strategic missions of one kind or another. The remaining 110 to 160 submarines are of older but still more or less serviceable types. They would be relatively easy to detect and sink with current weapons and sensors. However, it might be argued that the stockpile of modern ASW expendable sensors (principally sonobuoys) and weapons would not last too long. For example, published torpedo production figures suggest a run of about 10,000 lightweight weapons to serve throughout NATO. NATO in turn probably has about 400 ships carrying these weapons, and on average such a ship may require about 20. It would seem to follow that NATO has about one ship-fill worth of modern lightweight torpedoes (its standard surface ship and air ASW weapon); this estimate does not count torpedoes carried by aircraft, or emplaced in CapTor mines.

At first blush it might seem that the 10,000 torpedoes quite outnumber their likely targets. However, the ASW experience of the past, both in World War II and in the Falklands, suggests that many weapons will be expended against false contacts. In 1943–45, for example, the ratio between false and real contacts was about nine or ten to one: if two weapons are fired against each contact, that would mean 20 torpedoes per submarine actually detected. The modern torpedoes might be expended quite early, after which second-rate Soviet submarines would have a much better chance of survival. Moreover, the war itself would probably destroy a fair proportion of the most modern NATO ASW ships. Again, the older forces left after the first few weeks might find it much more difficult to deal with even second-rate Soviet submarines. Much would depend upon the state of stockpiles of older types of weapons, and on how fast new weapon production could begin.

These considerations suggest that it is extremely important for NATO to deal with Soviet submarine force as soon as possible. For example, if the newer craft survive past the phase in which modern weapons are expended, then they will be extremely effective.

It is also essential to distinguish between the total size of the current Soviet force, which is substantial, and the rate of new production of attack submarines, which is much less impressive. Cuts in the production rate must take many years to affect total force size. One might assign submarines an operational lifetime of 20 to 30 years, the higher figure pertaining to newer designs. In that case, a production rate of ten per year would suffice to maintain a 300-submarine force. Actual production in recent years has been lower, and it appears that most Soviet diesel submarines now being built are for export. However, even if the rate falls to five per year, that will take four years to cut the force to 280 boats, and even then the Soviets will probably choose to retain more than a few boats beyond their nominal lifetime.

The submarines and the bombers are the main open-ocean anti-shipping forces; coastal NATO navies would also have to deal with Soviet fast attack boats and with Soviet amphibious forces trying to turn the seaward flanks of NATO. US policy, which is concerned largely with the open-ocean threat, must balance off ASW and AAW, submarines and bombers. The usual perception is that the number of submarines is overwhelming, perhaps 300 compared to the 57 with which Hitler began his war in 1939. Moreover, in the face of weak convoy escorts, even a score of U-boats did terrible damage in World War II. However, NATO ASW defences are far stronger than those which the U-boats faced in 1939. Moreover, given their many concerns, Soviet commanders cannot afford to release many of their submarines to operate against the sea lanes of communication, at least at first.

After all, the purpose of the NATO submarine offensive to the north is to give them a reason to retain submarines there, quite aside from sinking Soviet submarines near their bases.[30]

As for the other main anti-shipping force, there are about 300 bombers, organised in regiments about 20 strong, and spread among the four Soviet fleets. For many years the bombers were considered primarily a means of attacking aircraft carriers, because their range was limited. Atlantic shipping, for example, could, in theory, be routed south of any realistic bomber radius of action. Even then, it was entirely possible that, in the course of a war, the Soviet Army would capture bases further forward and so apply the air threat to the sea lanes. That was certainly assumed in early NATO planning, in which sea-based fighters were an essential component of any naval operation off Norway or in the Mediterranean.

The current Soviet naval bomber, the Backfire, can fly further, at least at subsonic speed, and it is designed for inflight refuelling. Alternatively, it can fly supersonically or subsonically at very low altitude, to reduce warning time. Within a few years, the Soviet Navy can expect to receive a much larger, longer-ranged aircraft, the Blackjack, which will certainly be able to fly over much of the North Atlantic while carrying long-range anti-ship missiles.

It is obviously difficult to compare the anti-ship threats posed by the bombers and the submarines. To reach the open sea, the bombers must pass within long-range fighter range of several NATO countries. However, the record of fighters assigned to intercept such passing targets is mediocre at best. Moreover, although bombers attacking a battle force might find themselves in considerable difficulty, they would find other naval targets relatively easy. A cynic would suggest that they have received relatively little attention because land-based aircraft have only a subsidiary role in US naval thinking. However, anyone who experienced World War II German bomber attacks on convoys either to Murmansk or to Malta would consider them a real threat.

Any acceptable US maritime strategy, then, should deal with

both submarines *and* bombers. Otherwise it cannot pretend to guarantee sea control in the face of existing Soviet forces.

Notes

1. The most striking naval examples are submarines. The recent Tango class diesel submarine is essentially a modified version of the older Foxtrot, which in turn is an improved Zulu, a submarine designed about 1946 – which may incorporate some features of the prewar Soviet K class. At the very least, Tango could be described as a 1946 design (albeit vastly improved) still in production as late as 1982. Similarly, current Delta IV class strategic missile submarines are essentially modified versions of the first modern Soviet strategic submarine, the Yankee, which was probably designed about 1964, and whose basic design may well date from about 1960. The most important improvement in that quarter-century has been in the missiles, not in the submarine itself. This continuity is obscured by changes in the standard NATO designator of the submarine design, to reflect what, in retrospect, seem to have been largely external and weapon system improvements. Continuity in other classes is more likely to be restricted to major components, such as machinery. For example, Kresta almost certainly repeats the pressure-fired steam machinery introduced in the *Kynda* class, and the current *Sovremenny* uses the same plant.

2. The Kilo class diesel-electric submarine may be a case in point; it appears to have been designed specifically for export. Foxtrot production continued for many years after the Soviet Navy ceased to accept new boats, because Foxtrot was the standard export submarine.

3. Forced retirement is particularly unpleasant in the Soviet Union because most of the State-owned (or provided) perquisites of official life then vanish, leaving a senior man with only a small pension and a small apartment.

4. Khrushchev was ousted by a group representative of the interests he had slighted: it was led by Mikhail Suslov, the party ideologist (who would have objected to Khrushchev's attempt to dilute the Party establishment with younger men); it reportedly included Marshal Rodion Malinovsky (who certainly would have objected to the mass officer retirements); Leonid Brezhnev (who was closely connected to the defence industry, which suffered from the new crash programmes); and Alexander Shelepin of the KGB (who probably objected to the Khrushchev thaw). The anti-Khrushchev plotters are named by V Solovyov and E Klepnikova in *Behind the High Kremlin*

Walls (Berkley, 1986). Solovyov and Klepnikova are former Soviet journalists, and their somewhat sensationally-titled book is a compilation of what they were able to learn about the internal politics of the Soviet leadership. For an insider's account of the anger of the officer corps, see O V Penkovskiy, *The Penkovskiy Papers*; Colonel Penkovskiy was a General Staff officer. Although he makes much of his horror at Khrushchev's concentration on weapons of mass destruction, Penkovskiy seems to have been most angered by the dismissals of officers associated with the change in Soviet strategy. It seems clear from his account that the interest of the officer corps in personal careers far overshadowed any enthusiasm for a better hammer with which to smash the West.

5. Western analysts tend to distinguish between first-strike and retaliatory (second-strike) nuclear postures. The Soviets seem to see matters differently. They consider a pre-emptive posture, in which, given warning of a Western first-strike, they can limit damage to the Soviet Union by catching most of the strike on the ground. They therefore avoid the burden of choosing to shoot first, but gather the known benefits of doing so. The distinction is important, since both sides benefit most by not firing at all. It seems likely that the Soviets expect their intelligence apparatus to provide timely and reliable early warning. In the past they benefited from some extremely highly-placed agents. Moreover, in Europe they can expect considerable stereotyped message traffic to precede any NATO nuclear strike. Of course, they cannot expect the same thing for a US strategic strike.

6. These Soviet views are well known but, apparently, rarely considered for exploitation in the West, either from the point of view of forcing the Soviets to waste their non-nuclear forces in attack (by hardening or protecting nuclear systems) or of forcing the Soviets to waste their non-nuclear forces in defence. The sole current example seems to be the interest in attacking Soviet SSBN bastions, to reduce Soviet anti-shipping forces available for open-ocean work. One would speculate that it is very difficult for Western tacticians to see their nuclear forces as anything but a means of limiting escalation.

7. The reader should be careful not to connect action and reaction too closely; often the Soviets seem not to recognise a threat until they have some (at least marginally) practicable means of countering it. For example, the US Navy deployed nuclear weapons aboard its carriers in 1953 (and had a carrier-based delivery system as early as 1949), but anti-carrier measures seem to have achieved little prominence in official Soviet thinking before about 1959, when the navy first deployed large numbers of AS-1 Komet anti-ship missiles. On the other hand, it does appear that about 1955 the Soviets became intensely interested in counters to missile submarines off their coasts.

The United States did first deploy the Regulus strategic cruise missile at that time, but it may be much more significant that the Soviets were then testing their own early submarine-launched strategic missiles; Khrushchev may well have demanded a counter to what he saw as the weapon of the future. The 1955 date is deduced from the probable origins of the Alfa class submarine, which appears to have been conceived as a submarine interceptor. Alfa first appeared about 1970, and was therefore built under the 1966–70 Five Year Plan. It incorporated new technology (a titanium hull and a high-power-density reactor) which would have been developed under Khrushchev's new technology Seven Year Plan (1959–65). So much was required that preliminary work can surely be dated back to the preceding plan (ca.1955). By way of confirmation, Soviet interest in modern ASW (e.g., in homing torpedoes and in lower-frequency sonars) can be dated to the early 1960s, i.e., also to the 1959–65 Plan, with preparation during the preceding rump plan.

8. By way of contrast, Western oceanic navies generally do not maintain coastal defence craft in peacetime. They are expensive, and they do not contribute to the vital overseas presence mission. More fundamentally, Western policy is to carry the fight to the enemy, to retain the initiative so that coastal defence is not an issue. *The Soviets implicitly assume that the West will have the naval initiative.*

9. Note that the Soviet Strategic Rocket Forces are basically an outgrowth, not of an independent strategic air force (as in the United States, where the long-range land-based rockets are part of the air force), but of Soviet Army artillery. The US Army lost its fight for similar control of medium-range ballistic missiles in the late 1950s. The Soviets did develop an independent strategic air force in the 1930s, but its leading theoreticians were shot during the purges, and it had little role in World War II. The postwar long-range bomber force has had a very mixed history, and has recently been split up so that in wartime its aircraft would be subordinate to the unified (i.e., army) commanders of the various theatres of operations (TVDs). Very long-range bombers would be associated with a transoceanic TVD under the direct control of the General Staff, along with the land-based intercontinental rockets and the strategic submarines.

10. Admiral Gorshkov first publicly espoused the Third World mission in 1967. It is the only explicit Soviet military mission which is *not* tied to the classic Central Front scenario. One might associate it with the new *Kirov* class nuclear cruiser and possibly also with the full-deck carrier now fitting out. For example, the *Kirov* was laid down in 1973 (1971–1975 Plan), and was probably conceived sometime during the first post-Khrushchev Plan (1966–1970), when Brezhnev was allowing the services to go beyond Khrushchev's nuclear emphasis.

Gorshkov later pointed to the US decision not to intervene in Angola in 1974 as evidence of the value of his new naval mission: he claimed credit due to the presence of a Soviet naval patrol off Angola. He was, of course, careful to disregard the rather larger role of the recent US experience in Vietnam in discouraging another intervention.

11. Brezhnev reportedly had a personal connection with Gorshkov dating back to their World War II experience in the Black Sea. His style of leadership, moreover, was to avoid hard industrial choices and their inevitable political consequences; the Soviet bureaucracy enjoyed a kind of *laissez-faire*, as long as no one element became too greedy. Reportedly, too, as a result there was a general perception of stagnation, not to mention corruption. Andropov entered office determined to administer a reviving shock. Among other things, he fought his own campaign to unseat Brezhnev by attacking corrupt senior officials, and, once in office, he chose a police approach to improving productivity. As Brezhnev's longtime aide, Chernenko would have reverted to his former leader's style. Reportedly he achieved power as an interim measure, while Gorbachev and a rival, Romanov, fought out their competition for leadership. Both had been Andropov's protégés. However, Romanov had personal ties to the shipbuilding complex, because he was based in Leningrad. Gorbachev presumably would find it easier to make deep cuts in naval construction – just as Khrushchev did, in the 1950s. At the time of writing Admiral Gorshkov remains in uniform as an advisor.

12. The official claim has always been that the Soviets follow the "scientific" (hence correct) theory of war, whereas the West tends towards excessive pragmatism, and is insufficiently consistent. The Soviet "young school" of naval strategy was probably first described (in the West) in Robert Herrick's *Soviet Naval Strategy* (Annapolis: US Naval Institute, 1968). At the time, his view that the Soviet fleet was inherently defensive was quite controversial, but Herrick's basic thesis is now quite widely accepted.

13. Readers may object that Stalin actually built a high-seas fleet, or at least what looked like one. Note, however, that his larger ships carried out very few operations during World War II. Operations well outside Soviet home waters, which would have required numerous highly-trained men, were extremely unusual even during the first two postwar decades. It appears in retrospect that Stalin's big-ship fleet was more for show than for combat, on the theory that, to be a great power, the Soviet Union needed a large and powerful fleet. Certainly Stalin's successors quickly abandoned his programme of building large surface ships, and explicitly reverted to the prewar tactical ideas, albeit with postwar technological twists.

14. Wartime Soviet operations are organised by TVD, theatre of

operations. In the early 1980s the Soviet Navy pressed for the creation of a purely naval "oceanic TVD". At the same time Soviet naval writers began to refer to a "naval military science" distinct from the "military science" of land warfare, i.e., to argue that naval warfare really was different from land warfare. They were slapped down, and the oceanic TVD never became approved doctrine. These abstruse Soviet political arguments would seem not too different from the usual Western interservice fights.

15. The Soviet Army was also developing what it claimed were altogether new concepts of war at this time, in the form of Marshal Tukachevsky's *blitzkrieg*. In fact neither "new" idea was altogether new. The new naval strategy could be traced back to the French *jeune école* of the previous century, and Marshal Tukachevsky back to German ideas. In both, however, the degree of central control really was new.

16. This may explain Soviet fascination with operations analysis, which is the basis for so many *prearranged* tactical patterns. From a wider point of view, one might say that at present the Soviet Union is a *traditional society*, in which attention to ritual is more important than actual performance. The inverse is true in a *modern society*. The traditional aspect of Soviet life is particularly clear in the functioning of the Party; "agitation" (which often means giving boring speeches to sleeping audiences) is a prerequisite for advancement. Similarly, "following the book" would be nearly as important as actually killing the target. Moreover, risk-taking in combat would not be encouraged.

17. Readers of Soviet military periodicals are aware of numerous articles on the need for individual initiative. They would seem to present evidence that initiative is so very difficult to nurture in a society so averse to risk-taking on an individual level.

18. This concern also explains why the Soviets have provided back-up ocean reconnaissance satellites. The existence of the back-ups can be inferred from Soviet behaviour in international crises, when it is common for them to launch several extra tactical reconnaissance satellites, to observe a developing situation. The United States tends to build fewer (but much more durable) intelligence satellites, and since the Shuttle disaster it has become painfully clear that few, if any, back-ups exist.

19. This is the classic means of distant location as practised by navies from about 1914 onwards (albeit at different frequencies and at different ranges). D/F range is ultimately limited by the available triangulation baseline; for stations in the Soviet Union, D/F can probably track radio emitters out to ranges of about 1500 or even 2000 miles. Satellite-borne D/F (which the Soviets now have) would be needed for global coverage. Note that, unlike active location (by

reconnaissance), passive radio and D/F can be nullified by maintaining radio silence, or by transmitting over very short ranges or in directions not covered by the D/F net.

20. A future lock-on-after-launch mode would permit bombers to fire missiles without turning on their radars, using missile radars (data-linked back to the bomber) for target identification and designation. This method has been used for about a quarter-century by Soviet surface ships firing SS-N-3 and -12 missiles. Even in this case, however, it would be necessary for the bombers to be sure of their target before firing.

21. The names are Western phonetic letters, W and Z coming first, with the odd (queer) Q following. The Soviets designate their boats by Project numbers, e.g. Project 611 for Whiskey and 613 for Zulu. Of the later Western designators, a few had obvious significance: November (N) was the first Soviet nuclear attack submarine.

22. However, as in World War II, had the Soviets captured the Norwegian coast in some future war, the Whiskeys would have been quite effective in the Atlantic. Moreover, one might speculate that Stalin built his coast-defence submarines first, planning to switch over to mass production of open-ocean craft later. The chief limitation on such a shift would have been transportation from Gorky, the main mass production yard. Gorky is located on the Volga, and many of its submarines were transferred to the Northern Fleet by barges passing through the White Sea Canal.

23. The Kashin class missile destroyer, which appeared in 1963, can be seen as a transitional class, armed with an old-fashioned anti-ship weapon (the torpedo), but also with an anti-aircraft missile, SA-N-1, an adapted Army SA-3, which replaced the dual-purpose gun of earlier destroyers (SA-N-1 had a secondary anti-ship capability). Given the sequence of Five Year Plans, and the need to fix the characteristics of the missile before it could be included in a ship design, one might date the Kashin design from the abortive 1956–60 Five Year Plan, which in turn was probably drawn up about 1954–55 – just before Khrushchev assumed full power. The Kashin is also interesting as an example of "mission obsolescence". Although it was obviously designed as a classical destroyer, it was redesignated a "large ASW ship", in which capacity it could control groups of smaller sub-chasers, correlating their sonar outputs to estimate a submarine's position. This new role required very little modification: the addition of a simple computer and a data link.

24. Information on early Soviet anti-ship weapons is fragmentary. Komet, a beam-riding bomber weapon (designated AS-1 by NATO), was apparently based on wartime German work. Postwar, it was considered so important that, reportedly, Beria's son was placed in charge.

A coastal version (SSC-1) entered service, but a shipboard version was unsuccessful. A second shipboard missile, SS-N-1, was developed for service aboard Soviet destroyers, i.e., aboard the largest of the coast-defence craft. It actually saw limited service; it was guided by a director originally designed for main battery fire control. The self-guided SS-N-2 (Styx) appeared only late in the 1950s, as a replacement for existing torpedo boat weapons.

25. That this was a political choice, rather than a choice dictated by changing circumstances, is shown by the rather long history of the American carrier-based nuclear threat prior to 1959. The US Navy first showed intense interest in naval nuclear bombs in 1945, and from 1953 onwards it regularly carried such weapons at sea, aboard carriers equipped with nuclear bombers.

26. Kresta II illustrates the effect of Soviet industrial inertia: it was an ASW modification of the existing Kresta class anti-ship "cruiser," carrying a new stand-off ASW missile. Krivak was a new design, apparently designed to fill out ASW groups led by Kresta. Krivaks were later redesignated as "guardships" (SKR), recalling a Soviet category of offshore pickets.

27. Compared to a Kresta II, a Kara is somewhat larger and has a slightly heavier armament, including a secondary missile battery (SA-N-4). It has a variable-depth sonar, which the Kresta II lacks, and which would be particularly valuable in the difficult sonar conditions of the Mediterranean and the Pacific. It is powered by gas turbines rather than by steam turbines, and it has somewhat lower freeboard in relation to its length.

28. They do use fossil fuel to boost their power output for high speed, but such boosts would be relatively rare.

29. To refit a double-hulled submarine, the outer hull must be stripped away, a time-consuming process. The longer the necessary refit period, the smaller the operational force corresponding to a given total submarine force.

30. Underwater IFF is so ineffective that one might reasonably hope that intense Soviet ASW measures within the bastions would kill fairly large numbers of Soviet submarines themselves assigned to ASW. The rigidity and centralisation of Soviet command and control, and the natural application of Murphy's Law, would seem to make bastion defence a particularly likely ground for catastrophic Soviet IFF errors. After all, their submarines are probably far easier to detect than ours, and in the past badly frustrated ASW forces have often jumped at the opportunity to attack submarines they finally detected, even when the latter were friendlies operating in the supposed security of "no fire" zones.

7. The Maritime Strategy in Action

The Maritime Strategy, as developed explicitly since 1982, revives a classic equation: that sea control can most efficiently be seized and maintained through the early destruction of the enemy navy, i.e., through projecting sea power into his operating and base areas. Moreover, the threat of that projected power (against such valued assets as his strategic submarines) is intended to force the enemy into an early decisive battle. Promptness is important for two reasons. First, it prevents the enemy from dispersing his forces into the open ocean, where they can do enormous damage before they are tracked down and killed. Second, it frees up power projection forces to affect the land battle, which is almost certainly going to be part of the larger conflict in which the naval war is embedded.

For an application of the strategy, one might imagine a state of growing crisis between NATO and the Warsaw Pact. Both begin to mobilise, and the Soviets assemble their land forces for an attack. They pull naval forces back into bastion areas, to protect against the expected US naval offensive, and this pull back (a consequence of the declaratory aspect of the strategy) in itself eliminates the submarine threat to shipping in the North Atlantic for the first few weeks of hostilities. Similarly, because Soviet naval aircraft are held back to counter the expected forward movement of US carriers, it is possible to use short northern routes across the Atlantic. The pre-hostilities and early wartime build-up of NATO forces from North America is considerably accelerated. That in turn slows down the Soviet land offensive, when the latter materialises.

These advantages, however, may well be transitory, since the Soviets may reverse themselves and surge their anti-shipping submarines and aircraft out into the North Atlantic. Such a surge is particularly threatening very early in the war, as important, and possibly (temporarily) irreplaceable military cargoes approach Europe. The task of NATO naval forces is to make maximum use of the initially favourable situation, by pressing the Soviets back, and then by destroying their naval forces.

NATO mobilisation includes the movement of submarines towards the prospective Soviet bastions, as well as forward deployment of a battle force, which might include up to four carriers. Because such movements, at sea, tend to receive little or no publicity, they do not affect Western public opinion. Therefore they cannot contribute to war hysteria, which the NATO governments wish to avoid, and which might hinder their own mobilisation. On the other hand, the forward movement, which is (incompletely) detected by the Soviets, does convince them of the appropriateness of their decision to recall naval forces at sea, for defence of the bastions.

There is one important exception: some of the best of the Soviet attack submarines are probably assigned to lie off NATO SSBN bases in hopes of attacking the strategic submarines and thus of changing the strategic balance. That would probably amount to about 10 submarines in the Atlantic, to cover two US bases, one British, and one French. This amounts to about a fifth of the total modern Soviet attack submarine force. If one estimates that about half the Soviet submarines are really available at any one time, then, the anti-SSBN mission might consume as many as half of the most capable units – at least some of which would surely be operating in the Pacific.[1]

It is often suggested, too, that the Soviets habitually operate a substantial force of diesel submarines in the Mediterranean to counter allied SSBNs there. Even light area coverage probably requires at least ten boats at any one time, out of an available force of about 25 or 30.[2] It seems most unlikely that the Soviets would reduce their anti-SSBN patrols upon the outset of hostilities, since attempts to redress the strategic balance figure very prominently in their list of priorities. These activities would occur without any Western attempt to use the SSBNs to lure the Soviets out of other- wise harmful activities; no Western government is likely to admit even that its SSBNs are subject to attack.

The NATO SSBNs are peripheral to the tactics envisaged by the Maritime Strategy. They do serve one vital explicit role: they help to deter escalation to nuclear warfare, and hence help to justify the concentration on protracted non-nuclear combat. In addition, the extent to which the strategy relies on the threat to *Soviet* SSBNs suggests that at the least calculations should include the effects on *Soviet resources* of the Soviet threat to Western SSBNs.

Once hostilities begin, NATO submarines move into the bastion area, to hold back and kill their Soviet opposite numbers. En route, they try to roll back whatever submarine barriers the Soviets have erected against forward movement by the carriers, to limit carrier exposure to submarine attack. Given aerial refuelling, the carriers can probably launch strikes at Soviet air bases well before they encounter the Soviet submarine barrier; the Soviets in turn probably consider their own naval aircraft the first line of defence against such an attack.

The Soviets will be well aware of the dangers of attacking the carriers. However, they cannot happily forego such attacks. The carrier-based bombers are a very real threat since the four carriers may have a total of about 10,000 tons of bombs aboard. In addition, the Soviets may have good reason to imagine that they can penetrate effectively, since the submarines (both forward-deployed and directly supporting the battle group) may well have aboard Tomahawk missiles specifically intended to suppress defences, particularly surface to air missiles, which might otherwise stop the bombers.[3] If the bombers can penetrate unscathed, they can shuttle back and forth, delivering a substantial fraction of that 10,000 tons.

The carriers need not head directly into Soviet-controlled waters. They may make use of a temporary sanctuary, an area large enough to allow substantial manoeuvre, yet with narrow entrances which can be blocked against submarine penetration. Obvious examples are the Irish Sea and the big Norwegian fjords. In recent years some publicity has been accorded US carrier operations in the latter.[4] Both possibilities would limit the Soviets to air attacks, which the geography would make particularly hazardous. To reach carriers in the Irish Sea, Soviet bombers would have to beat off British air defence fighters. In a fjord, the surrounding mountains would tend to mask the radar image of the carrier, so the bombers would have to come closer before releasing their missiles, lengthening their exposure to defending fighters, perhaps even closing to within defensive missile range.[5]

Whatever they do, the carriers can expect to attract several regiments of attackers in sequence – the main air strength of the Soviet Northern Fleet. The whole of Soviet Naval Aviation, which must supply four fleets, operates about 300 long-range bombers. Allowing for aircraft not available for combat, it seems unlikely that any multi-carrier battle force would encounter more than about 80 in one series of attacks, and it might well be quite difficult for the Soviets to coordinate that many regiments. The Soviets are ultimately limited because they must face US carrier battle forces in at least three distinct areas: the Norwegian Sea, the Mediterranean, and the Far East. Given the sheer firepower of a three- or four-carrier battle force, it should be quite capable of destroying the three regiments it might be expected to face simultaneously.[6]

The Soviet Air Force also practices anti-ship tactics, but only as a secondary mission. Any major maritime war would be no more than one aspect of a wider war, and that larger war would surely absorb the attentions of the land-oriented Soviet Air Forces.

There are, of course, all those Soviet submarines. As long as US and allied submarines are invading the bastions, the Soviets cannot very cheerfully release their best craft to operate against ships in the open ocean. Moreover, the number of operational modern (and highly capable) Soviet attack submarines is limited. As for the battle force, its ASW escorts, including associated attack submarines, should be able to destroy numerous submarines. Operation in a temporary sanctuary might amplify the ASW power of the battle group, since it would, in effect, interpose new choke points between the battle force and the submarines.

A series of battle force and forward submarine operations should break the back of the Soviet submarine/bomber fleet. The destruction of a substantial (and essentially irreplaceable) fraction of their total force would probably greatly reduce any Soviet appetite for further open-ocean work, given the possibility that carriers would return or, worse, would strike elsewhere, as in the Mediterranean. Moreover, by killing off the Northern Fleet bombers very early in the war, and (by extension) by pinning down the others, an early carrier attack would minimise the effect (on maritime operations) of any Soviet land offensive which might provide the Soviets with bomber bases further south, and so which might add bombers to the open-ocean submarine threat. Nor would the Soviets find it easy to concentrate a substantial anti-carrier force in the Norwegian Sea or the North Atlantic for at least some months.

The Soviets might well prefer to conserve their open-ocean anti-shipping forces until their army had in fact seized the bases they need for full effectiveness. The object of the early allied naval offensive would be to force the Soviets to a series of decisive naval battles early enough that any of their army successes on land would not unduly change the situation at sea.

Once maritime superiority has been achieved, the carriers no longer need concentrate on air or, perhaps, on ASW defence. Within their nominal capacity of about 90 aircraft, then, they might carry many more heavy attack bombers. At the least, their F/A-18s could "swing" to the bomber role.

By this time the war on land might have stabilised, with very heavy losses to the tactical air arms on both sides. The 160 bombers of the carrier battle force would make a considerable difference, because instead of thousands of aircraft, each side might operate no more than a few tens. Submarine-launched Tomahawks might also make a difference, because they could approach enemy air defences from undefended arcs, e.g., from the rear. US attack submarines released from direct support of the carrier group could, for example, operate briefly in the Baltic in this role. The fleet could risk very heavy air attack while supporting Marine landings, because there would no longer be a need to face down massive Soviet anti-carrier (and therefore anti-ship) forces.

It would be unrealistic to imagine that, by itself, this particular campaign would win a major war. However, it would make possible valuable flanking operations early in a war, and they might well make a considerable difference to a hard-pressed NATO.

These operations exploit NATO geographical advantages: choke points which can be blocked, islands athwart the probable lines of advance of Soviet bombers. For example, land-based air force (E-3) airborne early warning aircraft based in Iceland can detect incoming Soviet bombers before they come within range of carrier-based E-2s. Differences in radar frequency between the two types of aircraft considerably complicate any Soviet attempt at jamming.[7]

The Mediterranean is a somewhat different maritime theatre. There is no nearby concentration of Soviet submarines, attack or strategic: the great bulk of Soviet Mediterranean submarines come from the Northern Fleet, through the Straits of Gibraltar, the primary choke point in the area. As in the Northern Fleet case, however, allied maritime operations are threatened by powerful bomber forces, in this case from the Black Sea Fleet. Again, as in the Atlantic, unless the bombers are destroyed early in the war, free passage through the Mediterranean, which is required for the support of the Southern Flank of NATO, is impossible. In this case, as in the North, carriers seem to be the most appropriate bait and trap; the Soviets also presumably fear amphibious operations into the Black Sea.

The Mediterranean also differs from the North in that it is more likely to be the scene of major Soviet ground offensive operations (beyond those valued for purely or obviously naval ends). The Dardanelles have been a Russian, and then a Soviet, objective for at least two centuries. To the extent that Soviet behaviour reflects Russian history, then, Turkey should be a major Soviet objective. In historical terms it is quite possibly as critical as security on the North German plain. These considerations alone should impel the Soviets to try to destroy the NATO long-range tactical air force concentrated in the Sixth Fleet carriers.

In peacetime the navy usually maintains two carriers in the Mediterranean. As in the Norwegian Sea, they can constitute a Strike Fleet. Early in a crisis, the carriers and their consorts might concentrate in the central or western Mediterranean, to make use of the choke points such as those represented by the Sicilian Straits and the Strait of Gibraltar for submarine defence, and to take advantage of land features which might complicate targeting. This location would increase the distance Soviet anti-ship bombers based in the Black Sea would have to fly to reach the carriers, and thus increases opportunities to intercept those bombers en route to the carriers. After all, as in the north, the bombers are primary targets.

The situation in the Mediterranean is complicated by the status of Libya and, to a lesser extent, Syria. To the extent that Libya is a Soviet ally, the Soviets can base anti-ship bombers on Libyan fields and so bring them quite close to the Sixth Fleet. However, given the Soviet failure to protect Libya against the Sixth Fleet air raids in 1986, it is by no means certain that such facilities would be made available. Similarly, to the extent that Syria would make air bases available to the Black Sea Fleet, the bombers would be brought closer to their targets. In each case the fleet would lose assistance to be expected from allied land-based fighters whose operating areas the bombers would otherwise have to overfly.

It is sometimes suggested that, to the extent that the southern and part of the eastern rim of the Mediterranean is held by unfriendly forces, a two-carrier Strike Fleet would not be viable in wartime. Four carriers would be needed to achieve local maritime air supremacy.

Within a week or ten days the two Sixth Fleet (Mediterranean) carriers could be joined by the two Second Fleet carriers based on the Atlantic Coast. The four carriers might join to operate first in one theatre and then in another (for example, first in the Mediterranean and then, after an initial ASW campaign, in the north). Alternatively, given sufficient support from land-based long-range fighters, two carriers might suffice in either theatre. Finally, carrier strength in the European area could be considerably augmented, given sufficient warning. The carrier scheduled to return from the Mediterranean to the United States for refit could be held there, joined by her replacement *and* by the two from Second Fleet, for a total of five. Additional carriers refitting could be rushed to completion.[8]

Sixth Fleet strength was actually increased to three carriers for the Libyan raid early in 1986 by retaining the ship scheduled to return to the United States to be refitted.

As in the north, carriers in the Mediterranean provide a significant fraction of local air defence, particularly at night and in bad weather, as well as local deep strike air power. Given such potential contributions to the ground campaign in both areas, neither "swing" choice is very attractive. However, total carrier battle forces are limited.

In peacetime the United States also maintains one or more Amphibious Ready Groups in the Mediterranean. They represent a threat to the strategic flank of the Soviet Union, since (at least in theory) they can pass through the Dardanelles into the Black Sea. Regular (though limited) US peacetime naval exercises in the Black Sea (which is an international waterway) help to emphasise this point. The existence of this threat would tend to encourage the Soviets to concentrate their surface naval forces in the Black Sea, at least at the outset, for local coastal defence. Once back in that area, they would have to pass through a NATO choke point, the Dardanelles, to return to interdict surface traffic through the Mediterranean. The amphibious threat may also force the Soviets routinely to maintain substantial army and tactical air units far from the Central Front.

Once the war begins, the striking force in the Mediterranean may move forward towards the Eastern Mediterranean, threatening early air attacks which would neutralise the bomber elements of the Soviet Black Sea Fleet, and hence eliminate the most potent sea-denial force in the area. As in the North, it seems likely that the Soviets will attack the carriers, and that the striking force will be able to do substantial damage to the incoming aircraft. Again, as in the north, land-based fighters and radar aircraft may be able to help, although the fighters may not necessarily be available.

The Pacific combines important features of the Atlantic and Mediterranean maritime theatres. In the North Pacific, as in the North Atlantic, the Soviets combine an SSBN bastion and powerful land-based bomber forces. Further south, as in the Mediterranean, the primary naval threat is probably the naval bomber. The most important strategic feature there is the concentration of Soviet ground and tactical air forces on the Sino-Soviet border, a concentration which detracts from Soviet efforts in Europe. Because of its inherent mobility, a Pacific carrier battle force can be expected to operate in both sub-theatres, although simultaneous operation would require it to split up and thus to lose effectiveness.[9]

Currently the United States forward bases one carrier, USS *Midway*, in Japan. Because she refits at Yokosuka, the ship is always close to her station; this proximity helps to make up for the reduced number of carriers (compared to the previous force of 15 or even 16) in recent years. One or two other carriers operate in the Western Pacific, backed by the carriers of the Third Fleet closer to the continental United States. In the past, the Seventh Fleet carriers have often operated simultaneously in two widely separated areas, the North Pacific and the South China Sea, ships in the latter area operating out of Subic Bay in the Philippines. Subic Bay also supports some deployments to the North Arabian Sea, off the Persian Gulf. Typically a total of three carriers are immediately available, backed by two in Third Fleet, and by additional carriers under refit. As in the Atlantic, ships departing to return for refit could be held over in the Far East, so that a force of up to six carriers could be assembled relatively easily.[10]

Thus the Third and Seventh Fleet carriers could meet to form one or two powerful battle forces. Long-range aircraft in the Aleutians could help support a carrier movement forward towards Petropavlovsk; Seventh Fleet submarines would be able to operate in and around Soviet SSBN bastions erected in the Sea of Okhotsk or further south in the Sea of Japan.

The tactical style of the maritime strategy would apply to the Pacific just as to the Atlantic, and the combination of threat and actual attack in the Pacific might be expected to have a considerable effect on the course of the battle in Europe (by forcing the Soviets to keep ground and tactical air forces in the Far East, prior to hostilities) and in the Atlantic. The Soviets could not afford to accept major naval losses in the Pacific, because so large a fraction of their total SSBN force is based there. Given the threat inherent in US submarines and carrier battle forces, that in turn should force the Soviets to maintain substantial attack submarine and anti-ship bomber forces in the Far East, forces which cannot be used in the Atlantic.

The mere potential for US naval and amphibious pressure on the Soviet Far East would have two other important effects. First, it can be expected to cause the Soviets to maintain large ground and tactical air forces in the area, outside of those required to hold the Sino-Soviet border. Soviet military resources, though large, are limited, and this drain might make it difficult for the Soviets to assemble sufficient forces to see through a European campaign. Thus the potential for pressure in the Far East would tend to make it more difficult for the Soviets to preplan an attack in Europe. That hardly rules out war in Europe, but it makes the Soviet *blitzkrieg* scenario much less likely. The more probable scenario is a limited Soviet attack in response to a limited problem, and that scenario is much more favourable to NATO and to NATO mobilisation – should NATO take advantage of its inherent economic and industrial strength.

Second, the presence of powerful and aggressive US naval forces in the Far East would tend to encourage such allied and associated powers as Japan and China. At the very least, whatever the official Chinese attitude, the Soviets would find it difficult to rely on any promise of Chinese neutrality. The presence of US forces would, therefore, make it difficult for the Soviets to withdraw large forces from the Sino-Soviet border once hostilities had begun, and therefore once the attacking Soviet ground force in the West had become depleted through attrition.

Moreover, because the fleet in the Far East could strike either the Soviet naval base complex in the north or areas near the Sino-Soviet border further south, the Soviets have to maintain ground and short-range tactical air forces against either contingency. In the latter (southern) case naval strike forces would be able to support Chinese operations on the border. Whatever the position of the PRC (which would probably prefer neutrality), the Soviets would be unable to dismiss the possibility that, given US assistance, the Chinese would try to regain the vast territories they surrendered to the Czarists and then to the Soviet Union.[11]

Such holding actions are worthwhile because Soviet resources are decidedly finite. The Soviet submarine and bomber fleets are large, but they are nothing like large enough to provide over-whelming power at each of several widely separated points. Similarly, Soviet ground forces resources are finite. For example, to the extent that US naval air forces in the Pacific can threaten their main land supply line, the Trans-Siberian Railroad, the Soviets must maintain very large masses of materiel for wartime support of ground forces in the Far East. This materiel cannot easily be moved back East. The troops might be flown back, but they still need heavy equipment. Recent experience suggests that munitions and equipment will be expended very rapidly in any future land war, so that anything which ties down large masses of it should prove quite troublesome to future Soviet wartime leaders.

All of this is quite apart from the vital US interest in free passage across the Pacific. Much of the West's current industrial base resides on the rim of Asia. Its products, which are essential to US military production, must cross the Pacific by ship. The US industries in turn can be expected to feed NATO forces in the field. Should a war be protracted, the Soviets would surely consider it important to interdict this traffic.

The plausible threat of a *combination* of forward Atlantic, Mediterranean, and Pacific operations should strain Soviet land and associated tactical air resources. Ideally, NATO and the other allied states should be able to wage simultaneous global forward operations (so the Soviets cannot withdraw from any area without losing it) from the beginning of any major war. In fact the best they can hope for, given basic economic realities, is sequential global operations beginning as early and as far forward as possible.

The Maritime Strategy, then, can be expressed as global, forward, allied, and joint, the latter because the full effects of maritime operations cannot be achieved unless ground and land-based air forces can seize and hold (or defend already held) territory of maritime significance, such as Iceland.[12]

These examples of possible operations show how limited even a 15-carrier force can be. The traditional forward deployment is only two carriers in the Mediterranean and two or three in the Far East, with similar numbers working up or returning from deployment on each coast, so that there are about 10 active ships out of a total force of up to 15. It might, then, be relatively easy to form a second two-carrier battle group for Norway, but much more difficult to form ideal four-carrier concentrations for both the Norwegian Sea and the Mediterranean. Politically it would be difficult to pull the existing pair of carriers out of the Mediterranean to join the two from the East Coast in the Norwegian Sea, even though it might be argued that the concentrated force could do the most good by "swinging" north and then south.

US planners currently recognise four possible areas of carrier operation: the North Atlantic/Norwegian Sea, the Mediterranean, the Western Pacific and, as a secondary theatre, the Indian Ocean. Even with all 15 carriers simultaneously operational, that leaves one area short a carrier (hence with reduced bomber-killing capacity). Even coverage of the three principal theatres (with only one battle force each) would be difficult, particularly if one observes that the Pacific is really two theatres (North and South).

Fifteen carriers, then, are what the nation can probably afford, not what is needed to meet a national strategic goal of meeting potentially simultaneous Soviet attacks anywhere. Moreover, the situation is worse than it was two decades ago because the United States has the only large fully-capable carriers in the West.

The Maritime Strategy and its Predecessors

The fundamental idea of the Maritime Strategy, that sea control and power projection can (though they need not) be two aspects of the same naval effort is not new. It does reverse the common wisdom of the 1970s, which held not only that sea control and power projection were very separate naval missions, but also that money invested in one would generally come at the cost of the other, given limited resources. In this context, sea control generally was taken to mean open-ocean ASW, and power projection meant carrier attack aircraft and marines.

Why, then, does the strategy seem so new? After World War II the United States enjoyed two advantages. First, wartime building programmes had been so fruitful that the overall limit on ship numbers was not nearly so obvious. Until about 1970, for example, there were over 200 destroyers; until about 1960 there were about 300 frigates. As new carriers were built, war-built carriers were transferred to sea control (ASW) service. Second, given the limited range of Soviet naval bombers, sea control was largely equated with ASW. These bombers really endangered only the strike carriers which had to come within their range.

This happy situation ended in the late 1960s, as the wartime fleet, worn out, had to be discarded. The United States was left with limited forces for power projection and for ASW. The ASW problem was somewhat mitigated by the rise of SOSUS and of nuclear submarines capable of blocking the choke points. However, there were insufficient power projection forces to cover Third World and peacetime presence requirements. Some solution was needed. It came out of US naval history.

Sea control in the Pacific during World War II was ultimately assured by precisely the current strategy (although it was couched in rather different words).

The Japanese certainly sought to achieve it by power projection: first by the destruction of the US fleet in harbour (at Pearl Harbor), and then by luring the remainder of the US fleet to destruction by attacking a valued US asset, Midway. Note that their defeat at Midway eliminated the surplus Japanese sea power which otherwise might have been used for further expansion, e.g., into the Indian Ocean.

Similarly, the United States enjoyed limited sea control in the central and eastern Pacific, but only because the Japanese did not contest it. Full sea control required the destruction of the Japanese fleet in a decisive battle. At the Philippine Sea, American power projection into a vital Japanese asset, Saipan, precipitated just such an engagement, the outcome of which was the loss of most of the Japanese naval air arm, the striking force of the Imperial Navy. Power projection into the Philippines themselves four months later drew out what was left of the Japanese fleet, much of which was eliminated.

Histories of World War II generally concentrate on the island campaigns, the islands seized as US forces progressed across the Pacific. However, the ultimate objective was the defeat of Japan, the defeat of a maritime empire bound together by sea lanes. With-out free use of those sea lanes, Japan could not sustain herself, let alone continue her aggression. The *strategic* objective, then, was the destruction of the Japanese navy and merchant fleet, partly by sea denial (by US submarines) in areas the Japanese nominally controlled, and partly by the physical destruction of the Japanese Navy – which was brought to battle by attacks on specific islands. These seizures also tended to enhance US sea control (to protect US lines of communication) because the Japanese might have used them as air or submarine bases.[13] The islands also served as useful advanced bases, so that the fleet did not have to take its train into combat with it; the great anchorage at Ulithi is the classic case in point.

The later anti-*Kamikaze* operations could be somewhat similarly characterised: the carriers projected power onto the *Kamikaze* airfields (to destroy them on the ground) and also tried to tempt them into flight (and to destruction) so that they would be unable to contest the landings scheduled for later in 1945. There was, of course, no single decisive battle, so the fleet was never completely freed for other tasks.

Similarly, in the Atlantic it was impossible to destroy the entire German U-boat force in anything resembling a single decisive engagement. However, one might think of the formation of a convoy as, in part, a means of forcing the submarines into battle with ASW forces. Perhaps more importantly, as submarine technology improved during and immediately after the war, and therefore as convoy seemed less and less viable, the US Navy turned towards power projection, in the form of "attack at source", as a solution.

All of this would seem quite obviously to lead directly to the present Maritime Strategy. However, concepts like "attack at source" and what amounted to maritime air superiority (air con-trol achieved by the destruction of the enemy air force) lost much of their currency as nuclear weapons multiplied during the 1950s, and the United States drew away from the concepts and costs of protracted or classical war. The shift was gradual, and it was not altogether consistent, as befitted a shift made quite implicitly. However, it does seem fair to say that maritime air superiority, as a means of protecting important sea lanes, became less and less important, perhaps partly as local NATO air forces grew stronger.

NATO itself never met the conventional force goals drawn up in 1952, and had to depend upon tactical nuclear weapons to balance the very large Soviet army facing it. War might be somewhat protracted, and the Atlantic sea routes remained extremely valuable[14]. However, carrier strike forces were more and more valued for their ability to supply tactical nuclear attacks on the enemy's flanks and, in the case of escalation, for their ability to strike the enemy's homeland.[15]

Strike Fleets, in the Mediterranean and in the North Atlantic, have been a fixture of NATO maritime strategy since the beginning of the Alliance.[16] The Northern Fleet task is to attack Soviet naval bases in the north (attack at source) and to assist in the battle for northern Norway. It was expected to intercept and destroy Soviet surface combatants which might otherwise break out to attack ASW escorts protecting convoys, and to achieve maritime air superiority. The anti-surface ship role recalled that of the World War II British Home Fleet, which provided distant anti-battleship cover for convoys to Murmansk. As initially conceived, the Strike Fleet consisted of the most powerful US and British carriers. When the Royal Navy gave up its large-deck carriers, it retained an important Strike Fleet role, supplying an ASW support group built around a VSTOL carrier. Thus the carrier battle force element of the US Maritime Strategy is entirely consistent with a classic theme of NATO naval operations. What the strategy adds is a more explicit justification of the Strike Fleet concept.

In the mid-1950s, US naval strategists emphasised ASW for another reason as well: protecting the United States against a new expected threat: Soviet strategic attack submarines.[17]

As might be expected of a period of extremely rapid technological change (particularly in strategic weapons), US national strategy was neither entirely internally consistent, nor consistent with that of NATO. By about 1956, the air force claimed that it could destroy the Soviet Union in a very few hours, using H-bombs. It could, therefore, apply much of its old nuclear *blitzkrieg* strategy to central (US-Soviet) war. US policy did require that some threshold be erected between minimal Soviet aggression and total nuclear war, if only to keep the Soviets from thinking that they could get away with minor acts clearly not worth the consequences of nuclear warfare. As a consequence, the United States could not entirely abandon its conventional forces.

Korea was (in effect) a case of this type, a clear act of aggression which did not, however, merit the use of nuclear weapons. Such "freak" wars were clearly a special case.

As for NATO, the theory was that tactical nuclear weapons in the theatre would be used to fight a battle to stop an oncoming Soviet army, that it might well not be necessary to have recourse to strategic weapons.

These ideas did not last very long, and their passing began a kind of dark age in US strategic thought. As early as the mid-1950s, even as Strategic Air Command was growing towards overwhelming strategic power, it became apparent that the Soviets might soon be able to present a sufficient strategic threat to keep the United States from attacking them. The two superpowers would find themselves stalemated, at least in the main theatre, Europe. In 1955 the US Navy formed a Long Range Objectives group, which concluded that this stalemate would shift the area of superpower rivalry to the rim of the Eurasian land mass, where Soviet proxies would challenge the United States in the Third World. They predicted, in effect, the war in Vietnam, although the North Vietnamese were more than Soviet proxies.[18] A few years later the new Kennedy Administration focused on counterinsurgency (COIN) for much the same reason.

NATO strategy was much more difficult to shift, because it had to be approved by all nations of the Alliance. This inertia probably saved NATO ASW forces during the US thermonuclear romance of the 1950s. By the 1960s, the United States was no longer an enthusiastic supporter of the early large-scale use of tactical nuclear weapons, because the Soviets were deploying their own; simultaneous use by both sides would have devastating results. The United States, therefore, pressed (ultimately successfully) for a modified posture, in which NATO would initially present a conventional defence while threatening nuclear escalation. The threat of escalation was essential given the numerical disparity between the NATO and Soviet forces.[19]

The new NATO doctrine, then, was to hold as long as possible with strengthened conventional forces; this might mean a period of days or a few weeks, but little more. This period would suffice to solve a problem which had led to an essentially accidental war, and also to reach a NATO decision on nuclear attack. The next step would be a warning of escalation, backed up by one or more demonstration weapons (the nuclear "shots across the bow"). Should that fail, NATO would fall back on its old tactic of large-scale tactical nuclear attack. Finally, the US, British, and French strategic forces promised a further escalation to Soviet national destruction.

Sea control could contribute to this new NATO strategy by supporting resistance on land, and so putting off the evil hour of nuclear escalation. On the other hand, there was no expectation that war would really be protracted; it was more a matter of damaging the Soviets badly enough to convince them to stop without risking nuclear war. That in turn meant that NATO (or at least US) civilian and ground planners could concentrate on the central front in Germany. The war probably would not last long enough for serious threats to develop on the flanks, although it was necessary to provide for their initial defence. The flanks were particularly important to the US Navy, because its carriers were likely to be the main source of tactical airpower in both the north (Norway) and the south (the Mediterranean).

Even so, the primary naval contribution to NATO came to be perceived, at least by civilians and army-dominated staffs in Europe and in Washington, as sea control, and that more and more to mean close-in ASW in the central Atlantic. The Soviet naval air threat to shipping seems to have been very largely discounted. Sea control thus defined was separated from power projection, which was seen as more or less temporary provision of naval air and marine amphibious forces in limited or "freak" wars in the Third World. It seems to have been assumed by civilians and soldiers that, because of their limited numbers, carrier-based aircraft could not make much of a contribution to tactical air warfare within Europe.

The Strategy and the US Programme

In principle, the strategy should determine the US naval programme. The level of forces needed depends on the assumed war
scenario and on approved answers to some larger strategic questions. For example, the Soviets can operate more or less simultaneously on several quite widely separated fronts, and naval forces
including carriers cannot easily be transferred between, say, the
Atlantic and Pacific. Thus the ideal would be to have a ready
carrier battle force in or near each of the four areas of concern:
the Norwegian Sea, the Mediterranean, the Indian Ocean, and the
North Pacific, a total of about 16 operational carriers. To maintain
such a force for any length of time, the Navy would need additional
carriers (to allow for refits, damage, etc), a total of perhaps 20 or
25 large carriers.

Similarly, ideally a substantial Marine amphibious force would
be maintained in each ocean, or perhaps in each of the four vital
areas. The type of offensive operations contemplated require a
combination of specialised assault ships (to carry the assault eche-
lon and to deliver it rapidly in the face of potential opposition) and
follow-up commercial-type shipping.

The carrier force and the amphibious force (and now the battleship force) in turn should determine the scale of missile cruisers,
destroyers, and replenishment ships.

The required number of attack submarines is nearly independent of the size of the surface fleet, since submarines generally
operate by themselves. Because they are the only US warships
which can easily operate in waters nominally controlled by the
Soviets, the submarines are required for many roles beyond ASW.
For example, they may conduct sustained reconnaissance, as US
submarines did in World War II, and as US submarines have
reportedly done since. It is impossible to form an estimate of the
number required on an unclassified basis, but some years ago a
representative of the Atlantic Fleet Submarine Force remarked
publicly that his war plan required about 150 submarines.

Both the submarines and the surface ships must be able to use
their ports and a variety of choke points at least relatively freely. If

the Soviets are granted the possibility of mining such attractive areas, then the strategy demands a sufficient mine counter-measures component. Its precise size will depend on the number of ports to be cleared, and on the estimated time to clear a usable channel out of a port. Mine-hunting is difficult and tedious, and past experience (as in the Red Sea in 1984) suggests that even small fields will take several weeks to clear. One might, then, imagine that about 100 minecraft would be needed to keep US ports clear; the NATO navies are responsible for their own areas.

The reality is that the Navy can generally hope for about 20 ships per year. Ships last about 30 years, although expensive refits can prolong the life of some of the larger ones. On the other hand, experience with amphibious ships built in the 1960s suggests that some classes will never serve past a quarter-century. The "600 ship navy", then, is what the United States can hope to afford, not what its naval strategy requires. All the strategy can do is to con-tain the problem, by making for the most efficient possible compro-mise. The resulting fleet must be able to execute, not only the campaign against the Soviets, but also the much more likely combi-nation of peacetime presence and limited war in the Third World. The Navy cannot hope to build or maintain very many ships which are limited to one or the other.

The two central numbers which determine the shape of the fleet are determined by affordability: 15 deployable carriers and 100 submarines. The Navy managed to maintain 15 or 16 attack carri-ers from the mid-1950s through the mid-1970s, together with up to ten ASW/limited attack carriers. It really needs more. As for the submarines, the goal of between 90 and 105 has remained constant since World War II. Again, it is a minimum, and affordable rather than an ideal figure.

The effect of the Maritime Strategy is for the Navy to fight for the maximum carrier force it can afford, 15 deployable ships, rather than to accept some much smaller force in order to buy more spe-cialised ASW ships in the name of sea control. Note that the stra-tegic analysis shows that these ships cannot, by themselves, achieve sea control because the Soviet bombers can destroy them.

The Maritime Strategy also clearly emphasises amphibious

operations. That has meant a conscious decision to build up to a previously-agreed (but not met) goal of sufficient lift for the assault echelons of one Marine Amphibious Forces (MAF) and one Marine Amphibious Brigade (MAB).[20] The force goal actually considerably predates the Maritime Strategy, dating back to about 1970. At that time US national policy called for the ability to fight "two and a half" wars simultaneously: one in Europe, one against China, and one against a Soviet Third-World proxy. The MAF was associated with the full war, and the MAB with the "half" war. Part of the post-Vietnam rundown was a reduction from two to one "whole" wars, i.e., to one-MAF lift. The reality was that when World War II-built amphibious ships were discarded, lift was reduced to something closer to the assault echelons of two MAB.

The goal of one MAF and one MAB is generally equated to about 75 amphibious ships. In 1982, for example, the navy had 61 active and four Naval Reserve Force amphibious ships, which were equated to lift for the assault echelons of 1.15 MAF. However, the nearly even division between the two oceans left each fleet with only enough lift for an MAB-size operation.

There has been a larger shift. The Carter Administration sought to build a US capability to react very rapidly to an emergency in Southwest Asia, which might mean Pakistan or the Persian Gulf, 8000 miles from the United States. It stationed a carrier in the Indian Ocean, but it could not maintain a substantial force of Marines on that station. Instead, the Marines formed an air-transportable MAB, the sea-transportable equipment of which would be held aboard Maritime Prepositioning Ships (MPS) based at Diego Garcia, much closer to the possible operational area. The Defense Department became interested in what it called strategic sealift to support such operations.

The Maritime Strategy transformed this concept. Sustained Marine landing operations would require, not only the dedicated amphibious ships, but also considerable follow-up. The MPS ships constituted a valuable opportunity. Some of them were based on the coasts of the United States, and they were earmarked for the follow-up mission, at the least as an alternative to the Indian Ocean. In addition, the Navy began to buy up idle merchant ships as a war reserve, a first gesture towards the problems of sustained naval warfare. These purchases were particularly economical because of the slump in world shipping.

The requirements of the Maritime Strategy also show themselves in subtler ways. If so much depends on early battle force operations, then it becomes important for the navy to be able to concentrate its carriers in peacetime, to "train the way it will fight", and to test the new tactics. In peacetime, however, the carriers are dispersed because to many allies they represent a guarantee of US concern. Their disposition is so completely determined by political requirements that it often requires a Cabinet-level decision to move a carrier from its station. Yet anything even remotely resembling a fixed carrier station is anathema from a wartime point of view. Similarly, the peacetime arrangement of fixed theatres of operation has little relevance to naval operations: there is no clear boundary marked in the sea between, say, NATO SOUTH and NATO ATLANTIC.

The boundaries and the politics make it difficult to concentrate three or four carriers, either in peace or in war. In peacetime, it takes approximately three carriers to keep one forward-deployed. The Indian Ocean deployment is even more difficult, because the carrier is required to maintain itself in a fairly limited area, so that time spent in transit between, say, the Pacific and that area does not count. As a result, a 15-carrier force can support only about five forward deployments: something less than two in the Mediterranean and in the Pacific and one in the Indian Ocean. Even this force level is not altogether satisfactory. For example, when a carrier had to be withdrawn from the Seventh (Western Pacific) Fleet to go to the Indian Ocean, public opinion in Japan was upset. It seemed that the United States was withdrawing even as the Soviets added a carrier (the vastly less capable *Minsk*) to their own Pacific Fleet. Similarly, the NATO allies were not altogether glad to see the Sixth Fleet commitment reduced so that one of its carriers could sometimes serve in the Indian Ocean.

The situation was bad enough when the United States had merely to display its naval power. The actual use of naval power requires more than one carrier. The ideal is to be able to move the carriers about much more freely. That would also make the carrier force less vulnerable to surprise attack, as it would be much more difficult for a potential enemy to predict carrier locations or even operating areas. The new concept, "flexops", or flexible operations, has had only limited success, because of the political limits on deployments.

The flexops problem touches on a major difference between naval warfare and land warfare. Naval forces are fundamentally mobile. They move from area to area, concentrating to destroy similarly mobile enemy naval forces and thus to achieve sea control, and then to exercise naval force projection. By way of contrast, land forces are fixed to their geographical areas. The current US system of theatre commands follows just such a geographical scheme. Each specified and unified commander (CinC) has particularly naval forces attached to him or at least assigned to him for war use, and it is difficult to imagine just how these assignments can be broken to achieve optimum use of naval forces. To the extent that recent changes in the US military structure have strengthened the hands of the CinCs – including naval CinCs – compared to the central power in Washington, they have aggravated this problem.

The recommissioned battleships somewhat simplify pressures on deployment. In peacetime, a battleship standing off a hostile coast can certainly project US power; her 16-inch guns are quite destructive. Peacetime presence is often more a matter of perceptions than of combat capability. Only a battleship even approaches a carrier in perceived naval presence, so only it can substitute, even on a limited basis. In fact the battleship may have an important advantage in very limited warfare, in that its shellfire is not subject to interception, hence cannot entail casualties or the capture of US pilots.[21]

The Strategy and US Naval Technology

The Maritime Strategy should also guide the development of US naval technology. To at least a considerable extent, the existence of the Aegis missile system motivated the modern concept of maritime superiority, which is the basis of the bait/trap battle force concept. That operational concept in turn emphasises the importance of the "outer air battle", the battle against the bombers rather than against their weapons (an idea often expressed as "shoot the archer rather than the arrow"). Many outer air battle concepts have been proposed, but all require the earliest possible warning. Recent approaches to improved early warning include the development of Relocatable Over The Horizon radars (ROTHR), which can be placed at choke points, and the decision to replace existing carrier-based EA-3 electronic reconnaissance aircraft, which may be able to locate Soviet missile bombers long before they appear on battle force radars. Early warning also explains the Navy's interest in data links with Air Force-operated AWACS (E-3) aircraft.

The related concepts of power projection as sea control and then of seizing sea control as early as possible explains interest in the "swing" of the air group, since the same carrier would have both to seize air superiority and then strike land targets. That explains both the importance of the F/A-18 "swing" aircraft and of the air-to-air capability being built into the A-6F.

The Maritime Strategy is part of a larger national strategy the recent development of which suggests that a future major war is more likely to be sustained than brief. That in turn makes survivability features in surface warships more valuable. In a brief war, almost any damage puts a ship out of action for the duration. There is little point in investing heavily so that the ship can return to service some months later. If the war is sustained, however, almost any hull which survives is worth repairing. Strategy-related technology therefore includes efforts to improve ship survivability, and the hardening of the new Arleigh Burke class destroyer expresses these concerns.[22]

The new Seawolf (SSN-21) class submarine, the only entirely new warship design begun under the current administration, exemplifies the forward submarine strategy concept within the Maritime Strategy. A submarine in a forward area will encounter numerous targets, so it will expend its weapons relatively rapidly. It will be at greatest risk after it attacks (since the opposition will surely search near the resulting "flaming datum"), and when it passes into and out of the operational zone, since the simplest and most effective (i.e., least dependent on IFF) Soviet ASW measure will be a barrier.

These considerations impose two characteristics: high silent speed, among other things to escape from the location of an attack; and large weapon capacity, to reduce the number of passages into and out of the operational area. Ideally, too, the forward-area submarine should have as many torpedo tubes as possible, to be able to engage several targets simultaneously in its target-rich environment. Forward operations also particularly stress submarine sensors and the associated combat system, since the submarine must be able to disentangle particularly complex tactical situations.

These considerations virtually described the Seawolf. It is not so much faster than the previous Los Angeles, but it has a much higher quiet speed, and it carries twice as many torpedoes and has twice as many tubes. It is also large enough to accommodate a new, and more highly automated, combat system.

Notes

1. This view is based on the difficulty of operating a diesel submarine (which might be assigned to ambush SSBNs) near a well-protected base; the submarine must periodically reveal herself by snorkelling. On the other hand, submarines in the Mediterranean would benefit from the presence of heavy merchant traffic, and they would be relatively sparsely distributed. They could, therefore, be diesels.
2. Soviet allies generally receive their diesel submarines in groups of three, which suggests that it requires three to maintain one operational submarine. The figure given is based on the assumption that the Soviets have a total of about 70 to 90 usable diesel submarines. Mediterranean coverage by diesel submarines would be predicated on a division of that limited sea area into finite patrol "boxes", inside each of which very little sustained movement would be needed. The Soviet ambushers would benefit from difficult acoustic conditions. On the other hand, nuclear power would probably be needed merely to survive in the approaches to a major SSBN base, and a watching submarine would probably find itself in a stern chase situation.
3. Submarine-launched missiles have a unique potential for defence

suppression because they provide so very little warning. An aircraft approaching at medium altitude, for example to deliver an anti-radar missile, is certainly detectable. At the least, its appearance constitutes early warning that a raid is approaching, and in many cases its direction of approach may even suggest the route and target of the raid. However, low-flying Tomahawks may well be detected only a few moments before they hit, and it may be difficult for defenders to decide what pattern they represent, since the submarines firing them will be quite far from the battle group. On the other hand, submarines operating in forward areas need torpedoes with which to engage other submarines. The combination of roles enforced by the Maritime Strategy makes the limited weapon capacity of submarines particularly critical, and helps explain the need for vertical launch tubes in later *Los Angeles* class submarines, and for additional weapon space in the new *Seawolf*.

4. For example, the *America* battle group operated in Vestfjord in September 1985, as part of the annual Ocean Safari exercise. See, e.g., C C Wright, "US Naval Operations in 1985," in *Naval Review 1986* (Annapolis: US Naval Institute, 1986).

5. The missile defence firepower provided by Aegis makes it possible for short-range land-based fighters to contribute to the destruction of the bombers, since it is not critical that the bombers be attacked before they fire. Without Aegis, missiles fired by bombers surviving long enough to fire would have a much better change of penetrating to their targets, and it might be necessary for defending fighters to chase missiles in towards the ships. The effect of mountains surrounding a fjord would be to reduce the bombers' radar observation range, and thus to force them to come closer before attacking, increasing their exposure to fighter attack.

6. With, of course, the major *caveat* of sufficient early warning, so that the bombers cannot fire their missiles from well beyond the defensive fighters. That seems reasonable, given heavy US investments in early warning and in tactics (and deceptive technology) which should make it difficult for the bombers to attack from great distances. Successful Soviet coordination of bombers and submarines would also complicate battle group defence, for example because close-in air defences would have to deal with submarine-launched missiles. However, it seems unlikely that the Soviets could achieve tactical coordination on this scale, given the problems of communicating with submarines underway.

7. One lesson of the analysis leading up to the Maritime Strategy was a new appreciation of the value of strategic islands, such as Iceland, the Aleutians, and the Azores. Marine or army units guarding these islands, especially with air defence units, then, contribute directly to

the success of the Maritime Strategy in gaining early naval superiority. Aircraft on the islands, particularly radar aircraft, contribute; US Air Force E-3 aircraft can now communicate directly with naval forces.

8. All of these options involve delays, and the delays define the degree of warning necessary to execute them. Steaming time between the GIUK Gap and the central Mediterranean is about six days at 20 knots; between the US Atlantic coast (Norfolk) and the central Mediterranean, about 10 days (seven days to the GIUK Gap).

9. It is sometimes suggested that this force "swing" into the Atlantic rather than exert itself in the Pacific. Powerful forces must be maintained in the Far East in peacetime in order to show solidarity with major allies and trading partners, so the Pacific concentration is unavoidable prior to any European war. Even once a war began in Europe, the force could not be expected to "swing" into Atlantic waters quickly enough to affect any early campaign; the question is how to employ it most effectively in the Pacific. At 20 knots, a carrier based on the US Pacific coast would take about 28 days to reach the GIUK Gap. Passage through the Panama Canal saves more than a week at this speed, but the canal is too narrow to admit modern carriers.

10. Distances are a problem, however. At 20 knots, carriers based on the US Pacific coast would take about nine days to reach Japan, or 24 days to reach the Persian Gulf – which is about the same time it would take a 20-knot force leaving the US Atlantic coast. However, the Atlantic force could save over five days by steaming through the Suez Canal, which is wide enough and deep enough for carriers. It is about 14 days between Japan (Yokosuka) and the Persian Gulf, which is why the Seventh Fleet so often supplies the Indian Ocean/North Arabian Sea carrier.

11. The present writer well recalls a museum in Harbin, near the Sino-Soviet border, in which maps of the lands lost to the "unequal treaties" were displayed, together with paintings showing the expulsion of Chinese civilians from those areas. The Chinese position is that the Soviets should merely admit that the treaties were unequal, and that the border requires minor rectification. The current (1987) Soviet position seems to be that any surrender of territory would only be the beginning of a long process of surrender.

12. Thus expressed, the Maritime Strategy mirrors many earlier attempts to deal with the Soviet Union and its Czarist predecessor. For Americans, the earliest such discussion is probably Alfred T Mahan's book *The Problem of Asia*, which appeared in 1900. It seems to have been similar to a British attempt to update Mahan's original book (1890) by showing how his principles applied to an earlier war

against Russia – the Crimean War (in which the Allies attacked in the Baltic, the Black Sea, and even in the Pacific). US war plans of the 1945–50 period show operations strikingly like those proposed under the current Maritime Strategy. A Soviet observer, Ginrikh Trofimenko, has suggested that the Maritime Strategy represents a revival of Mahan's 1900 ideas, in *The US Military Doctrine* (Moscow: Progress Publishers, 1986). It is most unlikely that any of the framers of the strategy had read Mahan's book, which is one of his more obscure works. For a typical early postwar strategy, see Anthony Cave Brown, *Dropshot: The American Plan for World War III Against Russia in 1957* (New York: The Dial Press/James Wade, 1978). Brown published, largely unedited, an original US document (which is more an analysis of the effect of budget cuts proposed in 1949 than a true war plan) with notes; unfortunately, as A D Rosenberg has shown, the notes are misleading. Even so, the book gives a clear idea of the extent to which current ideas mirror earlier ones. Dropshot was, after all, a non-nuclear way of dealing with an aggressive Soviet Union. So is current US policy.

13. The prewar Japanese Navy well understood that it would be the primary target in any Pacific War, since its destruction would permit the strangulation of Japan by blockade, as well as air attacks on Japanese cities. Japanese strategy called for air and submarine attacks on the US fleet as it passed through the chains of islands administered by Japan, en route to a decisive battle in Japanese home waters. This reduction strategy was necessary because the interwar treaties granted the United States a 5:3 advantage in several key ship categories. The island reduction strategy in turn led the Japanese Navy to develop long-range land-based bombers, such as the G3M "Nell" which sank the British *Prince of Wales* and *Repulse* in December 1941.

14. This is remarkable. During the early postwar period it was generally assumed that large numbers of Soviet shore-based bombers would attack convoys to Scandinavia and through the Mediterranean. Later it seems to have been assumed that specialist Soviet anti-ship bombers would be held back to deal with US carriers; no one seems to have been concerned with the possibility that, unless the carriers could somehow destroy the bombers, they would make themselves felt on the vital sea lanes. Ships en route to England could, to be sure, be sent south out of bomber range. However, that would be of little value for Norway. Moreover, Soviet seizure of Norway would bring anti-ship bombers far enough south to overcome this ploy. One would conclude, then, that the equation of sea control with ASW (i.e., the exclusion of the air dimensions) probably implies an expectation that war will be

brief, and that the initial battle on the central front (of Germany) will be decisive.

15. One might reasonably ask why this should not have been entirely an Air Force responsibility, given the heavy investment in the Strategic Air Command. One reason was that, because they would approach from different (and unpredictable) directions, and probably at very low (as compared to high) level, carrier bombers would enormously complicate Soviet air defence problems. This became truer as SAC was forced to vacate bases along the southern perimeter of the Soviet Union.

16. The relative balance between Mediterranean and North Atlantic changed over time. At the beginning of the Alliance, the Strike Fleet in the North was expected to attack Soviet submarine bases and to cover convoys to Scandinavia against air attack. The fleet in the Mediterranean provided air cover against what was expected to be very heavy Soviet air attack, as well as nuclear strike aircraft to attack the Southern Soviet Union. As the Soviet fleet shifted more of its assets to the Kola Peninsula, the Strike Fleet in the Norwegian Sea became more important.

17. There were long-standing rumours of Soviet interest in submarine-launched rockets; both the United States and the Soviet Union captured data on German projects for such weapons. US fears escalated as the US strategic missile submarine programme grew towards operational capability (with Regulus cruise missiles) in the early 1950s; it was assumed that the Soviets would follow suit. SAC was building towards what it claimed was the capability to destroy the Soviet Union altogether, and the United States maintained strong air defences against the Soviet equivalent. By 1954 the British feared that the United States would abandon oceanic sea control entirely in favor of what might now be called anti-strategic submarine measures. In 1957 the Gaither Committee on US strategic defence described SOSUS as a means of tracking Soviet missile submarines within range of US targets, although five years earlier it had been described as a sea control measure. It was seen as a means of protecting convoys largely by enabling them to avoid submarine operating areas.

18. Khrushchev had much the same idea, though he phrased it very differently. He began by seeing nuclear weapons as the most likely instruments of capitalist assault, since they alone seemed capable of actually defeating the Soviet Union. However, after a time he discovered that the threat of *Soviet* nuclear weapons could quite possibly deter the West from attacking at all. The resulting state of conflict by means other than major war was termed "peaceful coexistence". The Soviet Union would seek to increase its power by moving into the Third World, through the use of Soviet-armed proxies fighting "wars of national liberation". In his memoirs, Khrushchev connects the shift of

shipbuilding resources from warships to merchant ships (which could carry Soviet weapons and other aid to the Third World) to this development. Krushchev's form of deterrence was particularly attractive because it permitted drastic reductions in what he considered obsolete conventional forces, the money for which was released for the creation of nuclear forces.

19. This development can be dated from about 1967. Reportedly the Soviets saw matters differently. Still recovering from Khrushchev's cuts, they considered their army in Eastern Europe sufficient only to contain local instability while holding off a NATO attack, and saw significant offensive capability as a future rather than a present possibility.

20. The division/air wing MAF includes 52,300 men, 70 tanks, 157 fixed-wing aircraft, and 156 helicopters. The regiment/air group MAB includes 15,700 men, 17 tanks, 79 fixed-wing aircraft, and 100 aircraft. The Marines also operate a smaller unit, the MAU (battalion/squadron), with 2000 men, five tanks, six fixed-wing aircraft, and 22 helicopters. In addition, the Marines operate an air-transportable MAB whose equipment is pre-positioned at Diego Garcia. It is difficult to specify the shipping required to lift any of these formations, because many alternative combinations of standard amphibious ships will suffice. Usually lift is described in terms of troops, helicopters (and helicopter "spots" for near-simultaneous take-off), large landing craft (which have to be carried in floodable "wet wells" aboard LHAs, LPDs, and LSDs), "square" (footage for vehicles), "cube" (cubic footage of stores), and gallons of vehicle fuel.

The current LHA, the largest US amphibious ship, was conceived as sufficient to transport a reinforced Marine battalion. Nine were orginally ordered, but four had to be cancelled in 1971. They will be replaced by new LHDs, essentially LHAs redesigned to carry air-cushion landing craft and capable of supporting Sea Harriers in an alternative "sea control" mode of operation. The smaller LPH carries about as many men, but cannot accommodate cargo or landing craft; thus the LHA might be equated to an LPH (of which seven were built) plus one or more cargo/well deck ships.

The peacetime Amphibious Ready Group generally consists of a MAU lifted by three to five ships. The composition of this amphibious squadron varies between fleets; the Sixth Fleet usually employs a single LPH or LHA plus one (LHA) or two (LPH) dock (wet well) ships (LPD or LSD) and one or two (LPH) LSTs. The combination varies because the LHA incorporates its own wet well and substantially more cargo capacity (both square and cube) than an LPH. Pacific groups were larger, with an additional wet well ship and an additional LST, to support the approximate equivalent of two Battalion Landing Teams (BLTs), although generally only one helicopter carrier is assigned. For details of forces assigned in 1982 see C C Wright, "US Naval Operations in 1982" in *Naval Review 1983* (Annapolis: US Naval Institute, 1983).

Mr Wright's 1986 summary (in *Naval Review 1987*) shows that these patterns have persisted, except that in some cases an attack cargo ship (LKA) has been added (sometimes in place of the LST). Beyond this visible increase, the Atlantic fleet developed and began to deploy a special operations capability in its Amphibious Ready Groups, which thereby gained some considerable raiding capability.

Current expectations are that with the appearance of air cushion landing vehicles the LSTs, which beach to discharge their vehicles, will become much less important. Future construction, then, will consist of air-capable ships (LHDs) and wet-well ships capable of supporting LCACs (LHD and LSD), with details adjusted to provide the appropriate mix of capacity.

21. This was a major argument in favour of recommissioning the battleships: too many pilots had been lost in Vietnam, attacking targets within 16-inch gun range (then about 20 miles) of the coast. Experiments in 1967 showed that modified (sub-calibre) shells can reach as far as about 50 miles. Note that most Third World targets are within a few miles of the coast. For a description of the experiments, see N Friedman, *US Naval Weapons* (Annapolis: Naval Institute Press and London: Conway Maritime Press, 1983).

22. It would be idle to suggest that hardening became important only after about 1982. It is, however, fair to say that at the height of the nuclear-only period, in the early and mid-1960s, protection was virtually dismissed as irrelevant. From the mid-1970s on, it has gradually become more and more important. Examples include the widespread installation of Kevlar internal armour, partly to protect ships against "cheap kills" by small-calibre weapons (wielded, perhaps, by terrorists) and major improvements in fire-fighting. The improvement might be measured in the difference between the performance of HMS *Sheffield*, which lacked US-style survivability features, in the Falklands, and USS *Stark*, which was of much the same size and character, in the Persian Gulf five years later. US interest in survivability can also be traced to the experience of Vietnam, where it was clearly important and where several US and allied ships were disabled by relatively minor weapons, such as Shrike anti-radar missiles.

The abortive Strike Cruiser of the 1970s would have been hardened. Her proposed mission included virtually solitary Third World operations, from which she would have had to return even after suffering battle damage. Her war, then, would have been a protracted one.

8. The Future of Maritime Strategy

The US Maritime Strategy is based on three fundamental assumptions: that the highway aspect of the sea remains paramount, at least within NATO; that the sea remains so vast that the use of choke points and forward operations remains vastly preferable to hunting enemy sea denial forces in the open ocean; and that a concentrated battle fleet, capable of projecting force into the Third World, remains viable in the face of Soviet or other future maritime forces.

The basic strategy is predicated on the assumption that the Alliance can present threats, largely in the form of a survivable battle fleet, which the Soviets can meet only by concentrating (and thus exposing) their sea denial forces. This concentration in turn should tend to limit the effective threat to the sea lanes. The first point motivates the Maritime Strategy. The second explains why some form of main fleet strategy is needed. The last assumes that it is viable. The bait/trap concept defines the tactics – and the likely near-term technology – of the Maritime Strategy.

Perhaps most important of all, the strategy, or at least most of it, is *public*. The Soviets can read about it. They can watch tests of some of the tactics.[1] They may, therefore, seek means of circumventing it. How seriously should this possibility be taken? How valuable is the integrating or motivating effect of a public strategy, compared to the opportunity it affords the most likely potential enemy?

The integrating effect is certainly there. The effect of publicising outline war plans is to relax the security accorded classified war plans. Thus, over the past few years senior naval commanders, such as carrier group commanders, have enjoyed a much fuller understanding of their classified wartime assignments, and have therefore been able to prepare themselves and their commands much more effectively. The rationale has been that it is more important for US forces to understand what they will have to do than to prevent the Soviets from achieving any understanding at all.[2]

History provides some comfort here. By the late 1930s the basic outlines of the US ORANGE war plan against Japan were fairly well known. Major fleet exercises were widely reported, and several books described the concept of the fleet's projected wartime cruise to the Orient. Important details of the various versions of the strategy were not, of course, public. However, the Japanese had every opportunity to shape their own strategy to deal with ORANGE. Moreover, by monitoring fleet exercises, US intelligence analysts were able to guess approximately what the Japanese strategy was. In the end, both US and Japanese practice came close to prewar ideas, albeit with some important twists. The ORANGE plan succeeded, because it was so sound that it could easily deal with Japanese countermeasures. It seems likely that the US Navy benefited so enormously in having a stable base for planning and for elaboration that Japanese knowledge was virtually irrelevant.

In the current case, the question is whether or to what extent the Soviets can change their known prewar assumptions, either as a result of their knowledge of US naval thinking or as a result of early war experience. Much depends on whether the Soviets can somehow split off the means of neutralising the threat presented by the US fleet from the means of achieving see denial. At present it seems that neutralising the prospective US threat is a central motivation of Soviet naval development. However, whatever their initial naval priorities, the Soviets would surely be motivated to shift to sea denial in the course of a protracted non-nuclear war. The early destruction of Soviet naval forces would prevent the Soviets from realising that important sea denial option later in a war.

For the future, perhaps, the Soviets, facing the possibility of a protracted non-nuclear war, might ultimately come to consider sea denial an extremely valuable option in its own right. Would they develop a distinct sea denial force *which would not respond to the* kind of bait/trap tactic which is characteristic of the Maritime Strategy? That in turn would depend on whether the Soviets could develop what would amount to a more economical coast defence force. Given past Soviet practice, the most likely mechanism would be a dedicated land-based missile force.[3]

The chief counterargument is that the navy occupies so low a position in a traditional land power such as the Soviet Union. It is fashionable to imagine that the Soviets somehow learned the lesson of sea power during the Cuban debacle and therefore decided to build a high-seas navy, but the reality of Soviet practice and of observed Soviet naval force structure does not support such an assertion; the Soviet fleet is not, and in the past has not been, designed for sea control in any Western sense. Even sea denial seapower is very expensive, and the Soviet economy is severely burdened. It seems most likely, then, that if a land-based alternative to sea-based sea denial were to surface, then the Soviet Navy would suffer badly – a development which the army-oriented Soviet General Staff might rue, but only once a war were in progress.

Basic Premises

Most of this book has been based on the premise that, despite radical changes in technology, Maritime Strategy shows continuities so strong that historical experience and classical concepts remain valid; indeed, that new technology can best be evaluated within the context of this experience. It is reasonable to ask, then, whether developing technology, particularly information processing and information denial (stealth and jamming), is now moving in a direction which will radically change future maritime strategy, perhaps even make it irrelevant.

Much of naval warfare depends on information. Navies are fundamentally stealthy because it is so difficult to locate and identify ships against the vastness of the ocean. As a consquence, naval tactics are designed largely (though not entirely) to supply just that information, often by reducing the alternatives open to an enemy fleet (e.g., by occupying a choke point through which it must pass).

The new "stealth" technology is, in effect, an anti-information-processing mechanism, a means of overcoming improvements in information handling. For example, improved submarine silencing (stealth) is opposed by improved signal gathering and processing (anti-stealth).

An additional issue central to the US Maritime Strategy is whether concentrations of surface ships can continue to survive in the face of submarine and air attacks. Like the first issue, this one would seem to depend very much on the competing progress of information gathering/processing and stealth. Here information gathering and processing also includes the exchange and amalgamation of information gathered by individual, perhaps widely separated, units. For example, a single ship equipped with a passive detector can only determine (at least instantaneously) the *direction* to a target. Two ships, pooling their information, can locate the target precisely by triangulation, perhaps while denying the target information as to their own location, since they need not send any signals in its direction.

To what extent, then, can we depend upon cooperation between widely separated elements of a naval force? Weapon and platform speeds are increasing, and it would seem that battle volume must increase commensurately. For example, the faster the attacking bombers, the further out they must be detected in order for them to be intercepted. The larger the battle space, the greater the benefit to be achieved by linking individual widely separated units together. For example, if bombers must be intercepted beyond a ship's horizon, then the interception itself is best controlled by airborne radar aircraft relatively far from the ship. They in turn may guide aircraft (as at present) or very long range shipborne missiles (as sometimes proposed).

If the battle space becomes very large, then assets integral to the mobile fleet may no longer suffice, and the fleet may come to depend in part on very long range reconnaissance systems reporting to a higher-echelon commander on land. There is clearly a trade-off between the capability (and cost) of the deployed fleet and the combination of long-range sensor capability and the security of the communications links providing their output to the fleet.

One might think of some fraction of fleet capability as insurance against the failure of long-haul communications or of sensors feeding them.

For example, a battle group at sea must carry with it sufficient fighters to deal with some level of bomber attack. The size of the fighter force in turn depends upon the degree of early warning to be expected. The better the warning, the greater the degree to which a limited force can be concentrated against the attackers. The less accurate the warning, the greater the dispersion of the fighter force, to deal with an ill-defined threat axis. Really early warning might allow battle group fighters to fly out towards the attacking bombers, far beyond the range at which they can hope to drop their missiles. Similarly, SOSUS warning of a submarine concentration in the path of the battle group might translate into a pre-emptive attack by S-3s from the carrier. For a given degree of security against submarine attack, the alternative to reliable early warning would be increased numbers of close-in escorts, or perhaps better terminal defences.

Success at sea then may come to depend in large part on the speed, security, and reliability of the long-haul communications links, both within the fleet and between fleet and land-based sources of information. Such communication can reveal the fleet's position. Its channels, such as satellites, can be vulnerable either to physical destruction or to jamming. Given this vulnerability, a fleet can be designed for a greater or a lesser degree of autonomy.

For example, under most circumstances a carrier's F-14s are controlled by an E-2C radar aircraft perhaps a 100 miles away. The F-14 radar is powerful enough that it can retain some considerable effectiveness even in the face of heavy jamming. An alternative system, "forward pass", has often been proposed. Very long range missiles would be fired by a distant surface ship, and controlled by the radar aircraft. The advantage of the system is that it can deal with very numerous targets, since the ship can carry many more missiles than the F-14s. However, forward pass requires extremely reliable long-haul communications, over much greater ranges than those inherent in the F-14/E-2C system. Moreover, failure of communication between the E-2C and the missiles completely negates the system, whereas the F-14s retain some capability even if they cannot guide their own long-range missiles.

This type of issue may determine the future of the large-deck aircraft carrier. Forward pass has been proposed several times, but it has never been practical, because of the complexity of the communications involved. If it becomes practicable, large surface ships loaded with very long range surface to air missiles could take over the outer air battle anti-bomber role currently assigned to the carriers. It is even conceivable that the forward radar role could be taken over by satellites.[4]

Land vs. Sea Transportation

The highway aspect of the sea is the motivation for naval development. It has two quite distinct aspects: first, just how important is sea transportation within a given political or economic unit; second, given a need to transport materiel overseas, does transportation by sea remain pre-eminent?

At the turn of the present century, Sir Halford MacKinder, a founder of geopolitics, argued that improvements in land transportation (largely, in his day, railways) had a deep economic and strategic significance. In the past, it had been significantly cheaper to move materiel over oceans than over relatively short distances ashore. As a result, Britain, with her oceanic empire, had achieved enormous economic power. However, if transportation within a large and self-sufficient land nation (such as the United States or Russia) became cheap enough, that power should easily overtake Britain. After all, land transportation within a politically unified country should not partake of the hazards of transportation by sea, particularly in wartime. MacKinder argued, then, that the future belonged to the autarkic (self-sufficient) land powers, particularly Russia, which controlled the heart ("heartland") of the Eurasian land mass.[5]

It is certainly still true that the Soviet Union is largely autarkic, although it is also still true that land transportation between the well-developed industrial base in European Russia and the Soviet

Far East is somewhat tenuous. Thus the Soviets, more than most, seem to rely heavily on what amounts to coastal shipping, in the form of the Northern and Southern Sea Routes from the Western Soviet Union to the Far East.[6]

The experience of this century seems to show that highly efficient inland transportation can be a mixed blessing, as it can make invading armies extremely mobile. The Germans might have done much better against the Soviets in 1941 had they enjoyed good roads inside the Soviet Union. As it was, they had to stop when the autumn rains came, and washed out many of the roads on which they depended, and they could not begin their 1942 offensive until the roads had dried out. It is much more difficult to move a substantial invasion force over thousands of miles of open sea.

Moreover, recent economic patterns seem to contradict MacKinder's central assumption. It is substantially cheaper to ship semiconductors or cars from Japan to the United States than to ship them by truck or by rail within the United States. MacKinder would have predicted that lower shipping charges within the United States would more than balance lower production costs abroad. As a result, the West seems more and more interdependent, linked more by sea than by land routes. Certainly the United States is much less self-sufficient than it was, say, in 1900, or even in 1950. Current arguments about free trade and the export of jobs are really arguments over the extent to which the United States should return to the autarky of the past, or whether the primary economic (and, in future, political?) unit should be some trans-national organism. Quite aside from arguments about manufactured products, the West still seems to require raw materials from overseas, whatever the efficiency of its internal land routes of communication.

The West as a whole, then, is still very much a seaborne entity. Any superiority (or parity) to be expected from the land-based Soviet economy is as yet a future possibility. After all, the gross inefficiency of the Soviet economy would seem far more a consequence of politics than of technology.

For the West, then, transportation across the seas remains vital. Indeed, as manufacturing diffuses through the world, it may become entirely impossible for any Western nation to afford self-sufficiency, even as an ideal, and transportation across seas may become even more important.

In wartime, moreover, it is almost impossible for the West to project power against possible targets except by moving that power over seas. It is true that the European NATO nations are contiguous to the most likely enemy, the Warsaw Pact. However, they are not altogether self-sufficient, and sustained warfare in Europe would require material support from overseas, not to mention troops from abroad. Any attempt to outflank the Warsaw Pact would almost have to be seaborne.

Technologically, the current situation is that communication within land masses *along developed highways and railroads* is relatively easy; coastal shipping fleets, at least in the developed world, have declined quite sharply over the past three or four decades.[7] However, it is still quite difficult to move rapidly over land in directions not yet prepared by road or railway.

Moreover, only ships can easily move masses of heavy materiel overseas. No technology in sight can materially improve matters. Aircraft are still very limited in payload, and they require (and will continue to require) vast amounts of fuel per ton of payload per mile. Airships can lift heavy weights at a limited cost in fuel, but at a very great cost in bulk, which presumably means manufacturing cost, as well as operational limitations.[8]

The Future of Sea Reconnaissance

The second key is the effect of the vastness of the sea, or, more precisely, the difficulty of scanning that vastness rapidly enough to find specific ships within a reasonable period of time. This applies both to surface ships and to submarines, although the technologies involved are radically different. Sea denial (not necessarily sea control) would become much easier if all the potential targets could be continuously tracked, since they might be attacked by long-range land-based weapons.

It might be imagined that this problem has already been solved in the case of surface ships, because they are detectable by radar aboard aircraft or satellites. However, to detect a ship in, say, the North Atlantic is not to identify it as the target. At any one time, several thousand ships are at sea. The number of worthwhile targets is much smaller, perhaps in the hundreds or even in the tens or units. The problem, then, is to select them out of the mass of irrelevant data (in the sense of information theory, noise). At present the Soviets approach the problem by relying initially on signals the targets themselves make, such as unique radar emissions. As a result, it is reportedly possible for entire battle groups to "disappear" from the Soviet fleet plot for days or even weeks at a time.[9]

The case of sonar is not so very different in principle. It is theoretically possible to cover the entire world ocean with short-range (i.e., high-reliability) sonars[10], which would, in theory, detect every submarine. However, that would be prohibitively expensive. Similarly, it is possible to search the world's ocean using moving sonars or air-dropped sonobuoys. Again, because reliable range is relatively short, search would be extremely, prohibitively, expensive. Claims that "the ocean will soon be transparent" generally translate into a claim that some future exotic sensor will be capable of searching the volume of the ocean very much faster than is currently possible.

Some figures will make these statements clearer. The Pacific, the largest ocean, has a surface area of about 50,000,000 square nautical miles, and the world ocean covers about 104,000,000 square nautical miles altogether. Current active sonars have a reliable range, in deep water, of about 5 to 10 nautical miles; one high-powered low-frequency active sonar should, therefore, be able to surveil about 75 to 300 square nautical miles. The situation is much worse in shallow water and under adverse acoustic conditions, but even at best it would take well over 300,000 or more active sonars to maintain continuous coverage of the world ocean, so that no submarine could expect to operate undetected at any time.[11]

What is possible is to lay large numbers of short-range sonars to cover a particular area, such as a choke point, so that there is a high probability that any submarine passing through is detected and attacked. However, from a strategic point of view, that is only a new version of the existing choke point idea, which itself is a response to the problem of the scale of the ocean, and the impossibility of reliable ocean surveillance.

An aircraft lays a field of sonobuoys, in effect a series of small (mostly passive) sonars. Coverage will not be entirely solid, but it seems reasonable to imagine that such an aircraft can search a box 100 nautical miles on a side in an hour, so that it might be credited with a search rate of about 10,000 square nautical miles per hour. Then the area of the Pacific might be equated to about 5000 aircraft-hours of search. Air search requires that sonobuoys be expended, and it is unlikely that any aircraft could search more than two such boxes per flight. Then the Pacific search area could be equated to 2500 search flights. Since search depends on sonar performance, it might be argued that newer, quieter, submarines would drastically shrink effective search areas. For example, if the box were only 50 nautical miles on a side, the overall requirement would quadruple, to 10,000 flights. The flights, moreover, would have to be nearly simultaneous, to maintain full coverage, since a submarine might otherwise be able to evade detection by always occupying some area not being searched.

SOSUS operates on a very different principle: it stares continuously at a large swath of the ocean, so that there is a fair chance that any submarine entering that swath will be detected. However, because it depends on sounds emitted by the submarine, it is subject to silencing improvements – just as the Soviet ocean surveillance system is subject to tight control of radio and radar emissions by the ships it is supposed to track.

It is not difficult to imagine the sort of system which would dramatically change matters. It would have to have an extremely high search rate, so that a very few expensive detectors could cover the entire ocean more or less continuously, or at least continuously enough not to miss many submarines. A low altitude satellite, for example, completes an orbit about every 100 minutes. The world has a surface area of something over 200,000,000 square miles, and the satellite must search a substantial fraction of that area on each orbit, say 2% or 4,000,000 square miles. It must, then, search a swath about 160 miles wide.[12]

There is no evidence that anything like this sort of performance against submarines is within reach. Even were it to come to fruition, it is not clear that submarines (particularly strategic ones) would immediately become obsolete, because they would still be moving targets. The moving satellite would record submarine position at some point, and there would necessarily be a time delay while its information was sent home for processing and then for use. Most likely such a satellite would be associated with a land-based ballistic anti-submarine weapon, representing the minimum time delay between detection and attack. One might imagine that the total delay would be of the order of an hour, during which a submarine would move 20,000 yards at 10 knots. To the extent that its motion would be unpredictable (and the submarine could always zig-zag), the missile would arrive without knowing where in a circle of 20,000 yard radius the submarine was. That might be tolerable if the weapon carried a large nuclear warhead. However, to the extent that nuclear weapons seem less and less likely to be usable in the near future, the entire system might prove less than effective. That in turn would limit it to operation near friendly naval forces, which could be expected to re-detect and attack, much as they do at present in connection with SOSUS. Moreover, the detector would probably not be uniformly effective over the entire surface of the ocean, and submarines might well operate quite effectively in areas of ineffectiveness, such as shallow or particularly crowded water.

The current reality is that submarines are becoming quieter (stealthier) and that not only are they becoming more difficult to detect (by passive means), but also they are finding it more difficult to detect other quiet submarines. It is not clear whether improved signal processing will reverse this trend. If it continues, then at some point it will no longer be clear that submarines are effective ASW weapons, since they will be unable to detect their targets passively. Platforms which can use active sensors, such as active sonobuoys, may become more important, especially in home area ASW. This possible development would have serious consequences for the Maritime Strategy, since the Soviets would no longer be compelled to use their own submarine force to hunt down US submarines operating in their home areas. The submarine element of the bait/trap strategy might be much less effective, even though the US submarines would still expect to detect and kill numerous Soviet craft.

This conclusion is not altogether certain, because submarines have both quiet and noisy operating regimes. If the tactical situation forces them to move at high (noisy) speed, they are detectable (and attackable) at long ranges. For example, a submarine might be extremely quiet at 5 knots, but it would also make good only 120 miles per day. Out of a total endurance of (say) 50 days, it would lose 40 days transiting to and from a patrol area 2400 miles from base. The time loss would be shaved to a much more acceptable 10 days if the submarine transited at a much louder speed, 20 knots – but in that case it would also be vulnerable to attack.

Clearly radar satellites *can* detect surface ships at ranges of several hundred miles. They are limited by the sheer number of ships at sea; they need some means of picking out the ships of interest. That is a brutal information-processing problem. The satellite radar must somehow record enough details of the ships under surveillance to pick out the important ones. It can, for example, measure the length of the ships it sees, and reject all ships below a given size. After all, aircraft carriers are rather large. But they are not so much larger than big container ships, some of which may travel at carrier speed; and they are significantly smaller than big oil tankers. Moreover, with the advent of surface-ship launched deep strike weapons such as Tomahawk, it may be necessary for the satellites to detect, identify, and track much smaller ships, perhaps half or even a third the length of a carrier.

If length is not enough, then a sufficiently sophisticated satellite can observe the silhouette of the ship it detects. It (or its ground station) might then compare the silhouette to a library, and thus decide which ships were worth attacking. Even a very fast computer would find that time-consuming. Moreover, if the comparison is done on the ground, the satellite needs some means of storing up its silhouettes and rapidly transmitting them down, and that in turn requires an extremely capacious down-link, since it takes a considerable amount of information to characterise a silhouette.

It is conceivable that some future development in artificial intelligence would somewhat simplify these tasks, e.g. by substantially reducing the amount of data which the satellite would have to transmit down. However, that would not eliminate the basic problem, that there are relatively few targets immersed in a mass of fairly similar ships. The ratio of targets to non-targets matters because substantial resources must be concentrated to destroy any one target; resources cannot lightly be wasted on non-targets.

This very elaborate system, moreover, would be subject to simple countermeasures. In both world wars, the Royal Navy converted old merchant ships to resemble its major capital ships, specifically for strategic deception. A radar satellite would have to drastically simplify the silhouette images it transmitted, and as a result it would probably be much easier to deceive. It is entirely possible that relatively simple electronic countermeasures aboard ship could so change the perceived silhouette as to throw off even the most intelligent satellite-based reconnaissance system. After all, the ship has available much more weight, volume, and power for its electronic countermeasures, and there is no reason to imagine that, at a given level of electronic technology, it will be at a disadvantage.

Moreover, it might be imagined that the satellite would have to operate its radar at very high frequencies, to package a usable antenna into the available space. It seems likely that "stealth" materials will be most effective at such high frequencies, and therefore that it will be easiest to modify the signatures of ships as they are perceived by future radar imaging satellites.

Thus, although the situation for surface ships is not as easy to predict as is that for submarines, it seems unlikely that the vital tactical considerations imposed by the vastness of the sea will soon be overcome.

This is not to say that surface ships will be so very difficult to detect – they are fairly easy to detect right now – but rather that detection of one ship alone is insufficient. The attacker needs a reliable picture of all the shipping in a substantial area, since he needs to guard against deception and ambush. The situation is not too different from that found so often in scientific fraud. It is easy to be carried away by the sheer power of modern science – and to forget that clever deception, which is unsuspected, can negate all or most of that power. Science depends very heavily for its power on basic honesty. Many sensors depend on an absence of creative deception.[13]

Ship Survivability and the Effects of "Stealth"

It seems likely that the new stealth technology will be applied to surface warships. Details have never been released, but anti-radar design probably employs a combination of radar-absorbing material (which is likely to be most effective at relatively short wavelengths), special shaping (to reduce reflectance), and special countermeasures. For the modern ship designer, stealth is more a question of emphasis of known principles than a special technology. The Israelis, for example, applied radar-absorbing material to the superstructures of their missile boats so as to reduce their radar signatures.[14] Both the US *Arleigh Burke* and the Soviet *Kirov* have sloping superstructure sides; at least in the US case this was intended to reduce radar signature.

It is probably impossible to make a large ship appear to vanish. However, it probably is possible to reduce its signature to that compatible with a much smaller ship, so that a remote sensor cannot distinguish, say, a carrier from an escorting cruiser, or a carrier from a suitably rigged merchant ship. That raises interesting possibilities for cover and deception. A highly centralised Soviet-style command structure should be particularly susceptible to such tactics, with their promise of catastrophic IFF failures.

It seems likely, too, that stealth technology can be used to alter the details of ship radar signatures so as to guide missiles into relatively unimportant parts of a ship's structure. The larger the ship, the better her vitals can be dispersed (or duplicated), and the easier it is for her designer to arrange to guide missiles away from the vitals. For example, some analysts of the designs of recent Soviet surface ships suggest that radar-homing missiles would tend to concentrate on their massive tower masts, the insides of which contain the waveguides of their radars. Hits would tend to blind these ships – but not to sink them.

In its most complete manifestation, the first naval application of stealth will probably be to carrier aircraft. The efficiency of a carrier as an attack weapon depends upon the survivability of her aircraft: if they can all shuttle their weapons from ship to shore and return, they can deliver massive tonnages at a relatively low fixed cost. If stealth means survivability, then it should greatly enhance carrier strike capability.[15]

The advent of stealth has led some to the suggestion that future ships should all be submersible. After all, one might say that stealth is required to survive, and submarines are inherently stealthy (and perhaps becoming more so). There are three counterarguments. First, the fleet exists to carry out some mission, not merely to survive. Submergence may be inimical to that mission. Second, submarine communications with and beyond the surface are inherently poor. Third, submarines have an inherent limit on internal volume, hence on what they can carry per unit volume, or per unit cost.

At the least the fleet must be able to protect ships at sea from air-launched attacks. The ships it protects cannot possibly be made stealthy, because it is most unlikely either that commercial ship-owners or Western governments will pay for the wholesale replacement or reconstruction of merchant fleets. After all, they seem unwilling, right now, to pay even to maintain substantial numbers of drastically un-stealthy merchant ships under their own flags. As a consequence, stealth on the part of the fleet will not in itself guarantee the survival of shipping in the open sea. A stealthy fleet will guarantee that survival only if its stealth contributes directly to the destruction of the enemy's anti-shipping forces.

The alternative to killing off the enemy's anti-ship forces is to destroy his weapons as they approach their targets. That requires some means of sensing the approach of airborne weapons – and submarines are ill-designed for that task. It may be argued that they can somehow surface only when air attack is imminent, but that assumes both a degree of early warning and a reliability of communication which seem unrealistic.

Finally, there is internal space. The usable volume of a submarine is equivalent to that of a surface ship of about 30 to 40 per cent its displacement, because the surface ship has most of its volume above water, and because its deck area is usable. Quite aside from the sheer cost of submarine construction, this one deadly consideration has killed off numerous projects for submersible aircraft carriers.[16]

Given all of these considerations, surface ships will still be detected and attacked. Weapons are becoming faster (which reduces reaction time), and they are becoming more intelligent (which may make countermeasures more difficult). It is, however, still true that a 10,000-ton surface ship can accommodate a much greater weight of electronics, including countermeasures, than can a 100-ton bomber or a 500-ton fast-attack boat. Any single weapon carried by the bomber or attack boat must balance electronics (such as counter-countermeasures), propulsion (for high speed, to overcome defences, and for long range, so that it cannot be destroyed before launch), and the sheer size of its warhead within a relatively small envelope. For example, Western submarine torpedo tubes generally limit weapons to a diameter of 21 inches and a length of about 21 feet.

Moreover, should fast-reacting weapons such as directed energy beams become a reality, they should be possible to accommodate aboard ships, since large ships can carry their hundreds or thousands of tons relatively easily. It seems likely that future signal processing and artificial intelligence technologies would tend to enhance ship self defence.

From the strategic point of view, enhanced ship self defence should require an enemy to devote more of his sea-denial forces to the decisive battle against an oncoming battle fleet. There is one *caveat*. If the enemy's own air defence technology renders the fleet's land attack weapons ineffective, then the entire bait/trap strategy may be negated. The chief argument against this possibility is that the fleet can attack over a very wide area, against numerous targets. A level of air defence which is quite feasible in a concentrated fleet becomes entirely impractical when it has to cover numerous land targets, which can be attacked from virtually all directions. Moreover, artificial intelligence would seem to be a very attractive means of enhancing the capabilities of land-attack missiles, whose targets can be specified in advance in considerable detail.

It seems unlikely that the application of stealth technology to anti-ship weapons will radically change matters. The nature of "stealth" has not been disclosed, but it is almost certainly a combination of careful shaping, radar-absorbing materials, and special countermeasures. The materials and the shaping are more likely to be effective against shorter- than longer-wavelength radars. The sheer size of ships makes it practicable to provide them with high-resolution low-frequency radars, either on masts or on the hulls themselves (with electronic scanning). Similarly, a stealthy missile would use some form of low-probability-of-intercept radar. A ship could accommodate sufficient (and sufficiently sophisticated) electronics to have a reasonable chance of detection. Moreover, a coordinated fleet would enjoy the advantage of multiple detectors and multiple receivers, and therefore a higher net probability of detection.

Even so, once they are detected and attacked, ships will be hit. Sometimes they will not even be able to detect the weapons attacking them. This is being written just after the Exocet attack on the US frigate *Stark* in the Persian Gulf: she certainly did not detect the one or two incoming weapons.[17] On the other hand, she did survive their explosion, even though she was a small and, nominally, unarmoured warship. She had been designed well before the last previous naval missile battle, in the Falklands, but she incorporated much survivability technology, which, in the event, proved quite successful.

The key point for this study is that, despite considerable advertising, even the smartest non-nuclear bomb is unlikely to wipe out a properly designed and operated warship at a single blow. Current missiles strike above the waterline, causing direct destruction and fire, which the ship's structure (as in the case of the *Stark*) can be expected to limit, provided appropriate fire-fighting measures are taken. The only option for catastrophic damage is a hit in a large magazine. The resulting explosion should (in theory) be able to sink the ship. In the case of the *Stark*, the missile exploded near the ship's missile magazine. However, armour around the magazine prevented the hot metal splinters (which the explosion of the Exocet created) from penetrating the magazine itself.

Countermeasures to even a direct magazine hit are certainly conceivable. In a large enough ship, it should be possible to armour directly against incoming weapons; magazines can be buried well within a hull and also below the waterline, so that any warhead must travel some considerable distance before penetrating them. Armouring can probably extend to shaped-charge warheads (as in Soviet weapons). After all, tanks are now armoured against such explosives, and they are much smaller than warships. Other possible countermeasures would include very rapid flooding arrangements (to fight magazine fires) and the use of insensitive munitions, which might not explode even under the stress either of a magazine fire or of the explosion of nearby weapons.

Torpedoes either strike the structure of the ship or explode under it. In the former case, the designer can provide sufficient subdivision to contain flooding, as long as the ship herself is large enough. The only catastrophic case would be an explosion in or very close to a magazine. In a small ship, such an explosion tends to flood the magazine and thus need not be fatal (although it may be so large that the hull structure is destroyed). In a larger ship, the structure of the ship tends to contain a magazine fire, and explosion is quite possible.[18]

The under-the-keel case is more difficult, as the torpedo explosion creates an expanding sphere of gas, which bounces off the bottom of the ship. The hull tends to flex at each bounce, and after a few flexes it may break in two. The countermeasure is obvious: if the bottom is soft enough, the sphere will break through it, and the hull will not flex at all, or at least very much. The ship will flood, but that generally reduces the problem to that of the contact torpedo already described. The prerequisite for this kind of response would be a fairly radical change in hull structural design, so that a broken keel would not be catastrophic.

All of this is not intended to show that warships can be made unsinkable; that has never been true. It is, rather, to suggest that large ships can still be hardened, almost certainly without destroying their efficacy. Thus the continued viability of a fleet strategy need not rest on expectations that the presently favourable ratio of defence to offence will continue forever. Rather, surface ship technology will probably offer some considerable margin for future degradation of active and electromagnetic defence.

Scarcity and Sea Power: The Future of Mass Ship Production

The Maritime Strategy is predicated on scarcity: scarcity of ships to fight the war, so that if they are to make real use of the mobility of sea power, the same ships must also seize sea control; scarcity of merchant ships, so that attrition is not really an acceptable approach to ultimate sea control; scarcity of escorts, so that convoy is not really a fully effective strategy. Some new technologies promise to modify this basic condition by permitting sudden mobilisation of national resources. It should be stressed at the outset that mobilisation, as in the two world wars, is viable only in the context of a protracted conflict, in which catastrophe comes slowly if at all. Mobilisation means little more than increased weapon production in a shortish war, and in a very short war, no more than calling up reservists to match them to their weapons.

The first new technology is automated generalised production. It is now possible to design a factory which can easily shift from one product to a very different one, merely by reprogramming its software (and changing the material delivered to it). Ships can be built from modules which such factories can manufacture; the US Perry class frigate is a good example. A specialist yard is still needed, but the modules need not spend much time there. Thus existing yards can enormously expand their total capacity by making use of nominally non-naval manufacturers – if proper preparation has been made. This technology would seem to apply particularly to merchant ships, which are so much simpler than warships.

Data busing is a related future ship production technology. At present outfitting, particularly wiring, is a major, specialised, and time-consuming aspect of warship construction. Further wiring is required whenever a ship is refitted. However, high capacity data buses could easily accommodate the current wiring functions, leaving sufficient capacity for future growth. Individual sensors and weapons could tap the data stream flowing through them, just as they tap ship power supplies. Because they would be physically concentrated, data buses would probably be relatively easy to protect. Protection in turn should become more attractive in the context of the sort of protracted war implicit in the Maritime Strategy. In a short war, ships which are severely or perhaps even moderately damaged are as good as lost, since they cannot participate in later stages of the conflict. In a long war, it is probably well worthwhile to repair even major damage, and a ship's ultimate survival will often depend upon how well its combat system can withstand minor damage.

Finally, it may now be easier to mass-produce escorts, because the new towed-array sonar systems can function even in relatively noisy hulls, as they are towed well astern of most of that noise. That means that a merchant hull can be converted into an austere escort by fitting it with a specialised towed array, perhaps containerised, and also by equipping it with a helicopter (to prosecute array detections). The result will be far from satisfactory, but it will probably work. If appropriate preparation is done in peacetime, then, it might actually be possible to overcome the current drastic lack of escorts.[19]

This last approach requires the existence of large Western merchant fleets, to provide enough surplus hulls for escorts. Unfortunately, the Western fleets are declining rapidly. Partly that is because it is difficult to attract crews at competitive wages. partly, too, it is because owners have chosen to transfer their ships to flags of convenience, largely in the Third World. It is a matter of some controversy whether NATO governments will be able to force multinational corporations to make their ships available in time of war. Similarly, one might wonder whether the government of a flag of convenience state falling under Soviet domination (or becoming violently anti-Western) would not be able to prevent NATO from using ships nominally under its control.

The merchant ship mobilisation issue also arises in mine countermeasures and in coastal ASW. In both cases, the Third

World boundary condition on the Maritime Strategy prohibits vast investment in peacetime, as such craft are not useful in the naval presence mission. They can, hopefully, be improvised in wartime from existing coastal craft, assuming appropriate prewar preparation. That is the basis of the current US COOP (Craft Of Opportunity) harbour mine countermeasures programme.[20] Unfortunately coastal fishing fleets are limited, and declining in the face of foreign competition, both in the United States and in Europe.

Even given these somewhat pessimistic *caveats*, mobilisation promises to change wartime strategy in a protracted war – assuming that the standing fleet, at the outset, is able to achieve at least temporary sea control. It seems extremely unlikely that mobilisation production could be initiated in time to affect the earliest stages of a future war. However, it could begin at the outbreak of war, and it could be extremely important after the first few months – if appropriate preparation is made. That in turn requires a wider appreciation of the possibility that future war would be protracted and non-nuclear.

In the past, mobilisation has entirely changed the nature of conflict. For example, the United States Navy studied the problem of war with Japan from about 1907 onwards. It developed a plan, but it could not really meet the materiel and manpower requirements which flowed from it. As a result, versions of this ORANGE plan developed in the late 1930s became more and more pessimistic. Mobilisation – the mass production of ships and the mass enlistment of men, both in the army which was actually projected overseas – totally changed the situation, and made ORANGE altogether feasible.

Potential Strategy-Breakers

It seems appropriate to close with a short list of some factors which might threaten the viability of the Maritime Strategy.

First among them must be the prospect of nuclear war at sea. For reasons stated several times in this book, neither side would seem particularly anxious to escalate to the use of nuclear weapons. Moreover, sea control would become far more difficult in the face of nuclear attack, as even a single weapon might well destroy or disable numerous ships.[21] There is one obvious and ominous exception. NATO doctrine is to fire a nuclear "warning shot" before initiating large-scale tactical nuclear escalation. It is entirely possible that some misguided NATO statesmen will imagine that such a shot could be fired at sea, thus avoiding damage to or near their own soil. At present US policy is to deter the Soviets from initiating nuclear war at sea, and the Soviets presumably are willing to avoid such use because (i) they do not so highly value naval assets and (ii) they much fear escalation to the land. NATO initiation at sea would entirely remove this bar.

Second must be the possibility that the Soviet Army would seize so much of the NATO coastline on the flanks and islands, or Japan in the Pacific that the current geographical advantage of the Western Alliance would disappear. For example, the Soviets might be able not merely to fly their bombers further into the open ocean, but also to escort them in their attacks on battle forces. That would not merely vastly increase the number of air targets. It would might also cut down the number of defending fighters, particularly if the Soviets were able to mount successive waves of fighters and then bombers. This potential threat might be met by increasing outer air battle killing power, for example through providing large numbers of very long range ship-launched missiles.

A third disaster would be for the Soviets to abandon their bastions altogether, on the theory that they were indefensible. That seems unlikely, given past Soviet practice, but it is possible. In that case forward deployed submarines would still be useful, but they would only be another means of attrition, attacking submarines transiting outbound, or returning for repair or rearming. Convoy would probably become much more important, and much would depend on whether convoys and their escorts could be shielded from Soviet bombers, the one open-ocean threat that they could not really counter. The battle force idea, then, would probably remain important, but the nature of the ASW battle would change. Matters would be particularly difficult because SOSUS and the barriers would lose much of their effectiveness in the face of significantly quieter Soviet submarines.

The other potential disaster would be an effective mine offensive, not only in coastal waters but also in the strategic straits which the battle force must transit. Future rising mines might be almost impossible to hunt or to sweep, yet they might embody torpedoes capable of severely damaging large ships. Moreover, it seems unlikely that existing types of mine countermeasures craft could be carried with a high-speed fleet.

This particular threat can be overstated. Mines do not generally incorporate any sort of IFF, so they cannot readily be laid in areas the Soviets may wish to transit. Nor does it seem likely that a future rising mine could easily distinguish between surface and submarine targets. The Soviets might eschew *surface* use of a strategic strait, but it would be much more difficult for them to avoid submarine use. Moreover, mines probably cannot be laid long before the outbreak of hostilities, since it would be foolhardy to rely on a long preset arming delay; in any case, it seems unlikely that hostilities would break out as a result of very lengthy pre-planning. Thus one might quite reasonably argue that by moving forward prior to the actual outbreak of war, the fleet could evade any early strategic strait mining problem, although its supporting ships might be less fortunate.

Existing mines *can* upset amphibious operations, the threat of which is an element of the overall maritime strategy. There are two current counters. One is to use vehicles which are largely immune to mines for over-the-beach delivery of men and materiel: air cushion vehicles and helicopters. The other is to mount the assault from well offshore. Even though the seabed (say) 50 miles offshore can be mined, one might argue that it would be uneconomical or extremely difficult to do so over the very large area from which an over-the-horizon assault could be mounted.

One has to conclude that the Maritime Strategy does not answer all questions, does not solve all problems. That is not exactly surprising. The strategy is a pragmatic attempt to deal with some very difficult boundary conditions. More than that, it is a direction in which to go, not a final, finished biblical type of dogma. It defines the kinds of tactical and technological problems the US and NATO navies must solve if they are to face some of the likely scenarios of the future.

It seems best to close with by comparing the maritime strategy to the most successful US war plan of the past, ORANGE. ORANGE was first studied in 1907, and by 1914 the main alternatives had been laid out. They were all clearly unfeasible: the fleet lacked the endurance, it lacked forward bases, it lacked reconnaissance, it lacked the means of sustaining itself in Japanese waters. But the plan did lay out what the fleet needed, and for the next quarter-century it inspired a long series of innovations. By 1939, ORANGE was on the verge of feasibility, and mobilisation plans existed to bring it to full feasibility. ORANGE actually succeeded in 1942–45. That was why Admiral Chester Nimitz, who commanded the Pacific Theatre, could say that he had experienced no great tactical surprises (other than the *Kamikazes*) during World War II.

In these terms, it is probably about 1930 or, at the very latest, 1935. War is not very near, although the prospective enemy is well armed and aggressive. He is clearly enough the prospective enemy that we can concentrate attention on him. There is clearly time to develop answers to the problems the strategy raises. If they are properly worked through, 1941 may never come.

Notes

1. The United States Navy has, however, been able to reduce the effect of such observation by using the Second and Third Fleets to test tactics in waters it controls, rather than the Sixth and Seventh Fleets, in their much more public domains.
2. The value of secrecy can be overstated. First, excessive secrecy makes it difficult for staffs to develop detailed war plans. In some cases, senior officers may act without understanding how their actions affect overall plans, and their independence may be counterproductive. Second, official secrecy may induce a false sense of security. The history of peacetime military planning shows few if any major and long-standing strategic plans which never fell into the hands of prospective enemies. Official secrecy might cause planners not to revise plans sufficiently to take account of that probability. Recent lapses in US security tend to emphasise this problem. Finally, plans developed in excessive secrecy may well be flawed. *Within limits*, greater exposure should make for better planning.

3. There are indications that the SRF tried to take over the naval defense role, claiming that IRBMs could be used to attack carrier groups. For example, it is sometimes suggested that SS-11s in the Southern Soviet Union were assigned specifically to attack naval targets in the Mediterranean. Admiral Gorshkov specifically attacked this kind of assignment, and it is difficult to imagine how very long-range missiles could function in a non-nuclear context. Very long range would be essential, first to attack before the carriers could launch their aircraft, and second to realise reasonable economy. There is little question but that some form of defence against anti-ship ballistic missiles could be erected. However, from a strategic point of view the significance of a Soviet shift to land-based anti-ship missiles would be to separate the anti-carrier from the sea denial roles, and so to neutralise the bait/trap strategy. It would seem, then, extremely important for the United States to deny any such economy to the Soviets.

4. Martin Marietta proposed exactly this kind of system to fulfil an Outer Air Battle requirement. A very large surface ship loaded with numerous long-range cruise missiles and powerful SAMs could be equated with the carrier, in the bait/trap role. It would not be as flexible as a carrier, particularly in a limited war or cold war role, when it would be extremely important for possibly hostile aircraft to be positively identified. At present, moreover, it would take about 4000 cruise missiles to equal the offensive firepower of the carrier. The claimed advantages of the system are reduced manning and reduced costs (since the expensive aircraft are eliminated). It is by no means clear that this would represent a worthwhile bargain, but it seems useful to describe it in some detail.

5. From this point of view, Europe and Japan sit on the "rimland" of Eurasia. MacKinder's dictum was "he who controls the heartland, controls the rimland; he who controls the rimland, controls the world."

6. In a Sino-Soviet war, the Chinese might, in effect, blockade the Soviet Maritime Provinces by cutting both the Trans-Siberian Railroad and the Southern Sea Route. The Soviets have long recognised this vulnerability, which is why they built the BAM (Baikal-Amur Mainline) railroad north of the Chinese border. The Southern Sea Route raises another interesting possibility. If indeed the Soviets come to depend upon it, then a US threat would force them to maintain protective forces, the costs of which would detract from Soviet capabilities in such land theatres as Europe. The historical analogue would be the British sea route to India and the East. The need to protect this route explained such acquisitions as Aden. At one time some students of Soviet alliance policy claimed that the Soviets were bent on acquiring bases and allies specifically to protect the sea route through the

Indian Ocean. This need was used to explain Soviet interest in, and heavy naval investment in, India. Conversely, the Soviets might see US interest in Chinese (PRC) naval modernisation partly as a means of applying pressure to the Southern Sea Route. That is not presently the case, since the PRC would be able to use sea denial weapons equally well against the Soviets and against Taiwan; US policy has been to avoid selling the PRC the weapons it requires to deal with Taiwan.

7. However, that relatively easy communication is quite expensive in terms of fuel, which often does have to come from overseas.

8. The reason is that water is much denser than air, so that a relatively dense object, packed with cargo, can still be buoyant in water. However, the difference in density between air and hydrogen or helium is sufficiently small that it takes an enormous volume of airship to provide enough margin of buoyancy to lift a relatively small volume of cargo.

9. This situation is, then, not so very different from that in December 1941, when the Japanese carrier strike force managed to vanish from US plots by cutting off all radio traffic. The US Navy, like its contemporaries, relied heavily on a series of high-frequency radio direction finders, in its case surrounding the Pacific operational area.

10. For example, in deep water upward-looking active sonars can use the reliable acoustic path (RAP) to detect all targets within a radius of about ten miles. In shallower water, upward-looking sonars would have much shorter ranges. In theory, a dense enough array of such sonars could cover the entire ocean – but dense enough is very dense indeed.

11. Convergence zone detection does not count, because the convergence zone is only a ring around the sonar: there is a substantial gap between its inner edge and the outer edge of solid (direct path) detection. Other exotic propagation phenomena, such as bottom-bounce, can extend sonar solid-coverage range, but only under special conditions.

12. The important figure is the total surface area of the world, since the satellite, unlike the searching aircraft, cannot choose between time over land and time over water.

13. The present writer well remembers the reaction of a retired Israeli general to a computer-based intelligence fusion system proposed in the late 1970s, which would have deduced the axis of a Soviet land offensive by collating intelligence reports. He considered the entire system virtually an invitation to disaster through careful fabrication of false data. The problem of deducing the axis of advance was so difficult, and success so spectacular, that the effect of really large amounts of false data had never really been evaluated.

14. In the October 1973 Yom Kippur War the Israeli tactic was to turn

towards enemy missile boats, reducing the radar signatures of their own boats, and then to fire chaff, which incoming missiles would detect. Given the large chaff target and the small boat target, the missile would be seduced into the chaff.

15. It seems likely that stealthy anti-ship bombers and missiles will suffer because they will have to use active radars to locate their targets. Such radars may in turn give away their presence. A stealthy aircraft attacking a fixed land target could rely on totally passive sensors: inertial guidance and perhaps (if it flew at high altitude) stellar navigation. It seems unlikely that anti-ship weapons could rely entirely on command guidance, e.g., by a radar satellite, or on passive sensors (e.g., IR).

16. For example, about 1956 BuShips developed a series of radical new submarine projects. It soon concluded that a 20,000-ton submersible carrier – which could make all of 12 knots underwater – could carry no more than two or three aircraft, which would have to take off over a ski-jump, as it was unlikely that a submersible catapult would become available. It was easier to build a submarine to launch one-way nuclear missiles, as such a carrier could never efficiently launch non-nuclear attacks. A modern equivalent might be faster (reactors are now more compact), but it would not accommodate materially more aircraft.

17. It appears (as of late May, 1987) that the ship could not detect the low-altitude Exocet because the latter was flying in a radar "duct" (a signal-trapping layer) created by water evaporated from the surface of the hot Gulf. The ship's radars and radar signal detectors would have been well above the top of the duct. Such anomalous propagation phenomena are fairly common in areas such as the Gulf, the Eastern Mediterranean, and the Arabian Sea, at some times of the year; they are unavoidable. If the duct existed, then the missile was detectable only during its brief glide from airplane to cruising altitude, which might have occupied a period of no more than about 20 seconds. It would have appeared on radar scopes as a transient signal, and might well have been dismissed as a false alarm. The tactical situation made it impossible for the ship to react to such alarms. For more details of ducting and of radar operation, see N Friedman, *Naval Radar* (Annapolis: US Naval Institute and London: Conway Maritime Press, 1981).

18. Several US cruisers survived magazine explosions during World War II. Postwar investigation suggested the mechanism described here.

19. This approach might become less attractive as Soviet submarines become quieter, since existing towed arrays are passive. Several systems now under development associate a towed array with an active sound source (sometimes also towed), and therefore could

continue to function even against very quiet submarines.

20. COOP craft are commercial fishing vessels designated for wartime use. They would be used to monitor clear channels into vital US ports. In peacetime reservist COOP crews would use converted Naval Academy training craft, largely for bottom surveys of the wartime routes.

21. It is true that in the 1950s the US Navy did plan formations designed to minimise nuclear damage. However, they made sense only because large nuclear weapons were relatively scarce. For example, it is perfectly possible to disperse a three-carrier formation so that two will survive if one is hit or near-missed. However, nuclear weapons are now relatively plentiful, and it is not difficult to imagine an enemy using one or two per carrier, thus largely defeating the defensive (but not the deceptive) aspect of dispersal.

Index